The
Resurgence
of Race

The Resurgence of Race

**Black Social Theory
from Reconstruction to the
Pan-African Conferences**

William Toll

Temple University Press
Philadelphia

To Benjamin and Monroe,
the best companions

Library of Congress Cataloging in Publication Data

Toll, William.
    The resurgence of race.

    Includes bibliographical references and index.
        1. Afro-Americans—Race identity. 2. Afro-Americans—Intellectual
life. 3. Afro-Americans—Social conditions—To 1964. 4. Pan-Africanism.
I. Title.
E185.625.T64   301.45'19'6073   79-17843
ISBN 0-87722-167-7

Temple University Press, Philadelphia 19122
© 1979 by Temple University. All rights reserved
Published 1979
Printed in the United States of America

Contents

Preface

"And when I contemplated the area of No Man's Land into which the Negro minds in America had been shunted, I wondered if there had ever existed in all human history a more corroding and devastating attack upon the personalities of men than the idea of racial discrimination."

Richard Wright
American Hunger

On first encountering the writings of W. E. B. DuBois, I was intrigued by his ability to portray the dilemmas faced by an intellectual trying to speak for an ethnic minority in a culture dominated by a white Protestant majority. The more I read, however, the better I understood how Black intellectuals had become pivotal critics of American patterns of deference and of power. Because Blacks were judged to be inferior by the white majority, explanations by DuBois and others about the relationship between exploitation and "backward" behavior were dismissed as the rationalizations of an anomalous "mulatto" class. Before his analytic statements could be taken seriously, DuBois had to demonstrate that Black social life rested on a cultural tradition from which moral judgments could be made. DuBois, then, had to acquire the analytic tools of the white elite to conduct a cultural warfare against them. While he movingly expressed the dilemmas of intellectual leadership, he came to play a crucial historical role in challenging the cultural hegemony of the white Protestant elite. As I began to analyze DuBois' debate with Booker T. Washington, I came to believe that it had been seriously misinterpreted and had been in fact a major event in American *cultural* history. It turned not on tactics for fending off white power, but on defining the purposes for which Black power should be mobilized. The debate stretched back to antebellum days, and came to a head as free Negroes and freedmen pondered the meaning of Black life in a world dominated by the capitalist market system and the ideology of white supremacy. As the relationship between freedmen and free Negroes shifted, the elites trying to prescribe purposes for Black life shifted also. As politicians gave way to educators, and educators to urban intellectuals, the ideologies to rationalize a Black destiny became the subject of intense debate. The process by which one set of elites gave way to another and created rationalizing ideologies, demonstrated how Blacks struggled to salvage their sanity in a culture predisposed to destroy their identity. The observations by Richard Wright that head this Preface express all too clearly a major theme in this volume.

As the research and writing proceeded, I received a liberal education not only in the methods of exploitation that have been used to advance the market system in rural and urban America, but in the ways racism developed a life of its own. In the dining hall of the Harvard Club of New York City, as well as in the parks of Jacksonville and the streetcars and newspaper offices of Atlanta, Black minds were deemed incapable of serious thought. All too often, Black intellectuals expressed similar doubts while searching for the tools to counterattack. Yet by 1920, in intellectual circles at least, racism was on the defensive and the rudiments of a Black cultural perspective on which moral judgments could rest had been recognized. How this occurred, and its significance for American cultural history, became the major inquiry of the concluding portions of this study. After months of research in the papers of Booker T. Washington, the NAACP, Joel and Arthur Spingarn, Mary and Robert Terrell, Archibald Grimke, James Weldon Johnson, and others, I learned to respect the travail of Booker T. Washington and his friends. I learned also to understand the icy reserve of DuBois, and to see how it could melt in the company of sympathetic friends like Mary Ovington, John Hope, and James Weldon Johnson. Most of all, I think I have come to appreciate DuBois, not simply as a "minority group leader," but as an historical personage bent on liberating America from the effects of racism. He has been so viciously maligned by Cold Warriors and so narrowly interpreted by students of political affairs, however, that his capacity to interpret American thinking has remained obscure. While learning from him, I hope that I have kept my debt to him in scholarly perspective.

Over the years several people have encouraged and assisted me in this undertaking. I would like to thank Professor Kenneth Stampp, who first approved this subject in truncated form as a study of the Booker T. Washington-W. E. B. DuBois controversy. His patience has provided a model for any prospective teacher, and I hope that in some measure I have met his exacting standards of scholarship. I owe debts also to Berky Nelson, Raymond Wolters, Ron Takaki, and Frances Keller, who at crucial moments were willing to listen and to read. The National Endowment for the Humanities provided a summer stipend in 1973 to assist in the research for Chapter 5 and part of Chapter 1. The *Journal of Southern History* has kindly allowed me to use material in Chapter 1 which first appeared there. I would also like to thank Mrs. James Weldon Johnson for permitting full freedom to examine the papers of her late husband, and Dr. Herbert Aptheker for allowing me to examine the correspondence between DuBois and Mary White Ovington, which at that time was in his custody. George Cunningham, a graduate student at Yale in 1973, kindly gave me a copy of *The Autobiography of an Ex-Colored Man,* and only subsequently did I come to understand its importance in the development of the Black imagination. Michael Winston of Howard University also opened the Alain Locke Papers to me prior to their cataloguing. Allison Blakely shared his knowledge of Black consuls and broader subjects, and his hospitality, on many occasions. Finally, I owe a profound debt to Michael Ames of Temple University Press. Without his encouragement and patience this project would never have been completed.

The
Resurgence
of Race

Introduction

In 1903 W. E. B. DuBois published the most influential collection of essays ever written by a Black American, *The Souls of Black Folk.* The book ranged over many social, historical, and literary topics, but its most profound theme was the exposition of a distinct Black psychology. Blacks, DuBois argued, had the same hopes and desires as other peoples, but they had been treated as strangers in their own land. Subject to enslavement rather than free migration and to stigma rather than equal opportunity, they had been "born with a veil" and perceived the world through a maze of stereotypes imposed on them by white America. His essays, DuBois hoped, would reveal the human feelings and unique achievements of Blacks and demonstrate how they confronted their inner doubts. *The Souls of Black Folk* not only reflected the influence of DuBois's education at Harvard and Berlin, but also the intensive and growing debate among Blacks over their history and destiny. America produced the first stratum of Western educated Black intellectuals who reflected on the problems of colonial control and proposed various theories and strategies to combat it. Two dominant images of the freedmen emerged from their debates. The first, suggested by former slaves like Frederick Douglass and developed by T. Thomas Fortune and Booker T. Washington, depicted the freedmen as an impoverished peasantry in need of social rehabilitation to survive the Darwinian struggle. The second, developed primarily by formally educated free Blacks like Alexander Crummell and George Washington Williams and then stated in a more radical and sophisticated way by DuBois, saw Blacks as a nascent ethnic group in need of cultural revitalization to understand themselves.

The tension between those who promoted a theory of social rehabilitation and those who emphasized cultural revitalization provides a theme for interpreting the rise and decline of Black leadership elite from the 1870s through the 1920s. In the 1870s and 1880s when the intellectual stratum was thin and the overwhelming majority of Blacks were freedmen living in the countryside, the images remained indistinct. Because the qualities of Black people were so little appreciated, the importance of a cultural Renaissance was barely recognized. Men like Crummell and Williams, who discussed Black cultural achievements, were far less influential than writers like Douglass, Fortune, and especially Booker T. Washington, who drew shrewd analogies between the conditions and needs of the freedmen and the recently freed Russian serfs. However, as Blacks gradually migrated to cities, as their literate stratum became larger and better educated to the analytic modes of social science, as the achievements of Africans and Afro-Americans were better understood, and as the doctrine of rehabilitation failed to eradicate obstacles to opportunity, the protagonists of a more distinctive and aggressive Black personality gained a wider hearing.

As the African political scientist Ali A. Mazrui has noted, "The distinctiveness of the fate of black people is that they have been the most humiliated in recent times. . . . The restoration of black dignity is almost the ultimate measure of racial equality."[1] Writers like Paul L. Dunbar, William Ferris, James Weldon Johnson, and DuBois fully felt this stigma, and while they supported efforts at rehabilitation, they searched even more for an ethic of revitalization. Through their efforts and the disparate activities of Black writers and artists, they had eclipsed the ethic of rehabilitation even before World War I. Certainly the most influential Black writers had by then come to believe that a cultural Renaissance was necessary to overcome the legacy of white racism.

Explaining how leaders emphasizing rehabilitation gave way to those promoting cultural revitalization presents the most complex problem in this study. Unlike partisan politicians, literary figures do not lose their positions after an election defeat. Nor in most cases are their ideas suddenly and finally discredited in a dramatic cataclysm. James Weldon Johnson, for example, found his important novel, *The Autobiography of an Ex-Colored Man,* had a greater vogue by the mid-1920s than when it was first published in 1912.[2] *Up From Slavery* and *The Souls of Black Folk* have been continuously reprinted since the turn of the century.

Instead, a combination of social and intellectual changes enabled cliques of leaders with distinct ideologies and interests to succeed one another. In part the problems of particular decades, like the collapse of Reconstruction governments in the 1870s, inspired men and women to suggest new approaches to social reform. Momentous events, like the trench warfare of World War I, helped erode powerful assumptions such as the moral superiority of Western civilization. In the aftermath, the tentative suggestions of a few about the virtues of Black culture could become the ideology of a multitude. In part, also, cliques of cohorts simply aged, and the ideas and events that inspired one generation had less meaning to its successors. This occurred in the 1890s when many leading politicos from the era of Reconstruction died at the same time southern Blacks were becoming disfranchised. During World War I genteel social reformers were eclipsed by young artists and political activists enthused by a new Pan-African vision. In addition, the methods of one generation, like the application of formal social theory to economic problems, were reinterpreted and put to more radical purposes by their successors. As men and women experienced such patterns of change, their efforts were given coherence by a common concern for the welfare of Black people, which they addressed in a widening debate over the meaning of Black history and destiny. Were Blacks simply a class undergoing a "natural" evolutionary process? Or were they a people with a unique psychology and culture and with a perception of life as morally appropriate as that of old stock White Americans who designated themselves "Anglo-Saxons?" Each generation of Black leaders posed the question from a different point of view, and each emphasized a different set of answers.

The people and events discussed in this book have already received much attention from journalists and scholars. The controversy between Booker T. Washington and W. E. B. DuBois particularly was evaluated by many contemporaries, white as well as Black, who felt compelled to add to the debate. In the 1930s Ralph Bunche, in a series of monographs for Gunnar Myrdal's study of race relations, discussed ideology, tactics, and leadership in great detail. Bunche however, reflecting his training as a political scientist, minimized the importance of historical continuity and emphasized the tactical differences and the immediate objectives of the individuals and organizations.[3] He did not seek an underlying ideological theme or a central debate over the nature of Black people. In the 1950s August Meier wrote numerous articles and in 1963 published an encyclopedic book on the ideology of Black Americans in what he termed the "Age of Booker T. Washington." Elliot Rudwick produced a thoroughly researched study of the political writings and activities of W. E. B. DuBois, and Emma Lou Thornbrough and Stephen Fox have written sensitive portraits of T. Thomas Fortune and William Monroe Trotter, respectively. Most recently, Louis R. Harlan has continued in this vein with a definitive biography of Booker T. Washington.[4]

All of these volumes provide invaluable guides to the thoughts and programs of Black writers and activists, but they have generally followed the theoretical formulations of Bunche. They assume that most Black spokesmen hoped ultimately for a humane integration into white society and that they disagreed primarily over the most appropriate tactics. But Bunche, writing particularly to criticize his predecessors, saw in the idea of race loyalty a retreat from modern forms of social organization rather than an authentic expression of identity and self-esteem.[5] He lapsed into a serious contradiction by criticizing Washington for his tactics but DuBois for his ideals. Uncomfortable with the parallel between Washington's materialistic social philosophy and his own, he ignored Washington's ideals and criticized his opportunistic tactics. Annoyed with DuBois for his hold over Black writers and artists, Bunche ignored his tactics and attacked his effort to use culture and tradition rather than "class interest" as the basis for political assertiveness. By doing so, Bunche denatured an ideal of racial achievement that had inspired a generation.

Meier, looking beyond Bunche's emphasis on tactics, correctly notes that most Black spokesmen utilized "self-help and racial solidarity" as a rationale to improve their social or economic condition. Yet many Black intellectuals simply did not feel fulfilled acquiescing to the prevalent dogma of white cultural superiority. Like the freedmen studied by Nell Painter and Edwin Redkey,[6] writers like Crummell, Dunbar, and DuBois needed a moral alternative to "white society." Here they disagreed with Washington, Kelly Miller, and others, who envisioned Black Americans as pupils of the more advanced "Anglo-Saxons." They disagreed not merely over tactics for social integration but over the meaning of Black history and destiny. The depths of this disagreement led writers like DuBois and Ferris to look with increasing care into African and Afro-American history and led DuBois, Johnson, and others to look more analytically into the psychology of Black Americans.[7]

The importance of culture and the control of its definition as a political factor in Black history was recognized by Harold Cruse in his massive study, *The Crisis of the Negro Intellectual,* published in 1967, However opinionated, unevenly researched, and argumentative Cruse's analysis may be, it demonstrates conclusively the importance of DuBois's emphasis on cultural achievements for allowing a group to understand itself. Yet Cruse also notes the significance of Booker T. Washington, because he too recognized the masses had to organize apart from whites.[8] Cruse argues that where the successors of DuBois and Washington failed to define their own cultural objectives and to create their own institutions, they failed to create a Black personality that could countervail against the pervasive effects of racism. This study reinforces Cruse's assertion that both Washington and DuBois had strong—though very different—notions of Black nationality. It also recognized the irony that, while he evaluated Black literature and art by utilitarian criteria, his recognition as an educator revived Black morale and contributed to Black national consciousness. By examining the half century preceding that which Cruse has taken for his province, this study hopes to explain the debate from which a sense of Black ethnic identification emerged. It indicates how Black writers defined and debated concepts like race, culture, nonpartisanship, and reform—and how their use of those terms helped shape their changing leadership. It strives to explain how Black spokesmen responded to developments within their communities and to more general changes in leadership throughout the country. Without a half-century of debate over Black character and destiny to rest on, the writers of the 1920s would have had a much harder time convincing themselves that Black people were a vital force.

Although this study focuses on the ideas and organizations created by Black writers, it is not intellectual history in a classic sense. Its primary tools are drawn from social history rather than literary criticism. Rather than exploring the literary inspiration for the writings of men like Crummell, Charles Chestnutt, DuBois, Ferris, and others, it emphasizes how their ideas were related to one another through a debate over the meaning of Black America. Fine studies of the literary contributions of DuBois, Chestnutt, Crummell, and Johnson have begun to set these authors into their Anglo-American context.[9] This study rests in part on the literary judgments of those works, though occasionally it disagrees with the conclusions expressed by other authors. By examining intensively the correspondence as well as the publications of participants, this study relates the development of their ideas to the fate of their social circles. The book, then, focuses on that ground where social and intellectual history merge. It is primarily an analysis of the rise, interrelationship, and passage of the elite, who were tied together in part by a common ancestry but even more by a common desire to interpret the significance of that ancestry to their contemporaries. Collectively, they learned to defend the moral integrity of "the race" while simultaneously preparing it to survive in a modernized and interdependent world.

1 | Free Men, Freedmen, and Race: Black Social Theory in the Gilded Age

In the years after the American Civil War, Black Americans experienced a form of reunion. Some who had been living in the North as free people and the great majority who had been living as slaves or free Negroes in the South came together to help rebuild the southern social and political order.[1] Out of the meeting of the educated urban strata and the rural freedmen, however, came a disheartening recognition. Political repression, punctuated by frequent violence and pervasive economic exploitation, deprived rural freedmen of their local leadership and of the opportunity to become independent farmers. As Nell I. Painter, William W. Rogers, and Robert D. Ward described, in Louisiana, Mississippi, Alabama, and elsewhere. rural leaders were murdered or sought refuge in cities, while the crop-lien and convict-lease systems and even peonage reduced the freedmen to new terms of servitude.[2]

Educated urban Blacks, however, faced more subtle and perplexing obstacles in their effort to assist the freedmen. They observed substantial differences between their own norms of behavior and those of the freedmen, and they faced also a barrage of white propaganda that denied that the freedmen had the capacity to become citizens. Cultivated free Negroes from antebellum New Orleans and Charleston, for example, began to identify with the freedmen only when northern armies imposed

9

restrictions on all Blacks with little reference to prewar social distinctions.[3] In addition, as the Reconstruction governments were accused of corruption, the freedmen quite logically were depicted by southern whites as politically irresponsible.[4] The most important novel of Reconstruction, Albion Tourgee's *A Fool's Errand,* though written by a northerner who decried the vigilantism of southern whites, also portrayed the freedmen as too submissive and ignorant to serve as citizens. Political activists like Frederick Douglass denied the allegation of inherent Black inferiority and a sensitive young man, Charles Chestnutt, questioned the capacity of Tourgee to empathize with the freedmen.[5] But free Blacks were left with the image of the freedmen as persons deemed unfit for participation as equals in a modern society.

Furthermore, the intellectual atmosphere within which Black spokesmen had to work had become less friendly. While many white abolitionists and their children retained a strong interest in educational and other rehabilitory work in the South, theories of class and race competition had replaced a belief in Christian cooperation in educated white circles. Against the assumption of social conflict and often shorn of the protection of clerical good will, Black writers had to consider carefully how the freedmen might be assisted to modernize. Virtually all Black authors in the late nineteenth century saw the freedmen as a primitive social class in need of rehabilitation and agreed that some form of education must provide them with the skills to compete with the more aggressive whites.[6] August Meier has argued that virtually all Black activists during these years were sufficiently disillusioned with Reconstruction to emphasize community self-help and racial solidarity.[7] But the purpose of such community efforts and the ideals that should provide the basis for group cohesion were seriously debated. Some writers, particularly those with a secular education like T. Thomas Fortune and John Stephens Durham, emphasized the social disabilities of the freedmen and drew analogies between them and other recently emancipated classes. For them the proper application of technical training would transform the freedmen into modern farmers and craftsmen. Writers with a clerical education and missionary vocation, like George Washington Williams and Alexander Crummell, however, held a more grandiose image of Black destiny. For them the freedmen were a distinctive people with a spirit, a history, and loyalties that must be utilized to promote full psychological as well as material rehabilitation. Writers like Williams and Crummel also departed from evangelical emigrationists like Benjamin "Pap" Singleton and African Methodist Episcopal Church bishop, Henry McNeil Turner, who felt that physical separation from whites would be a necessary and sufficient guarantee of Black prosperity.[8] Instead they saw revitalized Blacks and more humane whites as vital partners in the creation of a more cosmopolitan world culture. Out of their disagreements with secularists like Fortune and Durham emerged by the late 1890s more complex and philosophical alternatives to guide spokesmen who desired a more unified Black America.

Reconstruction, Exodus, and a Meaning in Defeat

Reconstruction was perhaps the most frustrating era for Black Americans because the promise of freedom was thwarted by insufficient economic and political power and by an ambivalent attitude of free men toward freedmen. In New Orleans in 1865 the Creoles briefly organized the Freedmen's Aid Association to make loans to Black farmers, and in South Carolina a Land Commission acquired several thousand acres to sell exclusively to the freedmen. But even at the height of their influence in South Carolina and Louisiana, free Negroes could not redistribute land in large amounts or make credits readily available. In states like Tennessee and Alabama, where Blacks had far less political representation, the prospects for economic reform were even less. Urban Blacks might retain the vote, but as a small minority of the Black population and of the active electorate they could do little to relieve rural exploitation. Most of the economic pressures could only have been relieved by the federal government, which refused to confiscate land or provide freedmen safe access to homestead sites. The government also refused to increase the money supply to ease rural credits and even failed in most instances to protect the freedmen during federal elections.[9]

While Black spokesmen were stymied by political opposition, their own conception of political economy and their view of the freedmen limited their ability to deal imaginatively with local problems. Some owned substantial property and may have feared government precedents for confiscating and redistributing other men's land. T. T. Allain of Louisiana and Blanche K. Bruce and Isaiah Montgomery of Mississippi owned large plantations, and they insisted that the freedmen, with encouragement and fair treatment, should earn the money to buy their own land.[10] Furthermore, many Black political spokesmen defended the gold standard, protective tariff, and other "tight money" policies of the Republican party as strongly as did secretaries of the treasury, Hugh McCulloch or John Sherman. John M. Langston, who served in Congress from 1889 to 1891 from a district that had been agitated for ten years by the so-called Readjuster Movement, listed as his most illustrious colleagues not agrarian reformers but Congressmen Joseph Cannon, Thomas B. Reed, William McKinley, and Henry Cabot Lodge, all staunch defenders of Republican economic orthodoxy.[11]

Black spokesmen, moreover, felt clear class distinctions between themselves and the freedmen. Whether nurtured in Presbyterian and Methodist churches in the North or the Catholic church in New Orleans, many free Negroes had promoted moral reform and temperance before the War and created mutual benefit and literary societies during Reconstruction.[12] Narratives written by fugitive slaves in the twenty years before the War emphasized how slavery had degraded the victims and left them ill-prepared to exercise social responsibility, and writers from Frederick Douglass to Martin Delany found in Christianity and middle-class social decorum the highest expression of moral rectitude.[13] Many political leaders in Louisiana, South Carolina, Mississippi, and Alabama had either been born free or manumitted by a white father and had received an education in the North. Even those born as slaves but living in cities in the South became absorbed in urban problems like school desegregation or access to public facilities.[14] They defended the civil and political rights of the freedmen, but they formed very different social circles.

Educated Blacks in addition, encountered a large body of literature that pictured both their African ancestors and the freedmen as barbarians. The schools they attended, the religion they practiced, and the popular opinions they encountered agreed that civilization and advanced institutions had reached their highest expression in western Europe and the United States.[15] To some extent free Blacks, supported by white abolitionists, had countered the assertion that Africa had made no contribution to world civilization. They often did so, however, within the context of a *romantic racialism,* which patronizingly contrasted the African's "feminine" virtue of aesthetic imagination with the West's "masculine" achievements in rational thought and the technological mastery of power. In a world that had not yet developed the analytic mode of cultural relativism, educated Blacks stressed the peculiar virtues of African culture to assert their own capacity to participate fully in Anglo-America's "advanced civilization."[16]

Many Blacks who went South after 1862 to educate the freedmen combined a sense of noblesse oblige with wonder at the peculiar habits and beliefs they observed. The Reverend Henry M. Turner of Washington admonished his congregation for discussing African history merely to display their knowledge and urged them instead to assist the freedmen, "the race that we are inseparably identified with." The Reverend James Lynch, first missionary of the African Methodist Episcopal Church to the freedmen of South Carolina and later a leading Republican politican in Mississippi, exclaimed, "Oh, this work among the freedmen has a charm about it. . . . It has its difficulties, but they must melt away before a cool head and a warm heart." Charlotte Forten, the descendant of an elite Philadelphia mulatto family who became a teacher at Port Royal, South Carolina, in 1862 and who came to be revered by the freedmen, left a journal that combined the romantic fascination of the missionary for native customs with genuine affection for the individuals and the group that represented part of her ancestry.

She was amazed by the remarkable musical talents of "the Negroes," their "colorful headdresses," their swaying motions while singing and praying, and she was amused by their rudimentary comprehension of marriage sacraments. They displayed a "child-like" faith toward their teachers, she observed. "Had a nice long talk with some of the people this morning," she wrote, and "the more one knows of them the more interested one becomes in them."[17]

Although sensitive women like Miss Forten might move beyond romantic racialism to appreciate the freedmen, in part at least, as a unique cultural group, political activists like her brother-in-law Archibald Grimke, Douglass, and Langston judged the freedmen by standards similar to those employed by liberal white politcans like Carl Schurz and journalists like E. L. Godkin. They admitted that the freedmen had never absorbed the work habits and sense of civic responsibility necessary to act as citizens. Douglass, on a trip to Haiti in 1871, was appalled by the lack of progress toward economic modernization and democratic self-government that he observed. But while Godkin and Schurz denigrated the capacity of the freedmen for self-government, Black writers asserted that the freedmen had simply not received adequate incentives. To prove it, Langston in 1891 introduced a constitutional amendment to limit suffrage to those literate in English, and Isaiah Montgomery wrote that the freedmen needed proper guidance to acquire an education and efficient work habits.[18]

Black writers had become particularly anxious over the future of the race because white social critics had become so receptive to new European theories that depicted society as the product of perpetual conflict. In the 1840s and 1850s, when abolitionists had dramatized the retrogressive influences of slavery, American writers had emphasized the uniquely expansive character of American society and contrasted the nation's other institutions favorably with the decadence and class conflicts of contemporary Europe. During the Civil War, however, many intellectuals—chilled by the gruesome fratricide—rejected resounding ideals and concentrated instead on specific programs to assist the wounded, to educate the freedmen, or to improve the conditions of labor. By the 1870s, with slavery eradicated by a war that had sapped the nation's moral energy and with scandals illuminating the imperfections in American government, intellectuals were awakened to the rising conflicts between classes and nations. Searching for synthetic ideas that might explain the bitter struggles they observed, they turned to England, France, and Germany.[19] Writers like Herbert Spencer, August Comte, and popularizers of Hegel emphasized that nations would either undergo competitive social evolution, would fall to class warfare, or, if a farsighted but conservative elite retained control, could be managed scientifically.

While some scholars have warned that the popularity of social Darwinism in America in the late nineteenth century has been exaggerated,[20] it profoundly affected Black writers. However much Darwinian theory emphasized the gradual impact of environment on physical types, it nevertheless arranged species along a hierarchy that provided a new rationale for racial theorists. Although white writers discussed the development of societies from lower and simpler to higher and more complex stages, they actually traced the historical competition between races. Societies were merely the forms that races assumed during their evolution, and invariably the African peoples and their dispersed descendents were placed at the bottom of the evolutionary scale. As the Black educator William Crogman noted, white writers "persist in holding us up to this country as that abnormal child which never grows, which never can grow, and which the American people must nurse for all time."[21]

Most evolutionary theories further implied that the different races could not coexist in a single society unless the stronger dominated the weaker. Whites attributed the achievements of a Douglass or a Langston to their white ancestors and argued that without the protection of slavery "pure" Negroes would have died out. The census of 1870,which reported very small Negro population increase for the 1860s, was used to confirm the theory that Blacks lacked the capacity to survive as free men in open competition with whites. The "exodus of 1879," however, suggested that the freedmen could resist the remorseless "laws" that dictated their subordination and respond as a "normal" population would to economic and political repression. When the 1880 census revealed that the Black population had increased by 34 percent during the decade, the competence of the 1870 census and the theory of race subordination that it had allegedly proved were further challenged. As one social statistician was forced to report on Black population growth, "As it has taken place under freedom, it contravenes all the prejudices and upsets most of the philosophies. One would naturally have supposed from the reported bad treatment . . . and the preordained tendency of an inferior people to decline in the presence of a superior, that the colored race would be dying out."[22]

That the freedmen were surviving despite the trauma of enslavement and the terror of Reconstruction came as no surprise to Douglass and other Black intellectuals. They too believed in social evolution, but they assumed that the freedmen had unique adaptive capacities and that free Negroes had unique leadership skills. Alexander Crummell, at the time a clergyman in the District of Columbia, explained the unique pressures on Black Americans most clearly in a letter to his ministerial colleague J. W. Cromwell in 1877. Black Americans, he said, had to be organized to supercede the usual process that societies underwent after the collapse of slavery. "The history of mankind shows generally that after slavery comes a state of feudality. *That,* without doubt, is the aim of the leaders of society at the South. It is a natural desire, and we must not be angered at it. On the other hand, our aim should be for once to rob history of this consecutive link, and by organization, money, power and culture to lift our people up to the plane of ordinary social, moral and political life."[23] The social and moral basis upon which such a rehabilitation should rest, however, perplexed Black authors from the 1880s through the turn of the century.

While political experience and respectable opinion conspired to reinforce the primitive image of the freedmen, writers like Douglass and Langston did express subtle differences. From their varying emphases eventually emerged quite distinct perspectives on the strengths and deficiencies of the freedmen. The different attitudes can best be perceived in the conflicting evaluations of the highly publicized exodus of 1879, during which over four thousand Blacks moved in the late spring and early summer from Louisiana and Mississippi to the plains of Kansas. As Nell Painter has recently shown, the number of "Exodusters" has been greatly exaggerated. Their numbers were small compared with the decade-long migration of Blacks to Kansas from Kentucky, Tennessee, and elsewhere, and their motives were mixed. While many felt themselves on a pilgrimage of escape from the vigilantism of southern whites, others calculated their opportunities for economic improvement and brought some capital to buy small parcels or to settle in one of the small Black colonies that had been started during the decade.[24] Many Black spokesmen, however, saw in the migration the portent of major changes in race relations, as the freedmen seemed for the first time to be exercising initiative. When several thousand suddenly needed temporary financial assistance, emigrant aid societies were established in Baltimore, Philadelphia, and other eastern cities, and men like Langston and Douglass were asked for their views on the advisability of the exodus.

In responding to requests for their opinions, Black spokesmen not only discussed the practical consequences of the migration, but because of its allegedly momentous precedent, they expressed also their basic assumptions about the character and predilections of the freedmen. Three different views, all related but each with different social and political consequences, emerged. The freedmen were seen as citizens in search of their rights, as ignorant peasants in need of guidance, or as romantic evangels in search of a promised land. Each of these views foreshadowed a more carefully developed image of the freedmen that would be drawn after 1880, and each would also provide the ideological basis for major camps of Black spokesmen in the struggle for race leadership.

The view of the freedmen as citizens struggling for their rights was most forcefully expressed by men like Richard Greener and John M. Langston, who were themselves enmeshed in Republican party politics but who had little or no experience with slavery. Greener had been born and raised in New England, where he became Harvard's first Negro graduate, while Langston, though born in Virginia, the son of a plantation owner, had been raised in Ohio and graduated from Oberlin.[25] In a speech before the Emigrant Aid Society of Washington, D.C., in October, 1879, Langston combined a sophisticated analysis of the oppressive economic and political situation under which the freedmen suffered with a summary of what they as citizens had the right to expect in a free society.

For Langston the freedmen were a class similar in condition to the recently emancipated serfs of Russia and the freedmen of the Caribbean. After emancipation, he noted, such people had always suffered from the social and economic consequences of the slave regime. Not only did they lack land and capital, but they remained subordinate to the old master class, which assumed that the freedmen lacked the capacity to be anything but agricultural labor. Drawing very shrewd cross-cultural comparisons, Langston noted that the only precedents for freedmen to escape the grip of psychological and economic servitude occurred when they left the area of their enslavement. In Barbados, for example, Blacks still served at very low wages on the estates, but in Trinidad, where they had moved away from the estates to establish their own small farms, their social and economic condition was much improved. Langston did not expect the much larger American Black population to move great distances. But migrations similar to the exodus to Kansas would not only expose the freedmen to greater opportunities but would require the southern landlords to deal more respectfully with those who remained. Congress, he argued, had guaranteed freedom, civil rights, and the ballot to the freedmen, but "practical freedom" only came through migration from the locale of enslavement to an area where men, in the full vigor of their citizenship, could establish new institutions that would receive full protection under the law.[26]

Langston, like Greener in a similar talk to the American Social Science Association, expressed a common American faith in the virtues of frontier democracy and political agitation. He assumed that the freedmen, once separated from the power of the master class and inspired by the land in which John Brown had struck a blow against slavery, would develop new and self-confident personalities. Indeed, many Black families did thrive in Kansas, and a few were elected to public office in the 1880s.[27] But Langston had also noted "that centuries of enslavement imbed in the very soul of the enslaved the spirit of servility and dependence,"[28] and his discussion of Trinidad had conveniently neglected the unique social and economic changes, especially the importation of thousands of Indian laborers that enabled the freedmen there to improve their social status.

Frederick Douglass, who strongly opposed the exodus, seized precisely on these points. Though a leader of northern Black opinion since the 1840s, he had been raised in slavery and felt he understood the strengths and weaknesses of the freedmen all too well. Furthermore, as the victim of antebellum mob violence from northern working men and a frequent speaker at integrated labor conventions, he felt he understood the white comrades with whom the migrating freedmen would have to live in the North. Where Langston emphasized the rights of the freedmen as citizens, Douglass saw them primarily as a distinctive social type, "essentially southern men," who were as yet unprepared to compete with free white labor. Where Langston assumed the freedmen would soon slough off the effects of enslavement, Douglass felt that their "poverty, ignorance, and other repulsive incidents inherited from their former condition as slaves" would arouse new opposition among white workers and farmers among whom they would settle. Douglass, like Langston, argued that the freedmen had constitutional guarantees to full protection from the federal government, and he too discussed the economic exploitation and political terror to which they were subjected. But he believed that the exploitation would be temporary and that the freedmen must ultimately depend on their own social development to attain security. Indeed, he cited the acreage they had acquired, the farms they owned, and their familiarity with southern soil and production methods to demonstrate that they could succeed best in their "native land," the South.[29] While Nell Painter repeatedly asserts that Douglass was virtually unique among prominent Blacks in condemning the exodus,[30] she ignores his reasoning, especially his hard-bitten resignation based on his own experiences with racial discrimination and violence in the North. Indeed, while Langston's assertion of the rights of the freedmen would continue to appeal to Black politicians, Douglass's assessment of their social character and of northern conditions coincided with that of Black educators like Booker T. Washington and community organizers like Isaiah Montgomery, Charles Banks, and others.[31]

The third view of the migration dramatized its folk character by taking literally the biblical image of persecution and exodus. It became the most popular because it appealed to the romantic racialism that still adhered to the freedmen in the eyes of much of the sympathetic northern public. Black spokesmen with some clerical training like George Washington Williams, who visited Kansas in 1880 and 1881 were impressed by the spirit and achievements of the migrants. Williams's assessment of the economic and political causes of the exodus coincided with that of Langston and Douglass, and his cataloging of the progress the freedmen were making contradicted Douglass's dire warnings. But Williams contrasted the pathetic state of the migrants with their subsequent stability primarily to demonstrate their dogged religious nature. "The Exodus," he wrote, "was not a political movement. It was not inspired from without. It was but the natural operation of a divine law that moved whole communities of Negroes to turn their faces toward the setting sun."[32] Unlike the politically minded Langston, who drew analogies with classes in similar sociological situations, Williams compared the flight of the freedmen to other culturally distinctive people who had sought freedom in a righteous cause. In addition to the familiar typological reference to the Israelites, Williams also made comparisons with the more exotic Kalmuck Tartars, who had fled from the czars to China in 1770; the Huguenots, who had been driven from France; and the Acadians, who had been forced to flee Novia Scotia. The pathos of the Exodusters, he argued, was comparable, as were their achievements, which had been possible through the assistance of emigrant aid societies and white farmers among whom they settled. While Williams seemed merely to confirm Langston's justification of the exodus, his emphasis on its folk nature and the need of the migrants for Christian nurture reiterated the view that Black history would not merely chronicle secular events but would demonstrate higher moral purpose. When set into Williams's wider interpretation of Black history, his statements on the exodus contributed to a growing body of literature that related the distinctive characteristics of Blacks to a sense of their racial destiny.

Perhaps the attraction of the exodus to so many Black writers lay in the apparent willingness of the freedmen to challenge finally the pejorative stereotypes that had been spread about them and to begin to shape their destiny. Most Black writers until then had seen two divergent lines of racial development. The first traced the reduction of the majority to servility through the brutal methods that had been vividly described in slave narratives. The other line traced the rise of a fortunate few, who, through extraordinary initiative had made unique contributions to the nation as military or abolitionist heroes or who had built institutions to help stabilize free Black communities. The concurrent development of a free and slave group suggested, furthermore, that the freedmen needed a specially trained elite to help them replace the habits of slavery with the assertiveness of free men. As Langston noted, the freedmen had needed assistance from "the free colored class, which emancipated first and suitably prepared by its experience therefor, wrought now in example and effort to elevate and direct the thoughts and purposes of millions just passing the gateway of liberty."[33] The exodus demonstrated a religious faith and moral assertiveness which might provide the basis for social modernization. But *how* the freedmen were to be motivated and unified provided the basis for a discussion of their destiny.

The Material Meaning: The Freedmen as a Peasantry

Perhaps only within the artificial constructs of intellectual history can one say that a debate over the character and destiny of the freedmen began in response to the exodus of 1879. The exodus did call forth a set of conflicting interpretations, but it was rather a symptom of the collapse of the hopes that Reconstruction had borne. In its aftermath in the 1880s Black writers produced major works of history and political economy to try to deal more philosophically with the future of the freedmen. In many cases their histories and political and theological tracts were the first work of that type by a Black writer, and pride in the achievement often distracted commentators from the conflicting views of the freedmen that were emerging. W. E. B. DuBois, writing in 1913, noted that after the political turmoil of the 1870s, "in the eighties there are signs of unrest and different conflicting streams of thought."[34] But even he, the leading antagonist of his generation in a highly publicized debate over the future of Black Americans, distinguished for the 1880s only innovations in literary form. Nevertheless, while authors reached a consensus on the disabilities of the freedmen, they suggested different bases for binding the various strata of Black Americans to each other.

The underlying issue for Black writers in the 1880s and 1890s was not how skills might be purveyed to the freedmen, but how Blacks might understand themselves. As writers like Williams, Grimke, Durham, and Fortune developed as self-conscious "scientific" historians and political economists, they examined the causes of Black disabilities and class stratification in greater detail. They could no longer be content with drawing analogies, whether spiritual or sociological, with other peoples, but they examined instead more concrete relationships between Afro-American social classes, as well as Black relations with various white social classes and with Africans. The tools of scientific history,[35] the precise comparison of sociological variables, and the complex arguments of antimonopoly radicals were now applied to the history and current condition of Black Americans. Black writers, then, did not simply react to political conditions but developed historical and theoretical bases for directing the future of the race. While administrative heads of institutions like the young Booker T. Washington might pragmatically adjust to local political pressures, the authors of major books tried, with the scholarly tools then available, to identify the historical role of Black Americans and their appropriate bases of loyalty.

The most comprehensive and authoritative study of Black history to appear before World War I was George Washington William's *A History of the Negro Race in America from 1619 to 1880,* which was published in two volumes in 1883. Williams followed it with a detailed study of Black participation in the Civil War entitled *A History of the Negro Troops in the War of the Rebellion, 1861-1865.* The emphasis on military, legal, abolitionist, and Black church history reflected Williams's experience as a young soldier in the war and his postwar education as a minister and lawyer. But he kept before him an ultimate purpose—to demonstrate the capacity of Black people to contribute to a cosmopolitan world culture. As he confided to Henry Wadsworth Longfellow, he wished to assist the freedmen "to rise from their animal nature to live in the higher branches of manhood."[36] Williams was also quite consciously trying to write an accurate account that would conform to the latest canons of scholarly research. He visited archives throughout the country, interviewed survivors of major events, and corresponded with numerous informants. His appendices were filled with statistical and other information about Negro government employees, elected officials, colleges and other schools, bibliographies of books by Negro authors, letters of historical interest, and data on Black units that fought in the Civil War. Williams clearly bedecked the works with the scholarly paraphernalia needed to demonstrate that Black authors could write scientific, objective history.[37]

Not only the data but also the structure of Williams's histories departed radically from that of prior Black writers like William Nell, William Wells Brown, and his contemporary, William Simmons. They became models for Black histories that would be written for the next half-century. Prior scholars had focused primarily on individuals or events, but Williams sought to give form and purpose to the story of a race as it moved from provincial isolation to modernization and self-confident participation in world politics. He was not so much concerned with demonstrating the ability of Black individuals to succeed in a modern setting as to demonstrate how Blacks as a people had a distinctive role in the evolution of a more humane world civilization. Institutions such as slavery, abolitionist societies, and churches provided the social vehicles through which people expressed the instinctual sentiments of their respective races. The interaction between their institutions, however malevolently or violently expressed at times, would lead to a greater level of understanding between the peoples and a higher level of civilization. To say, as did Benjamin Brawley nearly forty years later, that Williams's "study of the legal aspects [of slavery] is not likely soon to be superceded" is to miss the architectonic he provided for Black history. It would be like commending Frederick Jackson Turner for his contributions to Western history, when in fact he provided both method and interpretative myth for understanding America as a developing society.[38]

In his preface, Williams noted that he included material on early African societies to satisfy the curiosity of young Blacks about the "antiquity," that is, the contributions, of Africans to ancient civilizations. Such interest, of course, sprang from the malignant stereotypes about Africans and their descendants as persons fit only for subjugation. If Africans, however, had organized their own kingdoms and contributed to Egyptian, Greek, and Roman societies, they had not only demonstrated independent cultural capacities but had also helped shape Western civilization. By combining stories of African achievements with detailed accounts of the slave codes in the colonies, the struggle for emancipation, and success in building Black churches, founding schools, and forming military companies to save the Union and to assist in Western expansion, Williams achieved two larger purposes.

First he demonstrated how slavery, through its uneven institutional and legal accretion, comprised an abnormal rather than an appropriate condition for Africans. In the various colonies, it had been defined to fit the shifting economic interests of the slave-holding classes. For Blacks slavery had not shaped an era of paternal guidance, but had rather despoiled them of their noble African social heritage. In his study of Black troops he argued that the slave "was sedulously kept in ignorance from the first, until ignorance had almost become a second nature to him. He was reduced to a machine. Calm and apparent contentment followed resistance and unrest." By contrast, the minority of Blacks who had lived in states that had abolished slavery, like Massachusetts, New York, and Pennsylvania, had contributed to the intellectual as well as the material development of their societies, just as Africans had contributed to the ancient Mediterranean civilizations.[39]

Second, Williams demonstrated how Blacks quickly came to understand the moral basis of American society, as measured both by its economic growth and the struggle against slavery. Both were part of the nation's effort to provide equal opportunity for all of its citizens, to allow industrial productivity and Christianity to bring material and spiritual comfort to mankind. If the purpose of America was to expand the meaning of freedom for mankind, then the purpose of Blacks in America was to call the nation's attention to the remnants of unfreedom within its borders and to lead in its eradication.[40]

The only flaw in Williams's story of progress remained the freedmen. In an analysis very similar to that of Tourgee, Williams concluded that efforts to reorganize the social order in the South could not succeed until the freedmen had undergone a psychological revitalization as well as a social transformation. Although Williams had observed Black troops in the West, many of whom had been recruited from the freedmen, behaving as brave soldiers, those freedmen who remained in the South generally lacked the initiative to function as citizens. The freedmen not only lacked individual intelligence and self-confidence, but they seemed to lack a collective purpose. The freedmen were hardly responsible for their deficiencies, because they had first been reduced to servility, then pressured by northern Republicans and southern Democrats without federal or state programs to increase their understanding of political issues. Nevertheless, Williams concluded, the freedmen had to acquire common schooling, land, and a stable family life before they could expect to participate in government. "The Negro will return to politics when he is qualified to govern." Williams concluded. "Than as taxpayer as well as tax gatherer, reading the ballot and choosing his own candidates, he will be equal to all the exigencies of American citizenship."[41]

Nevertheless, against his larger interpretation of Black history, Williams's assessment of the freedmen should not be taken as a condemnation nor as a capitulation to southern white opinion. He condemned contemporary whites as much for their indifference to the needs of the freedmen as he did their parents for having enslaved the original Africans. Instead, Williams saw in the freedmen the necessary field for Black evangelism. His chapters on the African Methodist Episcopal and the Baptist churches described their growth since the war and emphasized their capacity to bring enlightenment to the freedmen. He foresaw a reunion of freedmen, Africans, and educated Afro-Americans so that the race as an enlightened whole might make its distinctive contribution to mankind. As Nell Painter has recently reminded us, colonization carried no stigma in Europe and America in the late nineteenth century. At the end of the decade, still inspired by the notion that Black people had a special example of freedom to bring to the world, he sailed to Africa to preach the gospel in the Congo. There, unfortunately, he contracted a tropical disease and died a comparatively young man in 1890.[42]

In retrospect Williams's massive work seems a strange amalgam combining a mass of underinterpreted statistical data; an unbalanced, excessively legalistic treatment of slavery; a crude attempt to integrate heroic figures with general social patterns; and an extremely idiosyncratic treatment of various Black religious denominations. By failing to deal with slavery as a social institution, he was unable to identify the sources of cohesion among the rural freedmen, the capacity of the extended family and neighborhood networks to provide moral support, and the ability of local leaders to prepare for a Kansas exodus or the organization of a separate town.[43] However, once we allow for Williams's own success as a Christian soldier, his training as a lawyer rather than a sociologist, and his hurried accumulation of sources, we can account for his unbalanced presentation of data, his serious omissions, and his optimistic historical philosophy. His limited interest in the social life of the freedmen and his extensive treatment of white politics in the abolitionist movement and elsewhere, however, should not be confused with a belief in Black assimilation. Williams was neither a twentieth-century integrationist nor a cultural pluralist, but a nineteenth-century evangel with the experience, the energy, and vision to shape a Black history through its full extent as an element in the moral growth of Western civilization. He believed that while personal decorum should be shaped to one standard of integrity through Christian nurture, Blacks as a people with a distinctive history would have a unique contribution to make to the progress of Western society. He encouraged separate Black churches, as an expression of the spirit of Black life to which the brutalized freedmen would have to be reeducated. Indeed, the home mission of the Black churches should focus on the freedmen, just as the ultimate mission of Black America would be the evangelization of Africa. In his zeal for Black salvation, which he saw as a part of the transformation of all mortal life, he was prone to overlook the social strengths of the freedmen that were born through slavery and to exaggerate their weaknesses. But by setting them into the larger context of Black history he could present them as the victims of white exploitation, who would soon rise to an even higher moral state than had their African ancestors.

The image of the freedmen conveyed by Williams was largely reiterated in the early 1890s by Archibald Grimke in his biographies of William Lloyd Garrison and Charles Sumner. The studies were recognized quickly as major achievements in Black literature and added to Grimke's stature as a leading Black political spokesman. Unlike Williams, Grimke did not seek to analyze the institution of slavery or to recount the achievements of Black individuals. Instead, he glorified the abolitionist movement, particularly the "immediatist" leaders in Boston, whose rectitude illustrated for him the same moral force as did the rise of the Black churches for Williams. His volumes differed from those written by white New Englanders primarily because he emphasized the relationship between abolitionists and free Negroes, whose complete social equality and full civil rights both Garrison and Sumner considered an intergral part of the antislavery crusade. But because in his respected studies and in his many pamphlets published after 1900 he described the freedmen and prescribed means for resolving tension in the South, he added both authority to Williams's more detailed presentation and also variation to the proposed programs for social reform.[44]

Grimke received a liberal Harvard education and practiced law in Boston, and as S. P. Fullinwider has noted, he, like so many New England transcendentalists, believed that history progressed through a struggle between spiritual and material forces. Individuals and groups, however, were neither inherently nor absolutely good or evil. Human nature was grounded in "instinct," but individuals had the capacity to choose their fate. They might behave nobly or basely depending on whether they could subordinate their instincts for immediate gratification to their rational understanding of the long-term virtues of a just society. The antislavery crusade, for example—for Grimke as for Williams—constituted America's contribution to the international triumph of moral ideals. But as a social movement that expressed an enlightened spirit it drew to it persons with mixed interests. Grimke harbored no illusions about the motives of most northerners for supporting abolitionism, and he did not attribute to them a moral superiority to southerners. They came initially to oppose slavery, he believed, because they feared that anti-abolitionist mobs posed a threat to property. They had little sympathy for slaves, but opposed a labor system that threatened their own liberties. Nevertheless, Garrison, Sumner, and even Abraham Lincoln represented to Grimke a divine force working to promote the triumph of progressive ideals. The society for which they spoke rested on relations between labor and capital that offered workers greater opportunities than any in history. Indeed, to illustrate the existence of an ethical reserve in the northern public mind and to demonstrate the continuing influence of teleological thinking, he noted that many northerners believed that Preston Brooks, the South Carolina congressman who had caned Sumner and died shortly thereafter of a painful illness, had been the victim of divine retribution.[45]

Grimke's ethical and psychological assessment of abolitionism carried over to his analysis of the freedmen. Like Williams he noted in several places how slavery had brutalized intelligent Africans and had spawned race prejudice upon which the southern caste system then rested. But he saw the freedmen primarily as an integral component of a degraded southern society rather than as incipient members of an awakening and unified race. Terms like *African,* when applied by Sumner to free Blacks, seem to have denoted to Grimke only a remote sense of ancestry. Like Williams he assumed that education and religious instruction would improve living conditions, but more like Douglass he felt that men were shaped and derived a sense of destiny from the land in which they were raised. They must depend on an enlightened public opinion in their particular locales to legislate and enforce equal protection of the laws for all citizens. Change in the South, he argued at the conclusion of his study of Garrison, would not come through the imposition of federal power but only through the gradual social rehabilitation of the freedmen. "Genuine reconstruction of the South and the ultimate solution of the southern problem," he wrote, "had, in accordance with social law, to proceed from within, from the South itself, not . . . from Washington."[46]

While reinforcing Williams's image of the freedmen, Grimke represented primarily a synthesis of the views of Langston and Douglass. Despite his transcendental faith in human idealism, he did not idealize Negroes as a race nor assume that an international Black evangelism must provide the basis for racial enlightenment. Black Americans seemed to him a disconnected aggregate of diverse classes who shared some parentage and who should share civil and political rights with their white fellow citizens. Like Douglass he saw the freedmen as a class of southerners who were distinctive primarily because they had suffered enslavement. Like Langston he insisted that the state protect all citizens equally. He argued, finally, that enlightened citizens must forthrightly call attention to injustice and create a more honest and effective public opinion.

Williams in an evangelical context and Grimke in a moralistic political vein had emphasized the disabilities of the freedmen and prescribed methods for their revitalization. But several of their Black contemporaries, particularly T. Thomas Fortune and

John S. Durham, found in racial history a parochial view of the freedmen and in evangelism an insubstantial guide to action. For them, furthermore, moral suasion and political agitation were irrelevant to southern conditions because the region was so thoroughly backward that economic and social rehabilitation must precede fruitful political and spiritual revival. Fortune and Durham were neither conservative in their political thought nor unduly accomodationist in their relations with whites. Instead, they tried to analyze the needs and interests of the freedmen within the context of radical political economy and modern social science. For them southern history turned not only on race conflict as shaped by the master-slave relationship but also on a continuing class struggle for which slavery had provided a lengthy and formative, but nevertheless transient, initial phase. Poor whites constituted the bulk of southern society before, during, and after slavery, and in their presence, Durham and Fortune agreed, Black Americans would work out their destiny.[47] With the abolition of slavery the full effects of the narrow, extractive southern economy could be seen clearly. To those effects rather than to a racial or political crusade, Blacks, as members of a rural proletariat, must turn their full energies.

Fortune, born in Jackson County, Florida, in 1855, shared the experience of a childhood in slavery with Frederick Douglass and with his contemporary, Booker T. Washington. Like them he saw the freedmen as a rural proletariat desperately in need of psychological rehabilitation and basic agricultural skills that might allow them to become independent farmers. His father, as an outspoken local political leader during Reconstruction, was constantly harrassed by white vigilantism and through political contacts sent young Fortune out of the state to Howard University in Washington, D.C., for a higher education. Fortune—partly for financial reasons, partly for reasons that remain obscure—spent only a brief period among the capitol's elite Black Republicans. After a return sojourn of a few years in Florida, he launched a journalistic career in New York City.[48]

Despite his respect for many of the Black appointive officials, in New York Fortune found a more congenial and radical intellectual climate. where he was able to reassess the approach taken by many Black public officials to southern conditions. He met and read the tracts of the nation's most outspoken economic reformers who had been clustering since the early 1870s in the nation's largest and most cosmopolitan city. He came under the influence of many antimonopoly radicals, who saw in the control of land and capital by absentee landlords and speculators a threat to the economic opportunity and self-respect of small farmers and workers.[49] Fortune was influenced most by the prolific Henry George, who emphasized how railroads—particularly in California, where he had spent so much time—appropriated the largest share of agricultural profits. Railroads did so by inflating the cost of land, most of which they had received in federal grants for constructing the transcontinental trunk lines, which in turn monopolized the means of marketing products. Even worse, the railroads bred class conflict and undermined the ideal of the independent yeoman by forcing them, as squatters and homesteaders, off the land. Although American wealth might be increasing, George argued, manipulation by the monopolists kept farmers and workers on the edge of poverty. George hoped that the land might ultimately be held in common, but because the political parties rejected radical reform, he proposed a high "single tax" on uncultivated land. He hoped thereby to force speculators to sell their holdings at low prices to small farmers.[50]

The writings of George verified Fortune's own observations in Florida and provided ammunition to attack the system of land tenure and race relations. By publishing *Black and White, Land, Labor and Capital in the South* in 1884, Fortune became the most theoretically innovative Black writer of the late nineteenth century. Adapting George's analysis to southern conditions, Fortune argued that the struggle in the South was not so much between the races as between the landlords whether white or Black, and the tenants, whether Black or white. All societies, he argued, evolved through conflict between capital and labor, and the American South would follow this rule. Departing radically from the analysis of Langston and even Douglass, he stressed neither the citizenship rights nor the southern social traits of the freedmen. Instead, he focused on their structural position within the regional economy. The freedmen, Fortune believed, were entering a class situation similar to the one that had existed under the Roman Empire—and one that had contemporary parallels in eastern and central Europe. Unlike Langston, he did not so much see the freedmen struggling against static racial discrimination. Instead he emphasized how they were the most repressed of classes in a social order undergoing complete upheaval. With the defeat of the planter class, new men had come to power and a dynamic social evolution had begun. As some southern Blacks acquired land upon which they might employ renters, conflicts between Black landlords and tenants would occur much as they did among whites. Then all sharecroppers would see that race antagonism was simply a ruse devised by the owners of property to divide the dependent classes.[51]

    When applying theory to specific conditions, however, Fortune, like Douglass and George, had to consider specific situations and retreat to reform. Nevertheless, within the context of elite Black economic thought in the late nineteenth century, Fortune's policy proposals were at least as radical as those of George and the Populists among whites. He doubted, for example, that the idea of class as opposed to race interests would have much meaning to the freedmen until they could see enough Black plantation owners to understand how economic antagonism might cut across racial lines. Given the tension between condescension and cooperation within the Populist party over the treatment of Blacks, he was probably correct.[52] As he noted some years later in a different context, Blacks had been so often betrayed by whites since the Civil War that they had first to organize on their own behalf before they could form alliances with others. Consequently, in 1890 he launched a political gambit to call attention to the unique needs of Blacks as a class emerging from the degradation of enslavement. Grimke's moralistic idealism had allowed him to see a serious political alternative in Liberal Republicanism and Grover Cleveland Democracy and a major issue in civil service reform. Unlike Grimke, Fortune prepared a platform to break the cycle of rural indebtedness and dependence. His party, he asserted, should organize a Black-controlled central bank as a major lending institution, and, like the Populists, he called for a series of producer and consumer cooperatives. The economic and political thrust would create an independent Black electorate to which the major parties would then have to make concessions.[53] This radical alternative to Republican orthodoxy, however, was subverted by conventions of Black officeholders in Washington, desiring to assert their own influence with the party's cadre and by the insuperable difficulties in organizing the rural freedmen.[55]

Fortune, however, showed a far deeper understanding of economic theory and a greater willingness to explore political alternatives than any of his contemporaries among the Black elite. He propounded, furthermore, a thoroughly secular sense of the destiny of the freedmen; for Fortune their racial identity was simply an accident of history. They were, he argued in the 1890s, "Afro-Americans," persons of African origin who aspired to American social and political norms. "While we are classed as Africans, just as the Germans are classed as Germans, we are in all things American citizens, American freemen." Because of the prejudices of most whites against Blacks and the discrimination of the political parties and trade unions, however, Afro-Americans had to organize separately. Like Williams and others he believed that the freedmen had been given the responsibility for governing before they had acquired political acumen. He defended their theoretical rights to full citizenship, but he cautioned that the ballot, like the single tax, should not be interpeted as a panacea.[55] For typological comparisons to the Hebrews or cross-cultural analogies with the Russian serfs, he substituted economic and political reforms drawn from domestic agrarian insurgencies.

Fortune saved his greatest praise for the technical education and social rehabilitation provided at Hampton Institute, which had pioneered since 1869 in teaching the freedmen agricultural skills and modern family management. Here he provided the vital ideological bridge between the thinking of Frederick Douglass and that of the young principal, Booker T. Washington. Like Douglass, Fortune had not only engaged in radical journalism and political agitation but had also experienced the psychological trauma, the sense of disorganization and dependence, that slavery produced. He was neither convinced of the ultimate truth of a single strategy nor impressed by the power of evangelical analogies. While agitation might be necessary to protect basic freedoms, only an education suited to the freedmen would develop in them the capacity to exercise their rights.[56]

Many scholars have been puzzled by Fortune's frank criticism of whites and his embrace of radical reforms in his published writings, yet his close friendship with the apparent accomodationist Booker T. Washington. Some even suggested Fortune rejected his radicalism because of his chronic alcoholism and his need of financial support, which apparently only Washington was willing to provide. Such personalized explanations, however, overlook the early origins of this friendship and its very deep ideological basis. Fortune, like Douglass and Washington, was a thoroughly American pragmatist as well as a former American slave. Like them, he recognized a clear distinction between the political tactic of agitation and the need to rehabilitate the freedmen so they might function in the South as self-reliant citizens. Indeed, to emphasize the radical potential of industrial education, Fortune republished in *Black and White* a long report on Hampton prepared for the New York *Globe* by T. McCants Steward, a Black abolitionist who had recently returned as a missionary from Liberia. Stewart, Fortune noted, had formerly been a political agitator, but now emphasized the necessary preparation of the freedmen through vocational education. Indeed, Fortune wrote shortly thereafter, that the most successful work of the teachers during Reconstruction had been in educating farmers to the rudiments of a stable business and family life.[57] Without it they could never cope with the white majority among whom they lived.

Fortune's analysis of the freedmen as an evolving class of agricultural workers received more sophisticated treatment in the 1890s in the essays of John S. Durham. The son of a well-to-do Philadelphia mulatto family and well connected among the officeholder elite, Durham should presumably have adopted the political philosophy of a Langston or a Grimke and emphasized the importance of political agitation as the means to protect the freedmen. But Durham was educated initially as an engineer and then, after facing severe discrimination in employment, as a lawyer at the University of Pennsylvania. He seemed most impressed with the application of social science methods to the analysis of history. Thoroughly secular and nonteleological in his approach to human nature, he substituted a theory of specific historic conditioning for dreams about racial destiny. During his service as American consul in San Domingo and Haiti in the 1890s, he also learned to analyze comparatively the situation of the southern freedmen.[58] Where evangelists like Williams looked upon Africans and West Indians as objects of spiritual revitalization, Durham saw the masses as a series of peasantries in various states of demoralization, depending on their access to modern training.

Durham knew Fortune and his work and, like him, hoped to explain through historical analysis why the freedmen remained so impoverished. But like so many American reformers of the 1890s he utilized empirical social science to turn from Fortune's radical theorizing (typical of reformers of the 1880s) to a more technical analysis of conditions and more concrete rehabilitory proposals. Interested particularly in innovative education, he became acquainted with principals of industrial schools for Blacks like Hollis Frisell of Hampton and Booker T. Washington of Tuskegee. Both principals were sufficiently impressed by Durham to invite him to deliver a series of lectures, entitled *To Teach the Negro History,* to their senior classes in 1896. Washington informed Robert Ogden that the central theme of the lectures suggested that the work at Hampton and Tuskegee was "proceeding along the lines of nature." He asked if the John F. Slater Fund might not subsidize the publication of the talks and have Durham deliver them to the twelve schools over which the Fund held jurisdiction. Durham was "a strong man in all these race matters," Washington wrote, "and we should use him in larger measure than we have in the past."[59]

Washington was particularly struck by Durham's fusion of evolutionary theory with the actual patterns of American economic history. Drawing on his wide travels and readings in sociology, Durham identified specific variables that had historically promoted the evolution of dependent classes. He told his student audiences that "the development . . . of history as the basis of sociological research and generalizations, may, indeed, be said to be one of the advances of our own generation."[60] Through a careful study of American social history he could explain more precisely than Williams or Fortune how different means of organizing labor led to the evolution of distinct Black social types—each with unique psychological predilections. For Durham technological innovation, patterns of migration and settlement, and subsequent race and sex ratios combined to create unique labor demands and to open or constrict opportunities for technical training. Where Williams had described the legal evolution of slavery and the attitudes of the master class and Fortune analyzed rather generally the freedmen's class position, Durham explained how differential work options had created different types of Black people. Beginning as barbarous Africans, Durham argued, Black Americans had evolved into three primary and distinct social types: field hands, house servants, and craftsmen. Blacks everywhere had had the capacity to acquire the rudiments of a more civilized life, but the demography and economic setting of each colony determined how habits, values, and social institutions would actually develop. Where Blacks were few and posed no economic threat to white workers, many were able to learn trades and participate in the social élan that led to revolution. Where they were numerous and held on plantations, their ability to acquire skills was limited and they were policed in direct proportion to their numbers in the local population.[61]

Durham's division of Blacks into three social types not only diminished the significance of the traditional distinction between field hands and house servants, but provided the historical precedent for social rehabilitation. Each social type, he believed, had developed a different sense of itself and its relationship to the master class. The house servants, whose fidelity many white authors idealized, Durham condemned as a deluded class that had lost all sense of its true economic and social position. Their intimacy with whites, he argued, had led them to admire the planters' ostentatious social standards and had promoted a "mansion house morality" that only reinforced their dependence. The field hands, whose African superstitions were reinforced by illiteracy and provincial confinement, had become sullen. Nevertheless, they remained sufficiently separate from whites to avoid complete psychological dependence. "More hopeful was the natural demoralization of the quarters," Durham argued, "than the artificial corruption of the mansion house."[62]

Durham identified the craftsmen as the true leaders of the slave community because they nurtured their self-confidence through their mastery of technical skills. "Civilization's most fruitful germ lies in the mastery of a tool," he wrote, "While the mechanic was exposed to the cringing jealousy of other slaves, he commanded their respect. They looked up to him in spite of their envy, and he was the influential man among them." The mechanic had his own home with his wife and escaped both the slave quarters and the mansion house. Durham brought his analysis into the 1890s by arguing that both agricultural workers and service employees could best escape the habits of dependence by mastering those skills that would put their labor in greatest demand.[63]

Like Langston and Fortune, Durham emphasized that the freedmen were not unique from other emancipated agricultural classes. By learning to compare their social history systematically with that of peasants elsewhere, especially the evolution of Europe's dependent classes, American Blacks might understand their opportunities rather than lament their disabilities. They were above all, he said, citizens of an advanced nation and only temporarily members of a depressed class. Their evolution had brought them far from African barbarism and even set them apart from their contemporaries in the West Indies. Indeed, he condemned those Black historians who emphasized "race pride" because they seemed to encourage a narrow chauvinism and prevented their pupils from understanding how similar their evolution was with those of other peoples. Instead, Durham concluded, Blacks should be taught a history that explained how they had become in America a stratified people with the potential to participate as skilled individuals throughout the economy.[64]

The Alternative of Ethnic Consciousness

In addition to the writings of Williams and the emigrationist crusades of Bishop Turner in the early 1890s, Durham and Fortune also encountered efforts to promote a distinct sense of race identity in the writings of Alexander Crummell, the elderly pastor of St. Luke's Episcopal Church in Washington, D.C. For theorists like Durham, with a materialistic conception of history that rested on the latest empirical research, religious spokesmen seemed to base their programs for reform on vague and archaic notions of group loyalty. Whether Durham held the same contempt for most Black clergymen as did Washington and Fortune is not clear, though he had little regard for the views of Crummell's Liberian associate, Edward W. Blyden.[65] Durham never appreciated how the vision of ethnic distinctiveness, when shorn of its supernatural authorization and justified by a teleological interpretation of group suffering, might assuage the severe sense of Black psychological inferiority held by intellectuals and workers alike. Crummell may have been motivated by an antebellum vision of racial salvation, but he built continuously on his experiences in Africa, England, and America and encouraged young idealists to revive and unite a dispirited and dispersed race. With the stature of his age and learning, he could criticize Black politicians whose Reconstruction programs had failed, and he could provide young writers as well as clerics with a historic and mythic image of Black revitalization to compensate for thier humiliations. He asked them to transfer to the race a faith that he initially derived from a Christian God. Such a transferal under his aegis allowed young Black intellectuals to find precedent for their own roles as leaders over those of the tarnished politicoes and the pragmatic materialists.[66]

Unlike Williams, Fortune, and even Langston and Douglass, Crummell never wrote a major book to explain a systematic racial philosophy or to propose a comprehensive policy for race relations. Nevertheless, on the basis of his experience as an abolitionist, an exceptional education at Cambridge University between 1848 and 1853, and a twenty-year mission to Liberia, he published many pamphlets and collections of essays. His proposals fluctuated with the pressures of particular decades, as he advocated political agitation in the 1840s, became an emigrant in the depressing atmosphere of the 1850s, promoted vocational education in the 1880s, and encouraged social scientific scholarship in the 1890s. But he consistently tried to integrate the social rehabilitation of Black Americans with their moral revitalization. However disjointed his specific proposals might seem, beneath them lay a nineteenth-century faith in races as essential social organisms and in their sequential evolution as the Creator's process for the enlightenment of a cooperative mankind.

As Wilson J. Moses correctly notes, Crummell's romantic racialism sprung from an organic, conservative view of social process, but he was neither authoritarian by temperament nor inordinately mystical.[67] His abiding faith in the powers of the intellect led him to respect the orderliness of modern social science, though he abhorred the skepticism of Hume and Voltaire, which suggested in a world filled with injustice that life had no purpose. He encouraged a professionally trained rather than a hereditary elite to examine as carefully as possible the distinctive problems of Blacks. While Moses is again correct to argue that Crummell did distrust democracy and believed that societies "advance only by the force and energy of minorities," he never questioned the structure of American government or the capacity of the masses for improvement. For him race, as a primary loyalty for humanity, promised the readiest basis for mass enlightenment. So long as writers would bind specific reform programs to the general aim of spiritual revitalization, Crummell was prepared to entertain their ideas.[68]

Despite his antiquated rhetoric and aristocratic demeanor, Crummell became the most prescient Black social thinker of the late nineteenth century because he recognized that at the heart of Black exploitation lay systematic humiliation. As early as

1844 while only twenty-five-years old, he argued that Blacks had become so accustomed to social subordination that they unconsciously behaved as inferiors. "Hence has resulted to us the deepest degradation and the saddest debasement, affecting our well-being in all its social, civil and moral aspects." While Durham might appear modern by calling for the mastery of technical skills, he avoided the larger problems of psychological revitalization in a cosmopolitan world. Inculcation of efficient work habits might enable freedmen to compete in rural areas. But expertise and decorum alone would not enable literate Blacks to understand why their ancestors had not played a more creative role in modern history or to determine how they might compete with arrogant whites. His friend, the Episcopalian priest Josephus, epitomized Black tribulation when he wrote, "I do not intend to crawl for favor or friends to any white rascal—had enough of them. . . . You do not know the little humiliations I have silently endured. They may regret them some day. They don't know what is in this black brain." In a talk to the Working Men's Club of Philadelphia in 1881 that emphasized the dignity of skilled labor, Crummell specifically tied individual achievement to racial rebirth. His particular proposals—to learn trades, to work humbly when young, to save money, to buy farms—could have provided the philosophical basis for Booker T. Washington, who founded Tuskegee Institute in the same year. But Crummell combined the praise of skilled labor with the "natural right" of all persons to aspire to occupations commensurate with their talents. Blacks, he argued, must broaden the training of their youth to combat the West's racial stereotypes. Revitalization required that inculcation be coordinated with a central purpose defined by the race through its "natural leadership."[69]

The consistency in Crummell's thought from the 1840s through the 1890s can be attributed in part to his search for transcendental truths or "innate" characteristics of races. But he was also the only prominent Black abolitionist whose career was not deflected by the Civil War and Reconstruction, with their extensive interracial political and educational manipulations. Though he visited the United States in the early 1860s as part of a mission that obtained formal recognition of Liberian independence from the Lincoln administration, Monrovia remained his permanent residence until 1873.[70] He avoided the exhilaration of the Civil War's military crusade, which swept up Delany, Henry Highland Garnet, Langston, Douglass, and others, the promise of political power in conjunction with whites and the despair of Reconstruction's defeat. His prewar idealism was reinforced by twenty years of steady work among Liberian natives and was unperturbed by a similar period of American upheaval. Several scholars have noted Crummell's direct transfer of missionary views and experiences from the Liberian natives to the freedmen, but he did so not to be condescending. Unlike Durham, who found Black Americans more socially advanced than Africans and West Indians, Crummell believed that each branch of Pan-Africa must undergo similar and coordinated revitalization untainted by spurious relations with whites.[71]

In Liberia Crummell had observed Christian imperialism, American emigrationists, and African natives "in the raw," and he came to believe that the idea of progress for Blacks would have meaning only if driven by a Pan-African Renaissance. While he experienced sufficient discrimination and observed enough racist condescension within the Episcopal church to deny the moral superiority of white to Black men, he believed the Christian doctrine must refine and broaden the sensibilities of Africans. Christian nurture had brought him to Africa and prepared him to understand the historic relationship between the home of Black people and Western civilization, and this lesson, he felt, had to be propagated. He was appalled by the crude material culture and the occasional cruel customs of the natives, which Christian humanism must combat. But he was also impressed by the economic potential of Africa and the enormous dignity of its people. Upon that dignity a necessary reciprocal relationship must rest.

In a widely circulated essay entitled *The Relations and Duties of the Free Colored Men in America to Africa,* first published in 1861, he argued that American Blacks could never achieve psychological freedom until they, like the Irish, English, and Germans, acquired a deep respect for their ancestors. American Blacks—and not whites—must bring the gospel of Christ and modern skills to "develop" Africa, but they could acquire from Africans a sense of heritage and dignity. Not particular customs or beliefs but the example of flourishing villages, of carefully regulated families, of independent Black achievements would provide that orderly inspiration Crummell found at the basis of all "civilization." Indeed, because Crummell did try to preach to the natives and distrusted the economic schemes of the Afro-American oligarchy, he became the object of suspicion. He was warned by a friend that "you have sometimes allowed your interest in the pure black to mortally wound the *amour propre* of the mulattoes." Indeed he had acquired the reputation of championing blacks against mulattoes. He explained on several occasions, though, that he did not disapprove of mulattoes but only of the behavior of those who seemed intent on exploiting rather than assisting the natives. Dissociated from the ideal of a racial Renaissance, they had adopted the worst features of the white man's colonialism.[72]

When Crummell returned to the United States he found his antebellum observations of Afro-American psychology and his African experience of mulatto politics confirmed. He distrusted white abolitionists like Wendell Phillips and William Lloyd Garrison, whom Grimke elevated virtually to sainthood, as much as he did politicians like Rutherford B. Hayes. The abolitionists, however benign their motives, never encouraged distinctive Black schools or churches, while the politicians selected specific personages like Frederick Douglass or Richard Greener for patronage rewards and ignored the needs of the masses. And the major black politicians seemed to revel in their dependence because they lacked an appreciation of race. As he told John E. Bruce in the late 1890s, "Believe me there is no race of people on the American soil who have greater native genius than this race of ours. Our only difficulty has been opportunity. The mongrel everywhere inches forward . . . , the Negro, through the very instinct of his innate genius, modestly retires, and hence is rarely estimated at his true worth."[73]

After the death of Henry Highland Garnet in 1882, Black Episcopalian and Presbyterian ministers looked to Crummell as their spokesman to church councils, missionary meetings, and the literate public. He had helped organize such groups in Washington, D.C., into a ministerial conference that met weekly, and under their auspices he often gave public speeches. In a series of pamphlets, highlighted by a *Defense of the Negro Race in America* (1883), and culminating in the lengthy essay, *The Race Problem in America* (1889), he became the major proponent of a racial Renaissance. He denied, with ample reference to African and American Black achievements, that Blacks were incapable of acquiring the refinements of Western civilization, that they needed tutelage from whites, or that they would be absorbed by the more aggressive "Anglo-Saxon." They would survive and prosper, he argued, because "races, like families, are the organisms and ordinance of God, and the race feeling, like the family feeling, is of divine origin." Indeed, Blacks had already produced many trained teachers and ministers to prepare the race for its higher purposes. "The true leaders of the race," he reminded several arrogant white missionaries, "are men of that race; and any attempt to carry on missions opposed to this principle is sure to meet disasterous failure."[74]

While Durham had been correct to note that writers who emphasized race pride also lamented Black disabilities, Crummell had learned in Liberia that Negroes with skills, but no sense of race destiny, would not promote social rehabilitation. From people who believed that the battle against exploitation must begin with a revived Pan-African orientation and a paramount sense of race loyalty, Crummell hoped to recruit a new leadership. He respected old abolitionists like Douglass, but he condemned light skinned men like Fortune, Durham, and Greener who seemed to associate with whites to attain minor federal appointments, rather than working with blacks. He also distrusted educational reforms such as industrial schools, which, while teaching basic skills, did not promote a cultural basis for race cohesion and channeled young blacks into menial careers. While he promoted technical schooling in the 1880s, by the mid-1890s, he saw it as a "miserable fad" to limit Black intellectual growth. Crummell, no doubt, was attracted to men like himself, with university educations and intellectual predilections. But he was impressed most by men who also believed in an independent and distinctive black personality. His closest associates were ministers in Washington, notably Henry H. Garnet, J. W. Cromwell, William Crogman, and Francis Grimke, and clerical correspondents like Frazier Miller. But he also corresponded regularly with the journalist John E. Bruce, who knew many African and West Indian writers, and the poet Paul L. Dunbar, who struggled to present the creative qualities of Blacks to a white audience that demanded stereotypes.[75]

Gradually Crummell formulated plans to organize a Black cultural and intellectual elite. With the encouragement of his friends he tried to attract college-educated men who appreciated the intensive psychological and extensive international dimensions of Black rehabilitation. He was encouraged, he told Bruce, because younger scholars seemed to have a stronger sense of social responsibility than had their predecessors like Greener. On a visit to England he received support for a proposed Black journal from Dunbar. He then outlined plans for an academy where scholars would congregate to present papers on the Negro's social, economic, and cultural problems. He hoped for semi-annual meetings and publications to disseminate Black scholarly opinions and to win a wide audience for his notion of a racial renaissance.[76]

On his return to the United States, Crummell issued a prospectus for the American Negro Academy and called the first meeting for March 5, 1897, in Washington, D.C. He was elected president, but the other officers were younger men who would shape Black social thought and public discourse through World War I. The vice-president was social historian W. E. B. DuBois, whose paper on "The Conservation of Races" at the first session reflected Crummell's views. The treasurer was his close friend Francis Grimke, while the Howard University mathematician and sociologist Kelly Miller, and Archibald Grimke also held offices. In his inaugural address to the academy, Crummell described its mission as the assembly where the great philosophical questions of racial destiny and leadership were to be settled. The average Black American, Crummell had confided to Cromwell, "thinks that the creation of races was a superfluous act on the part of the Almighty," but the academy, he told the audience, "would provide the leader, the creative and organizing mind" to demonstrate how spiritual revitalization could direct modernization.[77] Academy members might well discuss technical changes, but they must first convince the freedmen—and all Blacks—of their unique destiny as a people because of their moral superiority to whites.

When Crummell died in September, 1898, the Washington *Bee,* the leading Black newspaper in the nation's most sophisticated Black community, noted his passing with a brief resume of his career as a scholar. The Washington *Colored American,* which had periodically noted his publications and activities, also assessed him as merely a prominent cleric.[78] These papers, however, featured the political maneuverings and social high life of the officeholding elite, and their editors, Calvin Chase and E. E. Cooper, vied with one other for the support of Republican administrations. They were hardly in a position to estimate the merits or influence of his work. Secular scholars like DuBois and Ferris and clerics like Crogman testified to Crummell's importance by emphasizing in their own works the need for a revitalization of Black consciousness within the general pattern of cosmopolitan modernization. Drawing on Crummell, they would argue that Blacks must not only understand the effects of racism on their personalities, but they must devise new standards to assess world history.[79] Through contacts with African and West Indian intellectuals and the promotion of cultural events, DuBois, John E. Bruce, and Ferris, along with clerics like Alexander Walters and Bishop Turner, gave substance to Crummell's vision of a revived Pan-African people.

By the mid-1890s a variety of theories had been presented by Black writers, each speaking for a somewhat different constituency, to interpret the history of Black Americans and to provide strategies for rehabilitation. A literature, which in the 1860s and 1870s had described the freedmen as cultural curiosities or pathetic peasants, by the 1890s identified a hierarchy of black classes with reciprocal relationships. Older political activists like Langston and Douglass still emphasized the primacy of citizenship rights, though Douglass, as a man raised in slavery, also stressed the the importance of restructing the personalities of the freedmen. The politicians presided over a large contingent of federal officeholders and journalists in Washington, who would keep the theme of partisanship as the basis of Black status alive into the early twentiety century. Secular theorists like Fortune and Durham, however, placed a new emphasis on the continuity of Black life from slavery to freedom. They suggested a more independent politics and they stressed programs modeled after those that had allowed other dependent classes to become "men of property." With substantial support from northern philanthropists, a new class of Black educators and small businessmen around Booker T. Washington, soon created a national network of support for this vision of petit-bourgeois independence.

Writers who examined more closely the basis of continuing black degradation, however, could not find in theories of class rehabilitation sufficient inspiration to attack the psychological core of racism. They called instead for revitalization of *all* black social classes and a new sense of history based on a Pan-African awakening. With support among an elite clergy and the new generation of college-educated writers and scholars (and drawing on certain folk beliefs of the freedmen), this vision would gain increasing support as international Black contacts increased just before World War I. The literature of the 1890s, then, projected a far more complex image of Blacks as a people of varied social origins and a revolutionary destiny. Whether they were primarily a class about to enter rural proprietorship or primarily members of an awakening Diaspora would be more articulately debated by the intellectuals of the twentieth century.

2 | Booker T. Washington and a Pedagogy for the Oppressed

Writing in 1903, the young Black scholar W. E. B. DuBois noted that, "easily the most striking thing in the history of the American Negro since 1876 is the ascendency of Mr. Booker T. Washington."[1] While Fortune and Crummell might propose more imaginative ideas to guide Black development, Washington's simple image of the freedmen as an underdeveloped peasantry, combined with his sophisticated pedagogy for their rehabilitation, gained the widest popular attention. Scholars who have emphasized the integrationist objectives of late nineteenth-century Black spokesmen and those who see it as a golden age of Black nationalism agree that Booker T. Washington was its dominant voice.[2] Washington synthesized integrationist and nationalist strains, but neither embodied his paramount objective. In fact, whether Black communities would ultimately integrate with or remain separate from whites was less important to Washington than was his concern for the modernization of hosts of individual farmers and workers. Like Crummell and the romantic nationalists, he sought to utilize the basic loyalties of Blacks so he might sweep them into a social evolution. The ultimate outcome of that process, however, remained vague. Washington combined a thoroughly pragmatic sense of tactics with a consistent theory of community rehabilitation led by technically trained educators and a petit-bourgeoisie. Harold Cruse is correct to assert that Washington was "the leading spokesman and theoretician of the New Negro capitalist whom he was trying to mold into existence."[3] By combining a pedagogy to build individual self-confidence through the inculcation of skills with an ideology that emphasized capital accumulation, Washington provided an image of Blacks entering the modern economy through the tactic of separate enterprise.[4]

In the years before his famous speech at the Atlanta and Southern States Cotton Exposition in 1895, Washington expended his energies on teaching and raising funds for his school at Tuskegee, Alabama. Unlike Fortune or Crummell, he did not write extensively then, and Louis Harlan is quite correct to note that he was not an "intellectual," a person who likes to analyze and generate ideas.[5] But the success of his pedagogy, which made Black development seem a normal part of national economic growth, won him a wide audience. By the mid-1890s he had become a master of the propaganda that played on many American prejudices—especially the view that politics was corrupt and that productive labor under expert guidance would provide the surest basis for national prosperity. His denigration of Black political agitation won for him, as C. VannWoodward and others have noted, wide support among white politicians, a few of whom even suggested he be appointed to William McKinley's cabinet.[6] But Washington minimized the significance of *all* political agitation and supported educational qualifications for the suffrage. In an age marked by Populist insurgency, large Catholic immigration, and labor violence, Washington's image of the freedmen as indigenous Americans struggling to become land owners, craftsmen, and store keepers gained for him respect among the northern public. His prolific publications (many ghostwritten) after 1898 promoting Black entrepreneurship and southern white as well as Black education won for him enormous philanthropic support.[7] Not as an original theorist but as a shrewd propagandist who applied ideas to an ever-expanding set of circumstances, Washington became the ultimate Black ideologist.

Washington became a popular figure because of his pedagogy, but a controversial one among Blacks because he promoted a new leadership clique to challenge the authority of the officeholding elite. His program was begun as a means of organizing and motivating rural freedmen, whom Black political activists like John M. Langston, John R. Lynch, P. B. S. Pinchback, and Richard Greener had largely abandoned. His fame allowed him to create a clique of Black educators and businessmen throughout the country who embodied his vision of separate Black community development coordinated with national economic growth. As Howard Brotz has noted, "The impression which has been permitted to grow about him that he was a compromiser who not only was prepared for the time being to give up equality but even accepted the white doctrine of the Negro's 'place' is in complete contradiction with what he actually said and did."[8] For Washington, as for Douglass, the freedmen were so thoroughly depressed and abandoned that assertion of their equal civil and political rights was simply rhetoric. The partisan manipulations of the Langstons and Lynches and the "good government" insurgency of an Archibald Grimke had little relationship to the grinding poverty of rural crossroads. As Washington was often reminded, his program was used by white political figures to justify their abuse of Black civil and political rights. But he, in turn, used whites to promote his doctrine of community development. As DuBois noted in his oral autobiography, Washington had no faith in whites and carefully fed them the information he wanted them to have.[9] His philosophy of economic modernization, he hoped, would unite rural freedmen and an urban bourgeoisie through the medium of his pedagogy.

Far from being a capitulation to white stereotypes or white power, Washington believed that his emphasis on the psychological effects of enslavement was long overdue. The elimination of the feeling of inferiority required every resource in Black communities, as well as assistance from sympathetic whites. He agreed with his contemporary, the Yale sociologist

William Graham Sumner, who wrote in the mid-1880s that "the progress of society is nothing but the slow and far remote result of steady, laborious, painstaking growth of individuals."[10] But the development of a class of former slaves into self-confident, assertive men in the face of enormous political, economic, and cultural oppression was a task more formidable than Sumner could imagine. Its achievement, as Harold Cruse again has noted, would have been more socially revolutionary than anything the Black politicos demanded. In a sense later recognized by radical writers and activists like Franz Fanon and Paulo Freire, Washington was trying to "enroll (the freedmen) in the search for self-affirmation" and to make them "men of property" in a society that had systematically denied them the substance of freedom.[11]

To argue that Washington placed the same emphasis on motivating the peasantry as have revolutionary theorists like Freire and Fanon is not to suggest that his political or pedagogical vision coincided with theirs. He did not desire a classless society nor one in which violence might play a legitimate role in freeing repressed rage or oppressed classes. He acceded to an insensate theory of Darwinian competition not a Marxian dialectics of purposive class warfare. Washington saw Blacks as a despised minority who must seize opportunity within an expanding capitalism, while Freire and Fanon urged an oppressed majority to overthrow a corrupt bourgeoisie, to replace a "dying colonialism" with a more humane socialist state. Above all, for Washington racial caste and generations of enslavement rather than more malleable class interests provided a pervasive obstacle to the freedmen. He had "felt the lash,"[12] as DuBois later noted; he could not see the individual personality spontaneously coming to comprehend class interests. Instead, he required that each person break the master-slave relationship within himself by accumulating sufficient skills to move with others silently and relentlessly, like Adam Smith's "invisible hand," against the consequences of caste. His tools for freedom were those traditionally available to dependent classes. As Louis Harlan has written, "He was forced from childhood to deceive, to simulate, to wear the mask,"[13] and unlike Freire and Fanon he lacked the temperament and intellectual tools to see the fulfillment of individual needs apart from the collective good of the race.

Nevertheless, like Freire and Fanon, his experience in rural districts convinced him that the peasantry must first be taught to scrutinize itself so it might develop the confidence to build economic power. All three men condemned urban intellectuals who ignored the psychology of the oppressed and who, from afar, incited rural people to senseless retaliation.[14] Not surprisingly, the leading Black political economist of the late nineteenth century, T. Thomas Fortune, when he was writing his most radical tracts, found a strong supporter and close friend in Washington. Politicoes, whose authority Washington challenged, buried his educational ideas beneath a barrage of condescension while condemning his personal motives and political contacts. But within the context of the South's extractive economy and oppressive caste system which were embedded in a rapidly expanding national economy, Washington's pedagogy had a more radical potential than it has been given credit for. Like men of a later age who have worked to free peasantries from tradition within a volatile political context, Washington placed first priority on reshaping personalities and creating a network of modern communities, at least as far as he understood modernization.

The Ideological Basis for Rehabilitation

Booker T. Washington encountered America's image of the freedmen at Hampton Institute in eastern Virginia, where he received most of his formal education and shaped his thinking on pedagogical and social issues. Washington became deeply devoted to its founder, General Samuel C. Armstrong, and to the Hampton faculty. He respected their professional judgement and through them became part of the educational and philanthropic network that over the next fifty years shaped southern Black education. Therefore, to understand how Washington organized and sustained his own institution at Tuskegee, one must briefly examine the psychological and pedagogical precepts of Armstrong's "Hampton Idea."

Armstrong had been born in Hawaii in 1839 to parents who were pioneers in preaching the gospel of piety and economic modernization to nonwhite peoples. His father had gone to Hawaii in 1830, under the aegis of the American Missionary Association, to preach the gospel of piety and modernization to the natives. His mother had been one of the first American students of Pestallozian kindergartens, which emphasized that children could learn best by being shown how to create things in their familiar environment. While Armstrong's father had taught the natives on Maui to till the soil and run saw mills, his mother had taught Chinese immigrant women in Honolulu's slums to cook and sew more efficiently. The skills of man and woman, they believed, should be coordinated to create a stable family life.[15]

As James McPherson has noted, Armstrong was not raised within the turmoil of the abolitionist agitation,[16] but he was even better prepared than the abolitionists to direct the practical education of people with a nonliterate tradition. He came to the United States after his father's death in 1860 to study at Williams College under Mark Hopkins, who also emphasized the practical application of philosophical and historical knowledge. Like many of his classmates, Armstrong enlisted in the Union Army after graduation in 1862, and given his experience with nonwhite peoples, he was particularly attracted to the Black troops who were recruited after the Emancipation Proclamation. He was appointed lieutenant colonel and rose to general of the Ninth United States Colored Troops, which were mustered from the "contrabands" in Maryland. His impression of the freedmen, therefore, grew from comparison with other "primitive peoples" and under the strictures of warfare, which required that all recruits be forcefully molded to survive in combat.[17]

Armstrong believed that the freedmen had distinctive racial characteristics, but he gave no credence to the romanticism that affected so many missionaries. "The whole darky business," he told Governor Lucius Fairchild of Wisconsin, "has been in the hands of women and sentimentalists." The unique affability and talents in music and plastic arts that made Blacks seem "charming," failed to impress Armstrong. Like Douglass he feared that whatever colorful habits the freedmen possessed would condemn them to impoverishment when they faced the competition of white labor. He stressed instead the freedmen's physical vigor that must be molded to inculcate habits of self-sufficiency. Some of their habits, especially the subservience and deception practiced in the presence of whites, Armstrong attributed to enslavement, but others remained from their original preliterate condition. Like the Hawaiians, the freedmen seemed to Armstrong primitive, innocent of modern notions of efficient production and of a world beyond their neighborhoods. "The darkies are so full of human nature and have to be more carefully watched over." he told a friend.[18] But they also lacked a heritage of nationhood and had become a brutalized peasantry that feared the white majority. They needed thousands of teachers who could appreciate and utilize their physical skills to create in them habits of independent judgement. With the assistance of the Freedmen's Bureau and the American Missionary Society, he began Hampton Institute as a model school where men and women could be molded to freedom by becoming efficient producers and consumers.

The image of the freedmen as a class with the potential to become modern workers challenged the rhetoric of southern paternalists, justified Armstrong's new pedagogy, and promised a realignment of North and South in a unified industrial nation. Blacks, Armstrong believed, had greater endurance than whites, and, as he told John Greenleaf Whittier, they "are plastic and take impressions easily, and they are earnest." To inculcate habits of self-discipline he set a rigid daily schedule that he believed whites could not survive. He wanted to accustom people who were already "fitted . . . for constant application and continuous effort at high tension" to self-control. Armstrong also insisted that Hampton be coeducational, with men and women performing craft skills and homemaking to simulate efficient family units. To impress upon his students the importance of concrete achievement and to make the school seem like a home of which they could be proud, he insisted that large brick buildings be erected even before enrollment justified them. Built with bricks from Hampton's own kilns, the structures were intended to impress students and potential donors with the Negro's ability to behave like efficient whites.[19]

Armstrong also developed a system of fund raising for his school similar to that of missionaries and presidents of major private colleges and universities founded after the war. However, he promoted and rationalized his venture on grounds peculiar to his sense of mission. He believed that the freedmen, like the Hawaiians, represented a burden placed before the evangelical middle class to test its moral stamina, but he saw in the struggle to rehabilitate the freedmen a special means for reuniting the sections. Educating the freedmen would become the ethical justification for the war. In July, 1869, he invited Mark Hopkins and Congressman James. A. Garfield to visit Hampton. Garfield had initially doubted that industrial education could invigorate the minds of young adults, but Armstrong convinced him that enslavement had created in the freedmen special educational needs. Writing to Governor Fairchild in 1872, Garfield stated that, "Whatever doubts there may be, and I admit there is ground for some, of the success of the manual labor school . . . the first want of the freed people of the South is to know how to live and how to work." Garfield joined Hampton's board of trustees in 1870 and remained until 1875. Armstrong also relied on prominent abolitionist families—like the Lowells of Boston, the Emersons of Concord, the Higginsons of Cambridge, and the Woolseys of New York—for small sums to support the school. In 1874 he urged Longfellow to visit by arguing that the presence of so prominent a New Englander would contribute to "a better feeling between North and South." To Whittier he wrote, "I only wish you could attend our anniversary and see with your own eyes the fulfillment of the things for which you have worked all your life." A class of modern workers was apparently being forged from a peasantry that had suffered both from primitivism and servility.[20]

When Washington arrived at Hampton in the fall of 1872, he encountered and was duly impressed by the first fruits of Armstrong's self-help program. Raised in what he recalled as the chaotic and filthy atmosphere of Malden, West Virginia, a coal mining town near Charleston, Washington was impressed at Hampton by precisely those features that Armstrong intended to affect Blacks: the physical plant and the invigorating routine. Washington was pleased to learn that Virginia Hall, the largest and most beautiful building he had ever seen, was to be his new home and that the "entrance requirements" were tests of his fortitude rather than his rote knowledge. As a sixteen-year-old, he was assumed to have adult responsibilities. To enable him to pay room and board, the school hired him as a janitor, and until he could earn sufficient credit to become a fulltime student, he enrolled in the night school. The discipline that characterized education at Hampton impressed Washington the most, because Armstrong set individual self-control into a pattern of communal organization. Washington often recounted the modes of self-discipline—like the ritual of the toothbrush, the meal, and the bath—that provided the fastitious decorum upon which to base self-respect. Because so many of the students were adults who planned to return to their home districts as teachers, they promoted Armstrong's emphasis on discipline as the basis for motivating entire communities. Washington imbibed this educational spirit and after his graduation in June, 1875, he returned to Malden, where for three years he conveyed to the freedmen his idea of education as social rehabilitation.[21]

In the fall of 1878 Washington received a stipend to study at Wayland Seminary, a small, prestigious Baptist school in Washington, D.C. His experience there, at the same time that young T. Thomas Fortune and George Washington Williams were encountering the Black political elite in its home base, left unsavory impressions. While Fortune went off to New York and radical ideologies and Williams into the archives to recreate a more satisfying image of Black historical progress, Washington reconfirmed his admiration for the Hampton Idea. Washington never theorized about his experience at Wayland, but his discussion of the students and especially the Black government clerks he met corresponded in tone with John S. Durham's analysis of the ante-bellum houseslaves and in substance with Franklin Frazier's subsequent condemnation of the salaried

"Black Bourgeoisie." The clerks and students, Washington believed, had become alienated from their roots and seemed to enjoy their dependency. They seemed uninterested in a wider race loyalty while fabricating an elevated social status. Several students at Wayland were more brilliant than any he had met at Hampton, but their classical education prepared them to participate in the life of the salaried city elite rather than to contribute to the rehabilitation of country districts. He saw in the clerks and officeholders persons who violated natural laws by being so detached from the productive labor and social demands of the Black masses. Indeed, he would later apply the term *artificial class* to his critics like William Monroe Trotter and W. E. B. DuBois because they seemed to have moved too rapidly beyond a norm of racial evolution and to have adopted the pretensions of aristocratic whites.[22]

Even more than Fortune and Williams, Washington rejected the Black elite in the nation's capital and turned to a profession that would allow him to influence rural people directly. In 1879, while still in his early twenties, he delivered the commencement address at Hampton, where he emphasized the need for individual initiative directed toward community development. The address was soon followed by an invitation from Armstrong to return as a teacher. Washington gladly accepted and was placed in charge of the night school. He was also asked to supervise a new experiment—the education of a small contingent of Indian youths sent from a federal prison in Florida. Washington characteristically went to his new task with enthusiasm and tact. From his contacts with the Indians he learned to compare the conditions of the freedmen to those of other "primitive people" and eventually to consider the universal applicability of his educational program. By the turn of the century missionaries would be writing to him from Japan, China, and Hawaii, as well as Africa, describing their efforts to implement his ideas.[23]

In May, 1881, Washington finally received an opportunity to apply his administrative talents to new educational work. A biracial group of businessmen and interested citizens of Tuskegee, Alabama, had asked General Armstrong to recommend a white man as principal of a new normal school for Negroes in their home town. Armstrong instead suggested Washington, and the Tuskegee group agreed. Though heading into the so-called Black Belt, an area less settled and less socially and economically diversified than eastern Virginia, Washington seems to have had no serious apprehension. He arrived under circumstances that conspired to favor his pedagogical alternative to Black political assertiveness. Somewhat later in the year President Garfield told a Black delegation from South Carolina headed by Robert Elliott that education provided the only tolerable means to improve the social standing of the freedmen. James G. Blaine, writing in 1886, argued that the most important consequence of the election of 1880 had been the consolidation of Democratic control of every former slave state, and despite continuing Black assertiveness in county elections, Alabama illustrated this point. In 1880 not one Republican, Black or white, sat in the legislature. Alabama Democrats, like those in most states, had come to power by balancing local terror against Blacks with promises of frugality in government. Democrats in Choctaw County, in August, 1882, lynched the local Black leader, Jack Turner, while the legislature cut the state's budget. However, appropriations for teacher training in "practical education" were increased, and more money was expended for the new state agriculture school for whites at Auburn than for the old liberal arts college at Montgomery. Teacher training schools for Blacks at Montgomery and at Normal, near Huntsville also received modest state subsidies. The appropriation of $2,000 for a third Negro normal school at Tuskegee was part of a pattern of modest state investment in economic growth. It was followed shortly thereafter by an amended Morrill Land Grant College Act, which sent small appropriations to each state for agricultural colleges, and by promotion in the Congress of bills to apportion money to states for education in proportion to their rates of illiteracy.[24]

In addition to local political and financial support for his work, Washington brought to Tuskegee a comprehensive image of the freedmen and a pedagogy designed to motivate them. His views—as expressed, for example, in his first speech to the

National Education Association in 1884, when he was still less than thirty-years-old—were carefully formulated from General Armstrong's precepts. They would become more comprehensive and be supported by more historical and sociological data over the years, but their general outline would not change until late in Washington's life. Like most Black and white Americans, Washington had learned from geography texts that the freedmen were descendants of barbarous Africans. The pilgrimages of prominent Black missionaries to Africa, far from heightening Washington's curiosity, reinforced the parallel between the Africans and the freedmen as victims of cultural isolation. Slavery had intensified the social primitivism of the Africans by enclosing them and their descendants in an economic system that prevented their intellectual and social maturity. Like Williams, Crummell, and Durham, Washington agreed that slavery had reduced the barbarous but proud Africans to subservience. He conceded the point made by southern white apologists that it had also taught them to appreciate a modern, humane religion and to adhere to disciplined labor. Nevertheless, like Douglass, he saw that enslavement had subjected Blacks to an inversion of the heroic American frontier experience by making disciplined labor seem pointless. While Yankee farmers and western yeomen had identified hard work as a means to freedom through the acquisition of a homestead, slaves had toiled through fear of the lash to enrich others.[25] The problem for Washington lay in taking what Blacks had learned as southern workers and transforming it into an ideology that would enable them to benefit from the modernization of the region.

The psychology of labor was to Washington the key to the rehabilitation of the freedmen. Like Fortune he understood the operations of land-tenure arrangements that had superceded slavery, but because he could not directly reform them, he hoped instead to change the habits of the mass of workers. In a manner that would later be utilized by theorists in many Third World countries, Washington made a crucial distinction between "working" and "being worked." "Work" indeed became Washington's operational definition of freedom, because it represented self-directed, rationalized procedures whose conception, execution, and product were planned by the freedmen themselves. Like Freire in Brazil and Fanon in Algeria, Washington sought to convince the freedmen that although they had toiled, they had never developed the discipline to work. Without a modern conception of labor, he argued, no rural people could ever acquire the property on which real freedom must rest. Without land, as the freedmen had complained many times during Reconstruction and as the Exodusters had dramatized, freedom was a sham.[26]

Indeed, Washington argued that the South as a region had to be liberated from a backwardness compounded of the social heritage of the Blacks and the economic system devised by the whites. Like many social scientists of a later day, he wished to avoid assessment of historical responsibility in order to expedite programs to eradicate the consequences of deprivation. Both violent politics and emotional religion, which abounded in Alabama, would only reinforce the provincial heritage that had developed under slavery and upon which continuing hostility between the races rested. He understood how slavery had inflated the self-esteem of whites, but he sought primarily to change the behavior of Blacks. As America's competitive society evolved, he noted, whites who judged men on irrational grounds would, like the slaveholders, disappear as anachronisms in the Darwinian struggle. By rehabilitating Blacks he would prepare them to compete with white labor and he would also eradicate the image of indolence upon which racial stereotypes largely rested. Blacks would then have achieved self-respect and would command the respect of younger whites who would never have known a servile Black caste.[27]

As at Hampton, Washington imposed at Tuskegee a rigid daily schedule to impress upon the students the need for order in their own lives and in the communities they served. Armstrong's daughter, describing the routine at Hampton in the 1870s, noted that study, shop work, and military drill filled a twelve-hour-day that "left little time for self-indulgence and indolence." Washington followed his routine closely, and his students appreciated the importance of the discipline. William Holtzclaw, who founded Utica Normal and Industrial Institute in Mississippi in 1903, noted how the rigid daily routine he imposed upon his students inculcated self-control and "good habits" in marked contrast to the apparent indolence of the local population.[28]

The rigid scheduling was based on the same pedagogical premises as that of the contemporary reform schools for delinquent youth. According to the report of the State Board of Charities and Corrections of California in 1904, the same pattern of early rising, exercise, rigid class schedules, training in crafts, and military drill was prescribed to alter the habit patterns and responses of the young offenders. Accepting the premises of what we would today call behavior modification, the state commissioners of education believed that systematic control of the pupils' habits would force them to devote full attention to labor and to acquire respect for virtues like efficiency, sobriety, and thrift. While Washington hardly believed the freedmen to be delinquent, he saw their rehabilitation in a broad social context rather than an individualized one. In 1908 he entreated the convention of the National Education Association to "help my race get well." Emmett Scott, Washington's private secretary observed, "The idea that education is a matter of personal habits, of cleanliness, industry, integrity, and right conduct, while of course not original with Booker T. Washington, was perhaps further developed and more effectively emphasized by him than by any other American educator."[29]

Washington, however, tempered the rigid daily schedule because he believed that students must come to appreciate the importance of approaching familiar items with a new sense of their utility. Like the advocates of progressive education, he believed that instruction beyond the classroom under proper supervision would teach youngsters to understand their own potential. A lesson in mathematics, for example, often involved taking students into the fields where they would measure off acres and calculate maximum yields. Lessons in public health emphasized how the natural growth of plants, animals, and people created an invigorating environment. Washington persistently admonished his staff to use natural resources imaginatively. He believed he would have to drill new teachers in his methods for two to three years before they could apply them satisfactorily. At the turn of the century he had to urge Joseph R. Lee, head of the academic department, to make his staff utilize the countryside more actively to supplement formal curriculum. "You will have to make a very strong and frank effort to bring them back to what really represents the Tuskegee Idea," he wrote.[30]

In many respects Washington participated in the effort to liberalize the classroom discipline that classical educators had maintained in the nineteenth century. Though he often used the word *inculcation* to mean *instruction,* several historians have noted that his emphasis on "learning by doing" corresponded with that of progressive educators like John Dewey and G. Stanley Hall. In contrast to southern Black colleges that retained the classical curriculum and rote-recitation longer than their New England models, Tuskegee became a paragon of a liberalized pedagogy. Washington's synthesis of discipline and spontaneity, however, differed from the progressives in at least one vital way. They worked primarily with students from "repressed" middle-class households and sought to reawaken their youthful spontaneity. Washington sought to bring order to students who often were older and who, he believed, lacked supervision and self-esteem. Both Washington and Dewey may have assessed education by its utility in producing "creative" people, but their methods differed almost as radically as did their pupils.[31]

Washington felt always that he was caught in a race with time. He believed that unless individual Blacks used their surroundings efficiently, Negroes as a group would fail to survive the Darwinian struggle. The imaginative flights of the poet, which Crummell and later DuBois and Ferris encouraged as vital to creative group leadership, seemed to Washington the self-indulgence of an idle elite. The wishes of individual students, therefore, had to be subordinated to the interests of the group. He feared, for example, the fascination young people had for "danger" and hoped to minimize the attraction of such "risks to their health" by emphasizing how the impairment of an individual's faculties might harm future generations. While he hoped to stimulate students by constant innovation in his teaching procedures, he disapproved of the spontaneous attraction students felt for the "vague, distant, and mysterious." In the end, he felt a profound distrust of himself and the people from whom he had sprung and a determination to transform them by emulating models provided by the powerful. As Richard Wright has noted, he was, perhaps more than any Black man of his generation, so hardened by rejection that he had become "impacted of feeling, choked of emotion."[32]

Washington's effort to popularize the distinction between working and being worked also determined his overall vision of Tuskegee Institute and his attitudes on broader social issues. He had been asked initially to organize a school for training Black teachers, but his conception of local needs required him to widen the purpose and expand the program of the school dramatically. Tuskegee, for Washington, should not merely impart pedagogical method or instruct persons in specific skills, but, like Hampton, should transform personalities and communities. To be free of local white control he sought private funding rather than rely on the parsimonious state legislature.[33] To dramatize his goal of community development he made an innovation over Hampton's organization so significant that he eventually felt justified in referring to his work as the "Tuskegee System." Not only did Tuskegee—unlike Hampton—have local Blacks on its board of trustees, but from the beginning its teaching staff was exclusively Black. The emphasis on Black administration to some extent reflected Alabama conditions. Lewis Adams, a local Black hardware-store owner, had been the leading promoter of a Negro normal school for Tuskegee, and the Black educator, William H. Councill, already headed a state-supported Black normal school. But Washington turned necessity to a pedagogical and ideological advantage. He respected dedicated white educators like General Armstrong and appreciated their broad background, but he believed that to change the consciousness of peasants the teaching cadre must share as many experiences with them as possible. Perhaps because none were available he never sought white instructors and solicited instead teachers from Negro schools. As DuBois later noted, Blacks resented Hampton's exclusively white faculty, and the social segregation of Black students from white teachers.[34]

For two specific reasons he came to argue that Blacks themselves had to fill positions of authority in institutions designated specifically for them. First, of course, the students would be inspired by the example teachers of their own race could set, and they would not feel the social distance between themselves and the white faculty as they did at Hampton. Second, and perhaps more important, Washington believed that Black teachers, particularly those from the South, would not impose pretentious ambitions on students. By respecting the student's smallest achievements, they would fortify his sense of efficacy. Robert Park, a white social scientist whom Washington employed as a research assistant, ghost-writer, and general advisor in the early twentieth century, provided keen insight into Washington's sense of purpose for rural schools in his reports from a tour of such institutions. After visiting a well-endowed school for Negroes in St. Helena, South Carolina, run by a dedicated white woman, he wrote that, "where the school fails is in the fact that it is away beyond and above the people. They could never create or produce anything like it and they cannot feel it is theirs . . ."[35]

Washington emphasized self-scrutiny and a close affinity between the teaching staff and the peasantry because he believed that all social groups must prepare themselves for a single goal: full participation in the industrial world. Like other Black writers of the age, Washington assumed that all groups emerging from primitive conditions had to learn from more advanced groups. Living in a country dominated by whites, Washington argued, Blacks could learn most effectively and disturb quaint prejudices the least by filtering technical knowledge through their own leadership. Separatism was for him not so much a social ideal as a strategy to allow the freedmen to develop the self-confidence to compete with whites. In a separate setting, Washington believed, he could most effectively convince Blacks that "economic efficiency was the foundation for every kind of success."[36]

Washington conceived of Tuskegee as a young and growing community, which—while dependent on outside capital—must strive to simulate self-sufficiency. He did not believe that products made by the pupils should pay for the upkeep of the school or that the school should operate at a profit. Such ideas about "manual trade schools" had been discredited before the Civil War.[37] But Tuskegee's students were to make enough of the school's physical necessities to defray operating costs and to lower costs of construction. Despite sporadic attendance and a graduation rate of only 14.1 percent as late as 1915, Washington believed his schooling had transformed a significant number of Blacks in the lower South. Students came from poorer families than those at Hampton and would have had to leave school under any circumstances. Under his program they had acquired the rudiments of a trade and the pedagogy to instruct their comrades. He instituted a one dollar entrance fee, which was subsequently raised to ten dollars to "weed out indifferent students." To defray the annual tuition of fifty dollars to make capital improvements, and to augment the endowment fund, he solicited donors. But unlike at Hampton and at most other southern schools, he insisted that students pay their own room and board either in cash or labor. By 1915 the cost amounted to ten dollars a month at a time when unskilled labor in the South received one dollar a day. As he explained to Seth Low, chairman of the board of trustees from 1906 through 1913, his policy limited the time many students could spend in school, "but in real education and character building we have thought it wiser to place responsibility for paying personal expenses upon the student. . . ."[38]

Washington also saw Tuskegee as the focus for exploiting traditional Black loyalties to transform communities from within. Initially, he cultivated the smallest gifts, even chickens from elderly ex-slaves, because he wanted local people to accept Tuskegee in their community. He romantically evoked a love of the soil and of the folk wisdom of independent Black farmers, and he brought some to Tuskegee for rest and relaxation. Once he had interested farmers, however, he hoped to demonstrate how the school could transform their lives. By 1893 he had begun the Tuskegee Farmer's Conference, which utilized the idea of Christian Witness to promote technological innovation. He began his conference by virtually preaching a sermon on the benefits of diversified agriculture, especially the corn-hog cycle practiced by farmers in the Ohio Valley, which provided alternate sources of cash income and of food. Washington may have begun diversified agriculture at Tuskegee itself to feed the students and to sell locally. Quite typically, though, he saw its larger social potential and incorporated it into his larger vision of community development. He called on the farmers to "testify" to their own efforts, however small, to practice the gospel he had preached. Those who had not performed such "good works" were admonished to "work" during the coming year so they too might testify to their faith in Washington's gospel. Though the audience grew, the format remained the same. In 1908, for example, the New York *Age* reported that, "These meetings in many respects resemble old time Methodist experience meetings. The delegates 'testify' as to their moral and material progress, not overlooking the spiritual in their oft-repeated insistence upon clean ministers and clean teachers."[39]

Unlike Crummell and the young W. E. B. DuBois, Washington believed that whatever unique cultural attributes Blacks possessed must be suppressed if they were to compete with whites. For him "race" consisted not of persons with "inherent traits" that induced mutual attraction but of individuals of common ancestry whose loyalties had been created by historical circumstances. As a race Blacks remained together because they faced a unique "condition." Despite their residence in a growing, progressive nation, they were perceived as incompetents and isolated from modern technology. To overcome this condition they must demonstrate the capacity to master skills. Like most entrepreneurs and educators of the late nineteenth century, Washington believed that "culture" denoted refined tastes and the capacity to express ideas or sentiments to enlighten an educated elite. Blacks who perfected the arts of music, painting, or dance were peripheral to the peasant's struggle, however ingenious as individuals they might be. Washington could appreciate the poetry of a Dunbar and even the paintings of a Henry Ossawa Tanner, whose most famous work Robert Ogden helped purchase for Hampton Institute. The writer Charles Chestnutt even submitted some of his later novels to Washington for criticism before having them published. Washington, however, treated such work not as aesthetic form conveying unique racial "gifts," but as ideological ammunition demonstrating further that Blacks could master the most sophisticated forms of expression in modern society.[40]

The most progressive and ennobling force in America, Washington argued, was the great corporate enterprise. John D. Rockefeller, Andrew Carnegie, Colis Huntington, and others had used capital to create thousands of jobs and to improve the standard of living for everyone, he observed. Washington successfully pursued such men to obtain large grants for Tuskegee's building and endowment funds and to have them serve on his board of trustees. His long and lucrative relationship with Andrew Carnegie was highlighted by a letter from the steel magnate that praised one of Washington's publications. Carnegie, like Washington, began as a poor apprentice in his trade and emerged as its leader because of his administrative genius and skills in publicity. He admired similar skills in others. As he told Washington, "One who has made so much out of life (more than any man living as far as I see taking into account the lowly start) must surely be able to tell us how to put the most into it."[41]

Washington admired most in Black men the same spirit of enterprise. He felt most at ease not only with other Negro educators like Holtzclaw and Robert R. Moton of Hampton, but with Negro businessmen like Robert A. Church of Memphis, J. C. Napier of Nashville, and Philip Payton of New York, who through their personal initiative, had created interlocking business networks. Although he questioned the honesty of the Richmond real estate dealer, Giles Jackson, and his Chicago counterpart, Jesse Bingha, he worked with them to promote Negro enterprise. He easily reconciled his romantic description of country life with his promotion of urban business by emphasizing how Blacks must accumulate property wherever they might reside. Like so many promoters of the virtues of country life at the turn of the century, Washington ignored its natural beauty and emphasized how its cultivation would yield stable and prosperous communities. The Black "cultural" level would then be elevated by inculcating in the farmers more sophisticated consumer demands. In 1907, for example, he told an audience at the Philadelphia Divinity School how he had been prodding a farmer's wife for years about acquiring a sewing machine. "I am not through with that family yet. I am going to work on that woman until through her I will get that old man to work five or six days of the week."[42]

The most promising example of accelerating Black production and consumption Washington saw in separate Black communities like Mound Bayou, Mississippi; Boley, Oklahoma; and other experiments in self-help. Mound Bayou had been founded formally in 1891 by a former slave of Jefferson Davis's brother and was located near the old Davis plantation in the Mississippi delta. Boley, as well as several other Oklahoma towns, were founded at the turn of the century by Blacks who had either worked on the railroad or had come there deliberately to farm. Black entrepreneurs like Charles Banks and Isaiah Montgomery who had founded these towns provided for Washington a powerful contrast to the clerks he had seen in the nation's capital. Here were men who used their education and practical experience to increase employment opportunities, generate capital for investment, and create mutual respect between local Blacks and whites. After the turn of the century Washington frequently visited these towns on railroad excursions and had Robert Park prepare articles about them for popular magazines. The towns encouraged separation of the races, which Washington did not see as a long-term goal but one that nonetheless demanded that Blacks rely on themselves for entrepreneurial, technical, and political skills. Washington, though arguing strongly that Blacks were first of all loyal Americans, concluded that "there is a temporary advantage to the Negro race in the building up of these race towns." Indeed, they seemed to Washington the fulfillment of the Tuskegee Idea. The mayor of

Brooklyn, Illinois, an unincorporated Black suburb of East St. Louis, expounded on the pride of his townsmen in following Washington's leadership. Blacks owned Brooklyn's stores, held all the elective offices, and had erected a brick school house for their children. The mayor felt he had best captured the Tuskegee spirit when he noted that Brooklyn had aspirations to become the "metropolis" of all the separate Black towns.[43]

Tuskegee graduates, of course, could rarely live in separate Black communities. At work they encountered whites who were occasionally organized into labor unions, and in racially mixed communities they encountered partisan political organizations. Washington saw both unions and political parties as agencies to alienate Blacks from their basic task of capital accumulation. He had first encountered unions in the coal fields of West Virginia, where he joined the Knights of Labor. Here he observed that a union seemed to consist of "walking delegates," men who did not themselves mine coal but who were dispatched from a central office to organize miners. They seemed to lure workers away from their jobs into a strike at the moment when the workers had accumulated enough savings to buy a home or start a small business. Usually losing the strike, the organizers departed and left the miners without savings and under even tighter control by the employers. Washington also observed that Blacks had been losing skilled jobs in the cities in direct proportion to the growth of unions. Data on racial discrimination by unions uncovered by Durham in the 1890s provided Washington with his greatest argument for advising Blacks to remain in the country districts.[44]

In his pragmatic pursuit of the nation's industrial magnates, Washington misrepresented the intentions of union organizers and the physical perils under which they worked. But the unspoken threat that unions presented to Washington was their emphasis on class rather than race loyalties. While the Tuskegee Idea did not envision any distinctive "race traits," it did see race as the basis of social and economic development. Unlike Fortune, Washington did not foresee that conflicts between labor and capital would supercede those between the races, at least not in the South for many generations. Instead, he sought to assuage racial tensions by encouraging Blacks to avoid biracial organizations, and he commended his graduates to employers as loyal Americans uninterested in unionization. Black involvement in conflicts between unions and management occasionally perplexed Washington. He did not reply to a labor leader in Birmingham who inquired why his graduates worked for a roofer who employed nonunion labor. When James Ferrier of Chicago asked what to do about Black scabs who had been fired after a teamsters' strike was settled in 1905, Washington wrote that he had no advice to offer. To the enthusiastic request from a Black union organizer in Spanish Town, Jamaica, for information about labor unions among American Blacks, Washington blandly replied that "we have no matter of this character for distribution."[45]

Considering himself both a Darwinian and a realist, Washington argued that partisan politics offered limited opportunities to anyone for improving social conditions. He agreed with DuBois and Douglass that free men should exercise the franchise, and he often said that Blacks must never relinquish their civil rights. After 1900 he reported violations of the fourteenth and fifteenth amendments to Oswald Garrison Villard, publicher of the New York *Evening Post* and to Ray S. Baker of *McClure's Magazine*, who he hoped would publicize such outrages. When he felt he might sway public officials he wrote letters to southern newspapers protesting disfranchisement maneuvers in state constitutional conventions and legislatures. He worked behind the scenes to try to prevent disfranchisement in Alabama and Georgia and was furious when local Blacks in Atlanta were unprepared to assist him properly. As late as 1914 he managed to use his influence with white officials in Montgomery to head off an effort to delimit a formal ghetto, a maneuver the Supreme Court ultimately found to be unconstitutional.[46]

But for Washington elective politics and officeholding were derivative vocations. Even presidents did not directly alter social relations but merely gave legal sanction to the decisions by which the great entrepreneurs organized productive power.

Washington was not an "economic determinist" because he believed that properly trained individuals could alter the course of a group's history and political participation could guarantee equal justice. But in any society those who controlled the factors of production held paramount power. Characteristically, both President McKinley's visit to Tuskegee in 1896 and Vice President Roosevelt's proposed trip in 1901 were planned by Washington jointly with the chambers of commerce of Montgomery, Mobile, and Atlanta.[47]

Washington's work at Tuskegee, however, had always required political contacts initially because part of the support came from the legislature and the rest had to be generated through endorsements. The network of philanthropists that General Armstrong had constructed included many prominent politicians who, like himself, were Union Army veterans. As Washington's fame grew, however, many white political figures and Blacks like Archibald Grimke began to adduce broad implications from his work and to seek his endorsement for their policies. Like Grimke, for example, Washington and Armstrong had opposed Senator Lodge's Force Bill and instead sought federal funds for agricultural education. While most Black politicoes resented his influence and decried his apparent hypocrisy for advising politicians, Washington typically combined pragmatic and ideological objectives. He used political contacts to gain support for his school and to promote entrepreneurship as the basis of Black community development. Between 1895 and 1905 he utilized contacts with governors, presidential advisors, and finally presidents to become, as Kelly Miller wrote, "referee at large . . . sole spokesman for the entire Negro race." The dual use of political influence for institutional and ideological purposes can best be seen in Washington's relationship with President Roosevelt, which was largely responsible for triggering so much opposition to him among Black politicians and intellectuals.[48]

The friendship with Roosevelt grew out of Washington's general search for endorsements. Since his famous speech at Atlanta calling for an end to political agitation and recommending separate but equal development for Blacks and whites,

Washington had delivered many other speeches where he had shared the platform with Presidents McKinley and Cleveland and other prominent persons. To gain the endorsement of the Spanish-American War hero and new vice president, Washington invited Roosevelt in April, 1901, on a good-will tour of the Gulf states, to include a stop at Tuskegee. Roosevelt, who had previously mentioned his admiration for Washington to T. Thomas Fortune, agreed, but preferred to wait until after the fall elections.[49] The assassination of President McKinley in September, 1901, forced Roosevelt to cancel his tour, but it magnified Washington's importance to him. Because Roosevelt was a neophyte in national politics he lacked contacts with the Republican party's cadre, and because he wanted to be nominated and elected in 1904, he needed a reliable source of information on its southern wing. Because Washington knew prominent Blacks throughout the South and had immense national prestige and no factional attachments, he seemed to Roosevelt the ideal informant. In addition, Roosevelt and Washington shared many personality traits. According to Kelly Miller, Roosevelt practiced a "strenuous" philosophy and spoke primarily of character, courage, and integrity. He saw few Negroes who embodied these characteristics until he observed Washington. On the day he became president, Roosevelt asked Washington to visit him in the White House as soon as possible to discuss patronage matters. Washington, after consulting with prominent Tuskegee trustees George Foster Peabody and Robert Ogden, and with President Hollis Frissell of Hampton, accepted the invitation. For him the relationship promised some influence on the president's southern policy and wider contacts for fundraising. Though Washington's initial visit to the White House became the center of a temporary controversy in the southern press, he and Roosevelt ignored the matter and it soon passed.[50]

Combining opportunity with ideology, Washington furthered both Roosevelt's political interests and his own social ideals. When consulted for patronage appointments, he disparaged traditional officeholders and recommended men with administrative experience in private business. In Georgia, for example, he found that two Black, incumbent internal revenue collectors, though appointed by McKinley, promised to support Roosevelt and "stand high in character with both races." In Alabama, Washington noted that a prospective appointee, though active in politics for many years, had as a druggist earned the respect of his neighbors. If Roosevelt wished to appoint other Negroes in Alabama, Washington suggested he select W. H. Pettiford, in whose bank Washington held token stock; George Lovejoy, a Mobile attorney; or Adam Wimbe, a planter from Greensboro. In Mississippi Washington designed an entire strategy for the president, again relying on successful Negro businessmen like W. E. Million and Isaiah Montgomery. The long-time Black Republican national committeeman, James Hill, Washington described as a "foul and corrupt politician." His description of Calvin Chase of the Washington *Bee* was little better. The best that he could say for Walter Cohen of New Orleans was that he represented a large contingent of local Blacks rather than "lily-white Republicans" and had brought some order to the administration of the local customs house.[51]

Washington vigorously supported the political aspirations of men with professional expertise like Robert L. Smith, principal of the Oakland, Texas, Normal School and a former member of the Texas legislature; Robert Terrell, a graduate of the Harvard Law School and a high school principal in Washington D.C.; and Charles Anderson, an appointive office-holder in New York City. Washington wrote almost a dozen letters to Roosevelt supporting Smith, who was finally appointed deputy marshal for eastern Texas in 1902 after he had visited the capital with Washington's letter of introduction. Under Washington's persistent urging, Terrell was appointed a federal judge. Anderson, who was appointed internal revenue collector for the Port of New York, Washington also hoped would be a delegate to the Republican national convention in 1904 to organize Black delegates for Roosevelt. According to Roosevelt though, Anderson's appointment was blocked by his old political nemesis, Senator Thomas Platt.[52]

As Roosevelt came to rely on Washington's consistency and logic for general racial policy, Washington expressed his views more vigorously. He pushed Roosevelt to condemn lynching and peonage, to oppose "lily-white factions" within southern Republican parties, and to oppose cynical efforts by politicians to enforce the franchise clause of the Fourteenth Amendment. From 1904 onward Washington was increasingly consulted on major speeches pertaining in any way to the South. He advised the president in July, 1904, to omit all references to the South in campaign speeches because of the inflamed relations between capital and labor then prevalent. The president, he wrote, should try to placate relations between labor and capital and between Blacks and whites because northern capitalists, who had invested heavily in the region, required peaceful conditions for their businesses and the region to prosper. If strikes continued and Blacks were recruited as scabs, Roosevelt might be called on to defend their right to work—thus losing support among union labor in the North. Roosevelt followed Washington's advice carefully. By 1906 he submitted pertinent sections of his State of the Union message to Washington for comments. Washington told a friend in the capital that he had convinced the president to modify the speech "quite a bit."[53]

Washington's new political role after 1901 challenged the entire officeholder class and led eventually to sustained opposition from other Black social strata as well. But it is important also to set it into his context—a combination of opportunism and ideological consistency to promote his educational ventures. The mastery of pedagogical, administrative, and diplomatic skills enabled Washington to make Tuskegee the best endowed private educational institution in the South by the year of his death in 1915. By creating an image of scientific pedagogy adapted to the peculiar needs of the freedmen, he raised an endowment that assured the school's long-term financial stability. In the absence of significant state funding, and with a desire to avoid state control, he followed Armstrong to raise "venture capital" among northern abolitionists and philanthropists. While visiting them in their homes, he found they would recapture past glories and see the concrete results of their efforts by contributing to Black social rehabilitation through education.

One man sent relics of John Brown all the way from California to inspire Tuskegee students, while others withdrew funds from missionary societies to support students at Tuskegee or to endow schools modeled after it.[54]

In the 1890s Washington turned to the incredible new wealth generated by industrialization to build Tuskegee's endowment. The spirit and the curriculum admirably met the demands of businessmen that schools prepare students as skilled workers and intelligent consumers. Washington shared the dissatisfaction of the industrialists with traditional colleges, which they felt denigrated labor, parsimony, and technology. To remedy these deficiencies new colleges of business and technology were founded and entrepreneurs and lawyers replaced clergymen on boards of trustees. The Wharton School of Finance and Commerce was founded in the same year as Tuskegee by a merchant family whose daughter took a particular interest in settlement work among Philadelphia's Blacks. By 1911, Tuskegee's board of trustees included Washington and Warren Logan (Tuskegee's Black secretary), three Tuskegee businessmen, two northern white ministers, eleven industrialists and bankers residing primarily in New York City, and Theodore Roosevelt. By 1914 the ministers had been replaced by two more industrialists.[55]

Washington raised funds to meet operating expenses, erect buildings, and increase the endowment, with tenacity and exact record keeping. He utilized his trustees to alert him to potential donors and to advise on prudent investment, while he managed resources at Tuskegee meticulously. In 1903 Carnegie assured Tuskegee's future and Washington's personal support with a gift of $600,000 to the endowment fund. The interest from $150,000 would support Washington and his wife for life, thus enabling their removal from the school's annual payroll. By 1909 annual operating expenses approached $200,000, but Washington had met them through annual contributions for every year but two since 1897. In addition, legacies due Tuskegee, some of which were already yielding income, had reached over $800,000. By 1915 the endowment fund exceeded $2,000,000. So efficiently had Washington organized the school's finances that by 1919, though enrollment had risen to almost eighteen hundred and a depression curtailed annual income, his successor, Robert R. Moton, was one of the few principals in the South to balance the budget without impairing the program.[56]

In promoting his program Washington received the support of many southern white educators who no doubt believed that Blacks should be confined to manual skills. W. N. Sheets, the Florida superintendent of education in 1900, asked Washington to recommend a man as principal of a school modeled after Tuskegee. Local Black educators, Sheets reported, felt it undignified to teach industrial skills, "but the mechanic arts and agriculture," he concluded, would benefit Blacks more in their current state of evolution than would a classical curriculum. To place Black men who agreed with his vision of economic development in positions of local authority, Washington cooperated with such white officials.

Occasionally Washington's pupils would assume control of schools that had had a classical curriculum. Their pedagogical innovations seemed to Washington the substitution of efficacy for obsolescence, but they often revealed social tensions within Black communities. When Washington sent Isaac Fisher, one of Tuskegee's most respected young graduates, to become principal of Branch Normal College for Negroes in Pine Bluffs, Arkansas, in 1902, segments of the local Black community bitterly objected. The retired principal had been a professor of classics and his assistant, whom local Blacks preferred for the job, was a college graduate. Fisher, however, received the support of the trustees and augmented the curriculum with courses in shop work and agriculture directly under his supervision. His success seemed assured when the trustees decided not to require him to take the state examination for school principals—a test that required knowledge of Latin and Greek. Fisher saw himself battling not primarily for his job but for Washington's educational philosophy. "If I can get a firm foothold in this school," he wrote, "I believe I can do much for the people here and for the prestige of Tuskegee. If I can succeed as the successor of a man who holds as many degrees as Professor Corbin holds and who has fought and is yet fighting our school and you, I think in a measure the tongues of our enemies will be silenced here."[57]

The Scope and Limits of Black Modernization

As Washington became involved with national figures, he saw how other Black institutions might contribute to his general strategy for race development. Many scholars, accepting the view of Washington's critics like DuBois and Trotter, have documented Washington's efforts to control the editorial policies of Black newspapers and representative bodies.[58] But despite his financial resources and prestige, Washington succeeded only moderately because the men with whom he worked did not sympathize sufficiently with his vision of modernization to implement his plans. Many, like E. E. Cooper and Fred Moore, were too absorbed in the traditions of partisan journalism to create independent newspapers that embodied Washington's vision of community development. Others, like Jesse Bingha, Lloyd Wheeler, and Philip Payton, represented the central contradiction of Washington's entreprenurial ethos. Much as Crummell and others had predicted, they became so absorbed in promoting their own enterprises that they lacked a communal spirit. Indeed, an examination of Washington's relations with newspapers and the National Negro Business League suggests the frustrations and the limits of Washington's philosophy rather than examples of his hegemony. His pedagogy for the oppressed became lost in the contradictions of urban enterprise.

Emma Lou Thornbrough has shown that prior to Washington's ascendency the Black press did not speak for communities but for factions of the Republican party. Black journalism and protest, which began on the fringe of politics with Frederick Douglass, Martin Delany, and others, had moved into the party system and failed to seek a wide Black constituency. As an institution, Washington found the press ideologically and professionally obsolete. Largely dependent on contributions from politicians, the newspapers necessarily equated patronage squabbles with racial needs and reported in detail the social life of the Black political elite. By 1900 editors like Fortune, Calvin

Chase of the Washington *Bee,* and George Knox of the Indianapolis *Freeman* had held their posts for at least a decade and along with Cooper, Moore, John E. Bruce, and Ralph Tyler cultivated a small audience for their precious style of political journalism. The increased cost of press equipment in the 1890s and limited retail advertising prevented them from enlarging their papers. But for Washington the fault lay with their desire to retain a style of life he had found repugnant during his initial stay in Washington in the late 1870s.[59]

Washington judged the Negro press by its failure to emulate the successful white newspapers, which had developed retail advertising and mass circulation to free their editors from partisan control. If Negro editors would substitute "boosterism" for partisanship, Washington believed, they too could win an audience among the Black and white middle class that might also help them gain support for the needs of the freedmen. Editors could succeed, he said, if they presented consistent opinions on local and national issues and promoted Negro achievements rather than defending parties or factions. When Knox, for example, allowed others to write editorials that diverged from the paper's general policy, Washington complained bitterly. The inconsistencies, he said, created doubts among the public over the integrity of the editor. The reporting could not be based on political gossip, and Black achievements must be publicized so that whites could see that the race could be "businesslike."[60]

To adapt Negro newspapers to his own standards, Washington provided guidelines and subsidized several papers with funds and copy. Fortune, Knox, Moore, and Cooper all received payments of from twenty to one-hundred-fifty dollars several times annually to meet pressing debts. Usually money was remitted to obtain specific placing of news stories, photographs, or publicity features. In addition, a special column, "Tuskegee Notes," prepared under Emmett Scott's direction, was circulated regularly. Scott, as the nation's only prominent Negro agent for the Associated Press, could make stories about Tuskegee available quickly and cheaply through the wire service. Although some critics found Washington's news releases fulsome, he explained to Francis J. Garrison, "legitimate advertising" for

Tuskegee consisted of publicizing achievements or honors that illustrated the success of the school and the acclaim given its ideals. If southern whites, for example, learned that Washington had been invited to a conference by the king of Belgium, they might see the provincialism of their opposition to his program.[61]

Washington's dilemma in developing a sophisticated and efficiently organized Negro press to publicize his views can best be illustrated in his relations with the Washington *Colored American* and the New York *Age*. The editors of these papers actively promoted Washington's views, but they still failed to produce a paper of which he approved because they could not free themselves from the traditions of partisan journalism. E. E. Cooper founded the *Colored American* in 1893 with the help of the Black journalist John E. Bruce, whose column, "Brucegrit," was widely circulated. Cooper had worked for over ten years as a journalist before founding the paper and was well known. He also admired Washington and in 1900 became secretary of the National Negro Business League. Washington appreciated that Cooper allocated less space than Calvin Chase's Washington *Bee* to partisan politics and reserved many columns to publicize Tuskegee. But Cooper could not alter his partisan attitude toward journalism nor divest himself of its obligations. He spent many evenings at banquets and parties with civil servants and office seekers, many of which were reported in the *Bee* and *Colored American*. In 1899 he devoted much time to obtaining appointments for Blacks as federal census takers. While he tried to impress Washington with the financial stringencies of editing a newspaper, Washington dismissed Cooper's behavior as typical of the frivolity of his social set.[62]

Cooper's training in partisan journalism also led him to transfer its apologetics from the politicians to Washington. A reader of the *Colored American* could not discern whether copy on Tuskegee appeared because it merited inclusion as news or because Cooper toadied to Washington as he had to Republican politicians. DuBois in fact concluded that Cooper lacked all independent judgment, and he complained that through the *Colored American* Washington sought to dominate the Negro press. But so incompetent did Cooper finally appear to

Washington that when the *Colored American* encountered financial difficulties in 1903 and 1904, he would not help. Despite Cooper's loyalty, Washington felt that he no longer needed a media outlet in the nation's political capital, where he already had the full attention of the president and the distrust of the "D.C. Crowd" of Black appointive officeholders. When Cooper's solicitation for funds to political appointees like Robert Terrell also went unanswered, the paper was discontinued in early 1905.[63]

Washington's relationship with T. Thomas Fortune, Fred Moore, and the New York *Age* was longer and more complex but perhaps more frustrating than his relationship with Cooper. Fortune had founded the paper as the New York *Globe* in 1881. By 1900, it had become the most respected Negro newspaper in the country because of Fortune's biting wit, the debates in the "Letters to the Editor" section, and the reporting from most major cities by prominent Negro professional people. Fortune's switch from the Republicans to the Democrats and back and his ideological flirtations with agrarian radicalism and nonpartisanship had defined the range of Black political options since the late 1880s. In the 1890s he had tried to develop the *Age* as a solvent business. He complained that local Black entrepreneurs failed to advertise enough to support newspapers, but the extant copies of the *Age* from 1905 through 1907 show advertising from Black businessmen in Manhattan, Brooklyn, and Jersey City. Although the proportion of the paper's income from advertising is unknown, it had a steady circulation of four thousand and in 1907 its stock was valued at over seven thousand dollars. Fortune also had a small, respectful if not always favorable white audience that included political figures like Senator Thomas Platt and Theodore Roosevelt. In the 1890s Fortune had also written a column on Negro life and politics for Richard H. Dana's New York *Sun*, and Washington suggested to Oswald Garrison Villard that he might increase the circulation of his New York *Evening Post* by adding a similar Fortune coulumn.[64]

Fortune had always supported industrial education as the basis for social rehabilitation and as the endowment for Tuskegee approached one million dollars, he dubbed Washington the "Wizard." Fortune, like Cooper, carried "Tuskegee Notes," featured stories about industrial schools, and reprinted many of Washington's speeches. Althouth he became personally indebted to Washington, he did retain his distinctive editorial style and occasionally criticized Washington in print for failing to appreciate the protest tradition of the Negro press. He insisted that as editor he retain jurisdiction over the paper's content and he was solely responsible for editorial views.[65] In early 1905, for example, the full debate over the enforcement of the disfranchisement clause of the Fourteenth Amendment, provided a real forum for the exchange of conflicting opinions. In the end Washington followed a position outlined by Fortune.[66]

While Washington lost interest in Cooper in the nation's political capital, he would have indefinitely subsidized Fortune in the nation's financial and philanthropic center. He told Fortune he wanted to make the *Age* a "national Negro paper, controlling the whole racial situation." Fortune, however, suffered from alcoholism, and the combined deterioration of his health and Washington's desire to have a stable medium to influence Negro businessmen and white philanthropists induced him to control the *Age* more directly. At the same time, he could not openly own the paper because he wanted to express his views on controversial subjects such as lynching, peonage, and segregation anonymously without losing support for Tuskegee from conservative philanthropists and southern whites. Washington still respected Fortune's editorial expertise, but he wanted a more reliable businessman to guarantee the paper's continuity. He suggested that Fortune sell his interest to an anonymous third party, who would insure the paper's financial stability while retaining Fortune on salary as editor. When Fortune refused to sell, Washington used Fred Moore, who had been editing the *Colored American Magazine* for him in Boston, to purchase the *Age*. Fortune bowed out as editor with the October 3, 1907, number.[67]

Washington believed he could now have unlimited and anonymous access to a respected newspaper. Between 1907 and 1915, however, Moore failed to create the type of journal for which Washington had hoped. Like Fortune, Moore shared Washington's enthusiasm for Negro business, but like Cooper he lacked imagination and skill in preparing consistent and well-written editorial pages and in retaining professionals like Archibald Grimke as correspondents. Until Fortune left for Chicago in December, 1907, Moore employed him as an editorial assistant. He then hired his son-in-law, Lester Walton, who had worked on white papers in St. Louis and New York and who had produced Black theatrical shows. By 1913, however, Walton became dissatisfied at not being consulted on newspaper policy and resigned. Moore then turned to James Weldon Johnson, a man of great literary skill and cosmopolitan tastes who had just returned after eight years as a consular official in Latin America. Although Johnson temporarily revived the paper's literary quality, the *Age* lacked the definitive style that Fortune had imparted to it.[68]

Moore, in addition, did not seem to understand how Washington and Emmett Scott wished the tone and content of the paper shaped to the spirit of enterprise. Constantly they had to remind him not to allow his political feuds with Charles Anderson and others to determine which events and personages he would cover and to prod him to publicize Black business successes. In 1910 Washington sent Moore a clipping on the improvement of economic conditions among Negroes in North Carolina, noting that "the Negro papers ought to give more time and attention to (business) and less to matters which have no permanent and practical value." In exasperation Scott chastised Walton in 1913 for not reporting the incorporation of the Standard Life Insurance Company of Atlanta, an event that had been duly lauded in the white Atlanta *Constitution*." This is really the biggest constructive thing that Negroes have done during the fifty years of freedom," Scott wrote, yet the *Age* had ignored it while publicizing patronage squabbles.[69]

The influence of the *Age* declined, however, not because Moore failed to attract readers but because he began to face competition. The weekly circulation of the *Age* more than trebled to fourteen thousand within three years after Moore became editor. But in late 1910, W. E. B. DuBois moved to New

York City to edit *Crisis,* a monthly journal affiliated with the NAACP. DuBois by then had become Washington's most respected critic, and within a year the circulation of *Crisis,* which featured publicity for Negro business, theatrical, and other achievements as well as news on civil and political matters, had equaled that of the *Age.* In 1911 a new weekly paper, the *Amsterdam News,* published in Harlem by Dr. P. M. H. Savory and catering to a West Indian readership, came into existence. Washington prodded Moore to adopt more aggressive advertising and sales techniques to meet his competitors. He suggested that he cooperate with the staff of the *Amsterdam News* and even that he move the offices of the *Age* to Harlem where he could become more closely involved in the life of the new Negro middle-class neighborhood. Moore, however, did not move the *Age* uptown until after Washington's death.[70]

While Washington did retain the benefit of expressing his views on southern matters anonymously in the *Age*, he became frustrated because he simply could not command its staff to obey him as he could employees at Tuskegee. He could not compel Moore as he could a teacher, and he could not devote enough attention to the paper to compensate for what he deemed the incompetence of individual staff members. Yet Washington himself undermined rapport among the staff because he could not tolerate the eccentricities that had marked successful Black editors and because he understood no better than they the changing interests of the urban public. In his desire for efficiency in administration he intrigued with friends in New York to purchase the *Age* behind the backs of both Fortune and Moore. He finally suggested that Moore rent the paper to Wilford Smith, his own business agent in New York City. Furthermore, Washington never appreciated how his small town boosterism reflected a style of journalism that could by 1910 have had very limited appeal to either Black or white urbanites. Ralph Tyler, on the basis of his knowledge of the New York press, advised Washington that some melodramatic stories would greatly expand circulation. Washington, though, condemned such sensationalism as much as he did excessive attention to the machinations of the old Black political clique. Without the flamboyance of an editor like

Fortune, the sensationalism of contemporary white metropolitan dailies, or the willingness to confront the political problems of discrimination in northern cities, no Negro newspaper could have attracted a large audience. While fighting one form of obsolescence, Washington in effect sought to impose one of his own.[71]

Washington's frustration with the Negro press reflected the cultural limitations of his program. They were even more fully revealed in the one publicity venture beyond Tuskegee itself to which he did devote full attention, the National Negro Business League. The league grew out of a report prepared by DuBois at Atlanta University in 1898 that demonstrated that Blacks had created almost two thousand successful businesses, most of which were located in the South. Inspired by this achievement and by some talks he held with DuBois in the spring of 1898, Washington conceived of a special Negro Exhibit in the American Pavillion at the World Exposition in Paris scheduled for the late summer, 1900, which he would coordinate with the founding of a permanent organization. To prepare the display he obtained through President McKinley the appointment of Jesse Lawson, a Black journalist in the Capital, to the American Commission to the Paris Exposition. Lawson then sent Andrew Hilyer, another Black journalist in Washington, D.C. to gather more data in Georgia, Tennessee, and the Carolinas, and sent Thomas Calloway, a Fisk graduate and close friend of DuBois, to supervise the display in Paris. DuBois and some of his students prepared charts, maps, and a text, which he then assembled at the last moment in Paris. In describing the exhibition, DuBois emphasized how Blacks had moved under their own direction from barbarism to all levels of civilization in a remarkably short period. The romantic racialism he had invoked under Crummell's influence at the initial meeting of the American Negro Academy two years previously was given concrete dramatization in the Paris display. Southern Blacks, he noted, were already "studying, examining and thinking of their own progress and prospects."[72]

While DuBois was presenting publicity to the world in Paris, Washington, with the help of E. E. Cooper, T. Thomas Fortune, Giles Jackson, Samuel Courtney (an old friend from

West Virginia then practicing medicine in Boston), and Louis Baldwin (a prosperous Black businessman in Boston), arranged a convention. Over three-hundred men and women met in Boston on August 23 and 24, 1900, to combine a holiday from southern weather with a serious effort to found a permanent national organization. Most of the delegates expressed the booster mentality that Washington desired, but they also believed they were generating the power to rejuvenate a whole race. Despite recent anti-Black riots in New Orleans, Wilmington, North Carolina and New York, delegates from Montgomery, Macon, and Pensacola reported the founding of local Negro Business Leagues amidst amicable race relations. Reports from Jacksonville, Tampa, and Selma asserted that business organizations could stabilize Black communities and mediate dealings with whites. Executives of the True Reformers Bank of Richmond and of the Penny Savings Bank of Birmingham noted how they had helped sustain their communities and improve race relations during the panic of 1893. J.C. Leftwich, the loquacious founder of the Black community of Klondike, Alabama, emphasized the social importance of Black enterprise even more directly. With increased unionization in the South, he noted, Black artisans faced increased discrimination in employment, and only the collective effort to build separate communities would give the freedmen and their children a new identity as men of property.[73]

To sustain the league, Washington became its president and obtained funds from Andrew Carnegie. His successor at Tuskegee, Robert R. Moton, also succeeded him as president of the league. Washington annually issued the call for league meetings, published letters of advice to local league officers in Negro newspapers, and had Emmett Scott handle the correspondence. He hired Fred Moore and Ralph Tyler as professional organizers with headquarters in New York City, and he continuously directed Moore to publicize the league in the *Age*. To encourage prominent local entrepreneurs he had the league meet in a different city each year. The 1902 meeting was under the auspices of the True Reformers and Giles Jackson in Richmond; the 1903 meeting was in Nashville under the auspices of Washington's friend, the banker J. C. Napier; and the 1912 meeting in Chicago was directed by the mercurial Jesse Bingha. To demonstrate race achievements and to influence potential critics, he invited men like Robert Terrell and the venerated president of Gammon Theological Seminary in Atlanta, J. W. E. Bowen, to address the 1902 meeting. The 1905 meeting was enlivened by the performance of the song, "Lift Every Voice," which soon became known as the Negro National Anthem. Washington enthusiastically thanked the authors, Bob Cole and James Weldon Johnson, for the race pride their work evoked.[74]

Contemporaries as well as historians have wondered why Washington should have promoted urban businesses so heavily while advising his students to remain in the country districts. His most strident contemporary critic, the native Bostonian and Harvard graduate William Monroe Trotter, thought that the league underlined Washington's cynicism. Trotter's exclusion from the Boston meeting, even though he had recently entered the real estate business, coupled with Washington's position as league president, confirmed his suspicion that it was intended less to promote business than to silence Washington's critics. Louis Harlan has recently argued that Washington organized the league, in part, because he was himself a businessman having greater net worth than most of those attending the Boston meeting and in part to provide a pleasant gathering for men who agreed with his emphasis on Black enterprise.[75]

Trotter was correct to believe that Washington despised him, and Harlan is correct to see the league as a vehicle for Washington's propaganda. But both men have not sufficiently emphasized how the league reflected Washington's southern booster mentality. Althouth Washington desired the league to operate nationally and to include various shades of business opinion, its format attracted primarily southerners. The most enthusiastic northern supporters had been raised in the South. With successful entrepreneurs testifying to their accumulation of assets, league conventions paralleled in form and tone the Tuskegee Farmer's Conference. Southerners dominated the first meeting and lightheartedly criticized the pomposity of Boston mannerisms. Promoters of separate Black rural communities brought personal greetings to Washington and hailed him as a "race leader" and "prophet" in a way that northern delegates never did. Washington, in turn, gave great publicity to local leagues in the South that sponsored his tours by train through the region. With their basis on entrepreneurship as the common tie between Black communities, Washington hoped the league could promote community growth in a way that had not been possible when politicoes had predominated as local Black spokesmen.[76]

With the league, however, as with the press, Washington encountered serious frustrations. Some difficulties arose because the league, despite its central headquarters, consisted of a loose federation of local associations. Its federated character underlined the basic flaw in its petit-bourgeois ideology, wherein entrepreneurs placed their own interests above that of the community. In Chicago, for example, prominent businessmen were willing to sponsor an occasional gala but not to use the league for community organization. The bulk of the organizational work fell to Washington's friend, the lawyer S. Laing Williams, and when he could not rally local support, Jesse Bingha provided some assistance. After the 1913 convention, however, the Chicago league disintegrated. In New York City Fred Moore, as salaried national organizer, managed to obtain the support of business friends of Washington like Charles Anderson and Philip Payton, Jr., But Washington had constantly to prod Moore into action, and the league developed a reputation as simply a clique of promoters who subordinated communal interests to their personal ambitions. Beyond the confines of southern towns where Blacks had far fewer institutions to express their interests, the business leagues and the philosophy they embodied seemed artificial.[77]

Although Washington began the league, according to Emmet Scott, to create "race consciousness and race pride," both men and Robert R. Moton seem to have envisioned a more direct political role for it. The league was reported to have taken a stand on certain bills before the Congress in 1912, though Scott refused to allow such information to appear in the press. In 1914, with the pressure of the successful organization of the National Association for the Advancement of Colored People undermining his support in the northern press, Washington saw the league as a vehicle for orderly protest. He told Moton to use the Business League in Virginia to complain about poor accommodations for Blacks on the Norfolk and Western Railroad. By 1915, Scott and Moton thought that the league might assume wider objectives and proposed a change of name to the Negro Organization Society. In addition to publicity and annual meetings, it would add mild forms of political protest. To further this objective, Scott urged numerous prominent Black businessmen from major cities to attend the annual meeting, though he never informed them of his plans to overhaul the league. The new plans were dropped, however, with Washington's fatal illness in the summer of 1915. Indeed an organization that depended on the social pressures of a small town to turn entrepreneurship into a force for community cohesion could hardly have functioned as a national protest organization.[78]

Given his sense of mission and his enormous energy, Washington's ventures with the Black press and with the Business League were logical extensions of his pedagogy of social rehabilitation. Contacts with editors, politicians and entrepreneurs, of course, followed opportunities rather than a master plan. But so carefully did Washington rationalize and measure the consequences of his acts that they sould be seen as components of an expanding vision of Black community. As he told Ray S. Baker in 1907, "I have long since made up my mind that the course to follow is to map out the work one is going to try to follow, then stick to it regardless of sentiment, always bearing in mind, however, to use common sense and not unnecessarily to anatagonize anyone."[79] But his efforts to transform institutions like the Black press that had grown out of elite politics and to mobilize a cadre of entrepreneurs to replace politicians as community spokesmen had their own limitations. Not only did repression continue in the South despite business leagues and increased accumulation of property by Blacks, but the major demographic trends among Blacks in the early twentieth century operated against him. Migration to northern cities led to unemployment that Black entrepreneurs could not relieve, while a new educated elite was not enthralled by an ethos of entrepreneurship. The migrants required representation of their interests through new forms of organization, and the cosmopolitan college graduates had more complex identity needs. New Black strata required alternatives to a pedagogy for the downtrodden.

3 | Non-partisanship, Ethnicity, and Opposition to Booker T. Washington

Many scholars have dicussed the development of Black opposition to Booker T. Washington, and his most persistent critics, W. E. B. DuBois and William Monroe Trotter, have both been the subject of biographies.[1] Historians, emphasizing Washington's role in reconciling North and South, have noted how his critics accused him of sacrificing Negro political and intellectual interests to advance his own program.[2] But scholars have not analyzed the sequential evolution of opposition to Washington and its relationship to broad changes in American social and intellectual leadership. Most of Washington's critics attacked different components of his political or educational strategies. But their debate with Washington was shaped by a wider search for an independent Black politics and a distinct Black voice in an era of third-party movements and of ethnic diversity in the American cities. Opposition to Washington was neither uniform nor unified but consisted of contending cliques facing the larger dilemmas of pluralistic politics and culture. To bring coherence to a discussion of the opposition to Washington and to see its relationship to a growing racial consciousness, one must examine two themes: nonpartisanship and Black ethnicity.

Scholars have assumed that Washinton's critics shared with him a vision of what Black people should become and disagreed with him primarily over tactics.[3] Washington and his critics promoted identical standards of personal decorum, business enterprise, and the virtues of American citizenship.[4] They also agreed that a major obstacle lay in the image of Blacks as plantation hands and slum-dwelling criminals. Washington countered those stereotypes with the ideal of efficient Blacks emulating white production, commercial, and family standards. Trotter, George Forbes—and men who were less critical of Washington like Archibald Grimke and Charles Chestnutt but who were also engaged in business—accepted Washington's cultural norms but emphasized instead the significance of citizenship in American identity. For such persons active participation in voluntary associations to defend rights and to purify political practices were an integral part of their public personality. Their opposition to Washington was based not only on tactical considerations. It was also a defense of the role of politics in their own social setting. Writers like Paul Dunbar, Chestnutt to some extent, DuBois, and musical artists like Will Marion Cook found still more serious dilemmas in Washington's prescription. In a world dominated by aggressive nationalism, Blacks, they argued, needed a distinctive identity to demonstrate their ethical parity with "the proud Anglo-Saxon" and to unify the disparate elements of the race. Just as Henry May discovered the origins of "the end of American innocence" even before World War I,[5] so many Black writers and artists sought a more distinctive and realistic meaning in *their* traditions in the generation before the Harlem Renaissance.[6]

The conflict between Washington and his critics, therefore, requires a broad social and cultural analysis. The consolidation of Washington's position as spokesman for social rehabilitation, and the development of an increasingly complex opposition, should be seen as the initial effort by Black writers to explore the full range of obstacles that thwarted their social equality in a modern society. Unlike the peregrinatious Black missionaries and Pan-Africanists of the nineteenth century, writers like Trotter, DuBois, J. Max Barber, Ida Wells-Barnet, and others lived within a society where they could directly influence the social ideals of a submerged but *mobile* people. America demanded rapid changes in the organization of labor, and Black leaders had to combine social theory, cultural awareness, and political strategies to improve the opportunities for their own people in the general scramble for security and status. The young, college-educated elite, therefore, assessed Washington's program against the background of settlement houses, political machines, ethnic diversity, discrimination, and romantic racialism. Indeed, in contrast to Washington the two major concerns for Black novelists, essayists, and sociologists were the class character of urban society and the complex relationship between race and class. To bring modernity to Blacks in a complex urban setting they gradually developed a new political ideology of nonpartisanship and an image of Black cultural uniqueness, which they felt would assault racism more effectively than an ethic of rehabilitation. The initial efforts to create a full alternative to Washington, like his own program, combined practical proposals and loosely organized groups, with a general intention to create distinctive Black institutions. As the Black urban population grew, however, the various intellectual and institutional efforts gained new publicity and gradually eclipsed Washington's simpler and more rustic vision of Black America. As Charles Valentine has recently argued, the assertion of Black ethnicity against the background of American racism was in many ways a revolutionary act,[7] despite the decorous setting in which it was initiated.

Political Agitation and the Search for Non-partisanship

The initial critics of Booker T. Washington came from a social stratum with established 'institutional and ideological commitments being displaced by rapid economic and political change. Aside from clergymen who disliked Washington because Tuskegee lacked sufficient denominational identification and evangelical fervor, the first sustained criticism of Washington came from a clique of Black political officeholders in the nation's Capital. Here a coterie of former elected officials like P. B. S. Pinchback and Blanche K. Bruce, political journalists like Calvin Chase and E. E. Cooper, and younger appointees in the civil service like Judson Lyons and W. T. Vernon vied for appointments. The older men represented the Reconstruction era when Blacks had played a dramatic part in southern politics, while the younger men had sought patronage initially through the former elected officials. These men by the late 1870s made Washington the mecca for young Blacks with social aspirations. For them any social philosophy that looked beyond the political arena for race leadership would betray the tradition upon which their own prestige rested.[8]

The officeholder elite became an ossified social enclave not only because they had lost touch with a supporting constituency but also because they lacked the expertise to resolve new economic and social problems contingent on the mobility of Black Americans after 1900. The deaths of Frederick Douglass, John M. Langston, and Blanche K. Bruce between February 1895, and March, 1898, symbolized the end of a heroic era in which one became a Black leader by agitating for citizenship rights. Not only had many southern states disfranchised Blacks, but some northern spokesmen like Archibald Grimke doubted the efficacy of a Force Bill, while many northern states had passed civil rights legislation. Agitation, therefore, was both dangerous and probably pointless in the South and lacked a clear focus in the North. In addition, new social types were emerging in Black communities. Kelly Miller, the Black sociologist at Howard University, noted that in the 1890s for the first time a major movement of Blacks to northern cities had begun, and DuBois shortly thereafter studied the first large stratum of Black college graduates. As the northern reading public shifted its perception of " the Negro problem" from that of southern stagnation to that urban resettlement, Black politicos residing in Washington were bound to lose their stature as experts to younger, professionally trained scholars residing in or near the problem areas.[9]

As Black officeholders discussed patronage they further revealed their awkward position. Without an active voting constituency, they conceived of their appointments as individual compensation for battles fought or opportunities denied in private industry. Patronage provided one of the few prestigious and suitable niches open to articulate and well-educated Black men. As John S. Durham, one of the most cosmopolitan of the officeholders, noted, young Black high school and college graduates could not obtain jobs as clerks in private firms, so government appointments provided an alternative. Though he felt private employment might yield a higher income, he accepted a consular position in the early 1890s and after 1900 sporadically sought other federal appointments. The poet Paul L. Dunbar, who held a minor post in Washington in the early 1890s, saw patronage as a socially appropriate and financially secure niche from which bright young men might launch literary careers. Like Durham, he believed that government positions should be available to compensate for racial discrimination in the private sector. When he relinquished his clerkship for a full-time literary career in 1897, he suggested to Republican functionaries a young man he believed to be a suitable replacement.[10]

To elite Blacks federal appointments still carried a patina of the success of the 1860s in gaining citizenship rights and symbolized a hope for widened political influence. In the 1890s Black politicians hailed as major advances for the race the appointment of Judson Lyons, Ralph Tyler, and Blanche K. Bruce in the treasury department and Walter Cohen, W. D. Crum, Charles Anderson, and John Dancy to local customs houses. James Weldon Johnson's appointment in 1906 as a consular agent in Venezuela provided the occasion for a gala banquet in New York and symbolized to the politicians that the younger generation of college-bred Blacks would carry forward the appointive political tradition. The officeholders "supping at the festive board" with Johnson believed themselves the embodiment of the civilized virtues.[11] But by succeeding according to the standards of a white elite they faced a dilemma. Racial discrimination in the civil service would limit the level of appointment to which they could aspire, while their lack of a constituency limited the political influence they could mount against discrimination. They had moved so far physically and culturally from the freedmen and the urban poor and showed so little interest in them that they were vulnerable to displacement as race spokesmen by those who could appear to understand the Black majority.

The D. C. Crowd, as Booker T. Washington contemptuously called them, developed in the 1890s serious doubts about its own political influence and the importance of its work. Many of them recognized that the expertise upon which race leadership could be built was shifting. Calvin Chase, the opportunistic editor of the Washington *Bee,* noted ruefully that in the twentieth century "new policies are to be formulated, new fields are to be made for the race." Leaders who understood social problems and who had political tact had to be found. His analysis pointed directly to Washington as a new race leader, but when Washington failed to support him for a federal judgeship in 1902, he became a vitriolic critic. Nevertheless, his logic led him to conclude that for social and economic rather than partisan reasons, "the colored politician is a nonentity now."[12] Indeed, as Washington gained influence, he became the particular focus for the discontent of the officeholders. In part because of his celebrated speech at Atlanta in 1895 and perhaps more importantly because of his network of contacts among abolitionist families still loyal to the Republican party, he had developed a wide following among the men to whom Black office seekers traditionally turned for appointments. As Durham, John E. Bruce, and others noted, Washington had gained the respect of shrewd political figures like Senator George F. Hoar of Massachusetts and James Clarkson of Iowa, and he seemed able to shape a political climate in which the freedmen might receive industrial opportunities and equal treatment before the law. Yet because whites saw in him greater knowledge of the social conditions in which the freedmen lived and to which philanthropic support was sent, he was replacing them as an authority on "the Negro problem."[13]

Specifically how Washington obtained national political influence remains obscure,[14] though by 1896 he had greatly impressed Clarkson and others. Southern governors and local officials were already asking him to intercede for them with the McKinley adminstration. He had been working vigorously to allay tensions between the races in Alabama by denigrating political and labor agitation. He supported conservative Republicans throughout the Populist embroglio and defended the gold standard. But spokesmen for the D. C. Crowd did the same; no more economically conservative Republican paper existed than Chase's Washington *Bee.* In addition to party loyalty however, Clarkson, Hoar, and young Theodore Roosevelt simply felt that Washington could speak more authoritatively about the needs of the freedmen and embodied progressive social values. Where the officeholders generally supported Senator Lodge's Force Bill, Washington asked for federal subsidies for agricultural demonstration projects. Where the officeholders adamantly opposed civil service reform, Washington wished to purify the entire electorate through literacy qualifications for the suffrage.[15] Many Black politicians accused Washington of hypocrisy for denigrating political agitation while functioning himself like a "boss." "Boss Booker" became a watchword among them, as men like Pinchback, John R. Lynch, Calvin Chase, and John E. Bruce observed their own influence erode. But other men like S. W. Bennett of South Carolina, Horace Cayton of Seattle, Whitefield McKinlay, and Robert Terrell recognized how ephemeral officeholding had become to Black social reform or political efficacy. They emphasized instead that Washington had faced the hard fact that in America influence rested on economic power and that appointive office had become a refuge from rather than a means to provide effective race leadership.[16]

Concern among Blacks over Washington's influence, however, was part of a larger debate over appropriate political loyalties and values that were expressed in the concept of nonpartisanship. As an ideology, nonpartisanship in the 1890s grew from *different* specific conditions but from a *similar* psychological impulse for Blacks and whites. For whites, nonpartisanship grew from the desire by a local elite to control expanding urban service monopolies and the political machines that serviced them. They hoped to do so by creating an informed middle-class citizenry that would abolish the ward system in local elections and bring professional expertise to the administration of government. To regain power at the local level, reformers hoped to encourage elite professionals and business-men to run on a nonpartisan ticket against machine candidates. Nonpartisanship would prevent national parties from influenc-ing local elections and would allow the elite to restore comity to the polity.[17] For Blacks, nonpartisanship to regain efficacy grew from a desire to retain influence in city governments and to secure citizenship rights for the freedmen. The Republican party nationally had abandoned them, while Democrats in several northern cities began to offer patronage. Good Govern-ment clubs in cities like Cincinnati and Cleveland accepted some like-minded Black professionals, but reformers in cities with large Black populations like Philadelphia and Baltimore rejected the Black elite. Realizing that they could rarely gain influence with reform elements in either party and unwilling to join the machines, Black professionals began to debate strategies for independent mobilization.[18]

Nonpartisanship had first been proposed by T. Thomas Fortune in the late 1880s, in reaction to the decrease in patron-age for Blacks from the Republicans and the failure of the party to provide economic support for the freedmen.[19] In 1892 Archibald Grimke had warned Massachusetts Republicans that local Democrats were offering patronage in exchange for a growing Negro vote, and by the mid-1890s Tammany Hall was providing Manhattan Blacks with minor appointments.[20] Journalists like Fortune and Chase then again raised the issue of nonpartisanship. Encouraged by Booker T. Washington, For-tune and Bishop Alexander Walters of Jersey City convened several meetings in 1898 and 1899 out of which emerged a new Afro-American Council.[21]

The new council represented the first phase in the new debate over nonpartisanship and reflected a shift in influence in the Black community. It included not only Washington and traditional office holders, but younger men with a bent for agitation like William Monroe Trotter and George Forbes. Washington, moreover, disagreed with many of the politicians who joined the council on the meaning of nonpartisanship. For them it meant dealing in a traditional way with more than one party, trading endorsements for patronage at successive elections. For Washington, it meant the selection of temporary officeholders on the basis of nonpolitical, primarily business, success. Like the white urban reformers promoting nonpartisanship, Washington believed that an appointee should demonstrate a standard of efficiency rather than simply party loyalty and should complement rather than vitiate civil service reform. His high regard for Charles Anderson of New York, for example, was based precisely on the latter's ability to meet that standard. Unwilling to accept this formula, officeholders like Judson Lyons, Pinchback, and Henry Cheatham resigned from the council and marched to political obscurity.[22] Trotter and Forbes, furthermore, developed still more radical views of nonpartisanship. They, like Bishop Alexander Walters of Jersey City, had ties to the northern wing of the Democratic party that eventually supported Woodrow Wilson. But they did not believe that nonpartisanship should mean a successive bartering of votes. Instead, they hoped to develop a new Black political agenda and they saw in the council the only available means for doing so. However much they may have come to criticize Washington after 1900, by working initially within the council they helped displace the older officeholder elite as effective spokesmen for the race.[23]

After 1901, debate in the Afro-American Council turned increasingly on Washington's political role because of his great influence with the new president, Theodore Roosevelt. Washington's work with the president coincided with his influence among southern white educators and northern philanthropists, who after 1901, established new funds to aid southern education.[24] The combination of his influence with philanthropists and the president enhanced his stature as an omnicompetent strategist. But it indicated to many Blacks that he had betrayed the idea of nonpartisanship by becoming a monopolist of power. To several members of the council, especially Trotter, Washington's enormous influence comprised the imposition of a highly partisan and decidedly southern strategy over a national situation. Nonpartisanship, Trotter believed, should allow for a full discussion of national problems and the selection of differing tactics to meet local situations. The rhetoric of attacks against Washington consistently depicted him as a "monopolist" who suppressed traditional American freedoms. Indeed, Washington did desire a tightly knit central agency that subordinated all action to the promotion of the Tuskegee Idea. The administrative structure promoted by his critics, on the other hand, consistently called for a loose federation of local associations coordinated by a secretary rather than a director. To his critics, Washington seemed to substitute Tuskegee for the Republican Party and to use nonpartisanship as a facade to cover his own interests.[25]

Specific criticism of the Tuskegee Program had been expressed at meetings of the Bethel Literary Society in the late 1890s. While no one attacked industrial education as such, speakers like the young Yale graduate William Ferris and Calvin Chase criticized the uses to which Washington put the program. In his zeal to promote his own school among New England philanthropists, Ferris reported, Washington insisted on the prior importance for Blacks of industrial over literary education. Washington, Ferris continued, seemed to support the contention of many whites, that Blacks lacked the capacity to absorb higher education. Chase then drew the logical conclusion that to deny the capacity of Blacks—even temporarily—to absorb the same education as whites was to affirm the legitimacy of Black subordination.[26] Other skeptics of industrial education in the 1890s like Crummell, Cromwell, and William Scarborough of Wilberforce University had not questioned Washington's motives. Indeed, Scarborough, a noted Latin and Greek scholar, became one of his staunchest defenders.[27] But as Ferris suggested, Black college graduates in the northeast had been increasingly irked by Washington's promotional schemes that lauded Tuskegee as the most useful recipient of philanthropy and suggested that the literary education they had received was not the best preparation for race leadership. Nevertheless, even when Washington reportedly criticized southern Negro colleges at the expense of Tuskegee, Black scholars like Kelly Miller, J. W. E. Bowen, and W. E. B. DuBois refrained from rejoinders so that philanthropists might be encouraged to increase their contributions. Washington's new relationship with Roosevelt and his new role with the Southern and General Education boards, however, crystallized the opposition of political agitators like Trotter and educators like DuBois and even Bowen. They could now see in Washington not simply a person advocating a different political strategy that might be legitimate in the South, but an ideologist attacking the values on which their own claims to racial leadership rested.[28]

The most vocal and persistent opposition to Washington came from young William Monroe Trotter, whose zeal became an embarrassment not only to Washington but to persons like DuBois, who while developing their own reservations to the Tuskegee Idea, were accustomed to a more genteel political style. Trotter's anti-Washington tirades, however, must be understood as part of his heritage of political agitation, which he inherited to some extent from Fortune and Chase. Trotter's father had been a Civil War veteran, and like Archibald Grimke a mugwump supporter of Grover Cleveland, for which he had received a political appointment in the Boston custom's house. Trotter had graduated from Harvard in 1895, where he had cultivated an "integrated" circle of friends from the Boston Latin School and had won a reputation as an aggressive advocate of social equality. After graduation he settled in Cambridge, where elite Blacks had been moving for a generation, sold real estate in a white firm, and took an active interest in efforts to reform Black politics. Indeed, that was what he had hoped for in the Afro-American Council, until Washington began to exercise more active control over it. As he later described the origins of his militancy to the white journalist Ray S. Baker, he found "it especially intolerable that a colored man, Booker T. Washington, should be ringing hurtful color prejudice, and the white newspapers should suppress colored men's criticism of his preachments."[29]

In 1901 Trotter, with George Forbes, founded the Boston *Guardian* and began to criticize Washington within the council. At the 1902 meeting in St. Paul he complained bitterly when Washington, through Fortune, manipulated the election of council officers to eliminate all persons who might challenge his views. If Washington had initially encouraged Fortune to reactivate the council to challenge the authority of the D. C. Crowd, he now felt compelled to control its political views to reinforce his influence with President Roosevelt. At the 1903 meeting in Louisville, where Washington delivered a major address condemning agitation and calling for "patience and forbearance" in relations between the races and the sections, Trotter led an even more vociferous protest. A few weeks later in Boston at a meeting at the Columbus Avenue Zion Church where Washington was scheduled to speak, Trotter organized in effect a continuation of the Louisville demonstration. Fortune, who was organizing the affair, knew in advance what Trotter had planned and had called the police, who arrested Trotter for disturbing the peace. Washington, in one of his less attractive moods, gleefully described how Trotter had been carried from the church by the police and how friends in Boston, led by the former Harvard football star and attorney, William Lewis, had pressed charges. Trotter languished in prison for thirty days but emerged by his own reckoning as a courageous opponent of "Boss Booker."[30]

Much attention has been paid to the dramatic incident at the Zion Church, but it ought hardly to be seen as the high point of Trotter's career. Instead it should be related to his more general effort to develop a nonpartisan rather than a simply anti-Washington political strategy. Trotter was groping for a modern political lobbying agency, but his understanding of options for a new program was limited by the attitudes and values of his journalistic and political circle. Though he lacked training in social science and economic theory, he was seeking a more comprehensive program around which an independent Black citizenry could rally. He believed that if Black reformers were to move beyond rhetoric they must do more than endorse candidates and platforms. They must also avoid the obligations of political appointment that had trapped Washington and develop a separate Black agenda. Many office seekers like Whitefield McKinlay rather cynically thought of Trotter as a Democrat advancing his own interests. John Durham, who, though a Washington supporter, had a more independent mind, was able to separate Trotter's tactics from his objectives. He had told Trotter that he disapproved of his methods and his attack on Washington. But he wrote to McKinlay, "So far as Trotter stands for the assertion of absolute equality, with no compromise or evasion, of course I stand for his views."[31]

When Washington gained control of the Afro-American Council, Trotter tried to create a new agency that would promote debate on how Blacks should become politically independent. Immediately after his arrest and release on bail pending trial, Trotter, with Forbes and others, organized the Boston Suffrage League to protest disfranchisement. Trotter became secretary and Archibald Grimke, a venerable advocate of nonpartisanship, became president. The Boston group, however, was part of a movement that had begun early in 1903 to protest racial discrimination in the laws of the southern states, and Trotter had to contend with the larger group's narrower concept of nonpartisanship. Calvin Chase headed the branch in the nation's capital and James Hayes, a Richmond attorney and former protégé of John M. Langston, acted as national publicity agent. Chase and the Reverend S. J. Corrothers of Washington, D.C., saw the Suffrage League not as a permanent lobbying agency but as an expedient to gain leverage with the Roosevelt administration. As Corrothers told the first meeting of the Boston league, "We mean to stand with either party that will give the best plank for the vote, but to hold ourselves independent." Chase also revealed his limited view of the league when he threatened to use it to lead Negro voters into the Democratic party. When Hayes, strongly influenced by Booker T. Washington, became a delegate to the Republican national convention, Trotter correctly concluded that he did not understand how the league might develop a truly nonpartisan Black electorate.[32]

The crisis over the meaning of nonpartisanship erupted in a convention of the league held in Washington in mid-December. In October and November Chase had used Trotter's imprisonment as a *cause célèbre* to gather support for the league. He publicized and attended a meeting in Boston celebrating Trotter's release and called the latter a "martyr for the manhood rights of the race." He reported regularly in the *Bee* on the organizational meetings of the local leagues in Pennsylvania, New England, and the District of Columbia and emphasized the need for a national convention. When the leagues convened, however, their leaders quarreled over political loyalties rather than discussing organizational plans, legal actions, or massive demonstrations. Corrothers now insisted that the convention endorse Theodore Roosevelt for president, while Trotter, Grimke, and Chase insisted that no partisan stand should be taken. The convention dissolved with no national organization achieved and no clear definition of nonpartisanship.[33]

With the collapse of the suffrage leagues, Trotter formed the National Independent Politicial League to continue the tactics of political pressure. As the Afro-American Council became moribund because Fortune could no longer afford the time or money to remain as president, the Political League gained publicity as it operated on the fringe of reform elements of the northern wing of the Democratic party.[34] Trotter, however, in addition to his virtriolic personality, lacked the funds and the knowledge to build a comprehensive lobbying agency. When the NAACP was finally organized in 1910, its firmest Black supporters were not politicians or journalists, but educators, social workers, and other professionals who could provide policy suggestions for social and legal problems. But however narrowly political was Trotter's understanding of nonpartisanship, he promoted more forcefully than any of his contemporaries the idea of organized opposition not only to Washington but to traditional political loyalties.

Expertise and the Search for Inner Strength

Nonpartisanship within the context of the Progressive era constituted a political philosophy, but it expressed also the interests of upper middle-class professionals, who joined to it broader attitudes toward social and even cultural reform. To advocate nonpartisanship in politics, therefore, often suggested that a person would demand professional analysis of social problems and rely on settlement workers, social scientists, and other local experts for leadership. In addition, among

Blacks, such persons might also feel that within the context of the ethnically heterogeneous cities of the North, they should find a distinctive voice to contend for status and power. Washington, as an educational expert, was perceived by supporters of nonpartisanship like Kelly Miller, Archibald Grimke, and DuBois as part of their reform movement. He, in turn, borrowed from their scholarly works, recommended them as experts on urban social problems, and even stayed at Miller's house on several visits to the Capital. He also enjoyed the performances of Black artists like Harry Burleigh and Bert Williams, who gave benefit performances for Tuskegee.[35]

Expertise, however, has limits of competence that Washington seemed increasingly to encroach. As DuBois and other Black scholars analyzed the impact of discrimination on Black communities and personalities, they encouraged many writers to reassess the consequences of Washington's policies. In addition to challenging Washington's political role, writers like DuBois and Charles Chestnutt and performers like Will Marion Cook began to raise questions about discrimination that Washington chose to ignore. Did Blacks, for example, not have a unique psychology and aesthetic sensitivity that, while stereotyped by whites, might also improve their ability to resist stigma? Black writers often used the term *caste* to describe their stigma and to imply an impenetrable and ambiguous barrier between themselves and white Americans. The barrier, however, not only limited Black opportunities but held Blacks together in distinct communities with cultural institutions of their own. To submerge Black personalities in economic roles, as Washington prescribed, would not only ignore persistent white exploitation but would drain the race of its vitality. As Paul L. Dunbar, a great admirer of both Washington and DuBois, noted of the middle-class Black man, "He has not—and I am not wholly sorry he has not—learned the repression of his emotions which is the mark of a high and dry civilization. He is impulsive, intense—and himself."[36]

While Dunbar may have been projecting his own personality over his social class, his celebration of a distinctive Black behavior would undermine the premises of Washington's program more than would any political strategy. Blacks, according to Dunbar, should be respected as much because of their cultural differences from whites as for the citizenship rights they shared. Race discrimination, therefore, was not simply an irrational act but a form of cultural warfare which, to be waged effectively, required continual protest and its own expertise.[37] Slowly, creative artists and scholars, as well as authorities on social welfare, developed the means to eclipse Washington as racial spokesmen.

The new social scientific view of Black Americans was crystallized best in the work of DuBois—though Kelly Miller at Howard University, R. R. Wright, Jr., in Philadelphia and Chicago, and William Bulkley, a high school principal in New York City, contributed also. Miller, Bulkley, and Wright called attention to the specific effects of racial discrimination, like the inadequacy of schools for Black children or the intense competition for employment that led to imbalanced Black sex ratios, strikes, and the use of Blacks as scab labor. DuBois, however, developed a comprehensive model of the Black class structure and analyzed the pervasive effects of discrimination on individual psyches, the institutional life of Black communities, and the strained relations between classes. He answered the call of Samuel McCune Lindsay, a white sociologist at the University of Pennsylvania, for an "American Charles Booth who will do for [urban Negroes] what has been done so successfully for the people of London."[38]

DuBois published his major scholarly monograph, *The Philadelphia Negro: A Social Study,* in 1899. He prepared for this work by completing a Ph.D. in history at Harvard, with two-years' study in Berlin. After two additional years of teaching at Wilberforce University, the college of the African Methodist Episcopal Church, where he suffered under the provincialism of the evangelical regime, he accepted a fellowship to investigate the living conditions of Blacks in Philadelphia's poorest quarter. DuBois envisioned the project as the first of many studies of Black social conditions he felt would contribute to the betterment of urban Blacks as the work of Washington contributed to that of rural people. For lack of funding, and insufficient numbers of trained successors, his study became the only sociologically systematic analysis of a Black community until the publication of Horace Cayton's and St. Clair Drake's *Black Metropolis* in 1944.[39]

DuBois's work announced a new era in Black literature and community leadership because it demonstrated the capacity of Blacks to master the new social sciences in defense of the race. It was a skill that would entitle its practitioners to an audience among the new college-educated white and Black elite. To a large extent in method, logic, and purpose it became a response to Frederick L. Hoffman's *Race Traits and Tendencies of the American Negro,* which appeared in 1896 and asserted that Negroes as a race were doomed to decline because of weak genetic material. In a clinical review for the *Annals* of the American Academy of Political and Social Science, DuBois argued that Hoffman, a statistician for the Prudential Insurance Company, lacked the professional training to interpret his data. He misunderstood the Black class structure, social organization, and regional differences that had developed since Emancipation, and he ignored relevant comparative data. In his comparisons, for example, Hoffman failed to utilize health and criminal statistics from European cities with which urban Blacks compared favorably; in his conclusions he ignored information on Black achievements since Emancipation; he attributed to the race as a whole deficiencies attached only to specific strata; and—most egregiously—he inferred causes of behavior from alleged "race traits" rather than equally plausible "conditions of life." In a criticism reminiscent of those leveled by contemporary social historians against zealous cliometricians, DuBois concluded that "the proper interpretation of apparently contradictory social facts is a matter requiring careful study and deep insight." The power to define and prescribe solutions for urban problems was not to be a white monopoly, as Samuel Lindsay, Leo Rowe, Jane Addams, and others quickly recognized.[40]

DuBois's work in Philadelphia had two specific purposes. He hoped first to demonstrate to white sociologists like Hoffman that environment, not race traits, created unique problems for Blacks. Second and more specifically, he hoped to disprove charges by whites that crime in Philadelphia was caused primarily by the Blacks of the Seventh Ward. Combining the historical research techniques acquired at Harvard and the sociological methods he had learned at Berlin, and through extensive reading in settlement house monographs, DuBois prepared an elaborate investigative schema to satisfy the highest canons of modern scholarship. His lengthy questionnaires, intensive mapping of neighborhood structures to recreate the physical setting, his use of local records—and his concern for the theoretical meaning of his findings—allowed him to resolve two questions he had set for himself. He concluded, first, that if the conditions of Black life were unique, the causes lay in the treatment of the Black minority by the overwhelming white majority. Second, if Blacks turned to crime, they were reacting to the frustrations of city life rather than expressing inherent traits they had brought from the countryside.[41]

The tenor of Black community life, DuBois demonstrated, was determined by the same sociological phenomena that affected whites: class structure and migration. Negroes in Philadelphia had since the early nineteenth century created distinct social networks based on family ties, residential clusterings, occupations, and education. The community, however, suffered persistent disruptions from demographic pressures that were intensified by racial discrimination. While most whites seemed to believe that Philadelphia's Blacks were congenital criminals, DuBois emphasized that their class structure was quite varied and that most were immigrants or the children of immigrants from the Virginia and Carolina countryside. Older Black families, like those of whites, had scattered through the city, even though whites identified Blacks with the slum districts. Many other families, however, had encountered discrimination that prevented them from finding the housing and neighbors they desired. The newcomers had clustered in the Seventh Ward, where employment was not always available and where philanthropic institutions could not meet their needs. The criminal element consisted of a small minority, most of whom had been embittered by discrimination.[42]

Throughout the study DuBois tried to strike a balance between the achievements of Blacks and the problems they faced because of social disruption. In a more systematic and integrated fashion than George Washington Williams, DuBois balanced a history of church and lodge growth, which expressed the needs of the stable elements in the community, with the effects of pervasive discrimination. The Black class structure, he noted, had been built up much like that of white Philadelphia, with older elements having created the vast African Methodist Episcopal Church, several schools, social clubs, and important businesses. But discrimination had prevented the Black elite from participating as equals in community leadership, and Black immigrants saw no reason to accept them as legitimate spokesmen. Consequently, the Black community contained frustrated and mutually antagonistic social classes. Because the elite had retreated into a reticent enclave, white Philadelphians saw only the poor, and their stereotypes about Blacks were reinforced.[43]

In addition to his path-breaking analysis of Black class structure and the dilemmas of the elite, DuBois also contributed a sensitive description of the immigrants. To understand their expectations and motivations he spent the summer of 1897 in Prince Edward County, Virginia, about sixty miles southwest of Richmond, to analyze the prevalent occupational, family, and social experiences of migrants from a typical rural area. He could then determine how city life modified their behavior. DuBois, like Fortune and Williams a decade earlier, noted the ignorance of rural Blacks but he characterized them with a certain romance and moral sensibility prior scholars had ignored. His sociology had a humane tone, like that of Jane Addams, who saw in immigrants contributors to—rather than deviants from—appropriate urban norms. He found rural Blacks to be a religious, humble, and brave peasantry who brought to the city a spiritual heritage that might counter the dislocation and materialism of the Gilded Age. Encountering discrimination rather than equal opportunity, however, many migrants became depressed and often cynical, and they betrayed the moral heritage upon which they had been nurtured. People who had created churches and lodges, who were accustomed to hard work, who honored the monogomous family, and who wanted better education for their children had been betrayed by the very environment in which they had sought widened opportunities.[44]

Politically, however, DuBois did not follow Washington and counsel Blacks to remain in the countryside. Like many sociologists after him, he saw the migration North as the first major effort by Blacks to participate as equals in the American drama of self-directed social mobility. He believed with Washington that the community must organize itself, but rural counties provided insufficient opportunities and the peasantry itself had determined to join the national move to the cities. The Negro problem, he noted, had become national rather than southern, and citizens everywhere could now see in their own locales the need to honor the constitutional commitment to equal protection for all citizens.[45] On the basis of his work in Philadelphia, therefore, he searched for ways to invigorate the Black community so the elite might lead, the youth might avoid despair, and the resilient rural spirit might be utilized to sustain the migrants. The implication of DuBois's monograph was that neither traditional political leaders nor southern educators could provide the new leadership the race obviously needed.

Technical expertise, however, did not make DuBois a potential spokesman for the opposition to Washington. He expressed the same distrust of the D.C. Crowd, of agitation and emotional religion, and the same insistence on careful social analysis as did Washington. As he was completing his Philadelphia study he assisted Washington on several projects, spoke in public with him on several occasions, and considered accepting a position at Tuskegee. By 1900, though, he wondered how much he might be needed at the school. His wife, who apparently harbored no professional idealism, felt he would be used simply to write Washington's speeches, and in 1900 DuBois declined an offer to come to Tuskegee. He then held a position teaching and directing a modest research program at Atlanta University, which he found a more attractive locale than the rural confines of Tuskegee. He told Washington, "I think to be sure I would be of use there, but after all would it not be a rather ornamental use than fundamental necessity?"[46] Despite his willingness to work with Washington, he had clearly identified the limitations for leadership that might be provided by a rural educator. Within the confines of cities, complex Black communities had more varied internal organization and required more frank relations with whites than Washington counseled. They had to draw on cultural traditions not simply entrepreneurial spirit to develop political power. The greater the migration became, the more would cultural and political strengths have to be cultivated to support economic endeavors.

Those Black writers who at the turn of the century discussed in episodic fashion themes DuBois set into a more comprehensive theoretical context were also ambivalent toward Booker T. Washington. Kelly Miller, Archibald Grimke, and Mary Church Terrell, all appreciated Washington's work and understood the political pressures upon him. Yet they all felt compelled to supplement his view of the needs of Black Americans. While Mrs. Terrell entertained him in her home, she perceived a deterioration of Black social status in the Capital itself that required protest. In an anonymous article in the *Independent* in 1907 she noted the same despair among young people over the lack of suitable occupations as DuBois had found in Philadelphia. In an article in a British magazine she called for federal intervention in the South to protect Negro lives and civil rights. Miller, while emphasizing the historical conditions that seemed to require a Black spokesman like Washington who would accommodate some white demands, still felt that he failed to inspire racial pride. Like DuBois, Miller saw in Washington's calculating temperament a lack of confidence in Black capacities. Grimke, in a number of articles, emphasized the importance of obtaining economic opportunities but noted too that only through the assertion of citizenship rights could such opportunities be defended. Nick Chiles, managing editor of the successful Negro newspaper, the Topeka *Plaindealer,* responded forcefully to Washington's criticism of an editorial urging Black resistance to white violence. "Your line of leadership may be all right for the South," Chiles wrote, "but ours is decidedly right for the entire world." He then cited Blacks in South Carolina and Mississippi who had successfully resisted white violence by counterattacking.[47]

To some extent the personal intercourse of elite Blacks with Washington was marked by cultural incompatabilities. Mrs. Terrell's relatives, for example, considered him crudely educated, and Washington made no secret of his discomfort and distrust of college-educated Blacks. He had asked his friend, the businessman J. C. Napier, virtually to exclude them from the audience when he spoke in Nashville in 1906. Hallie Queen, a Cornell graduate, a friend of Mrs. Terrell, and an intense admirer of DuBois, accepted a teaching position at Tuskegee but quickly resigned. "Have you ever been in a crowd of Hampton and other graduates where it is a crime for you to say 'college,' or if you happened to mention 'degree' you were termed an egoistic pendant," she inquired of Mrs. Terrell.[48] The snobbery of the college elite and the countersnobbery of the self-made entrepreneurs played itself out in the confrontation between Washington and his critics.

The psychological humiliations under which Blacks lived and the extent to which Washington ignored them was best described by the Boston lawyer Edward E. Wilson, who published a sardonic article in the *Atlantic Monthly* in 1906 entitled "The Joys of Being a Negro." Wilson argued that Blacks had the same ambitions, feelings, and rights as whites but that discrimination had created for them a more complex sense of themselves. While the descendant of the European immigrant, Wilson noted, "pools each his individuality in Americanism," Blacks were forced to remain apart pondering the reasons for their exclusion. He recounted sarcastically how the exclusion kept whites out of Black neighborhoods and relieved Negroes of the anxieties of the rich and the responsibilities for governing. "In fact, the Negro is the rustic of America," Wilson mused. "Of the doings of this great and busy nation he is a spectator." Since Blacks received no encouragement, they had to strive for perfection even harder than did whites, and should they reach such levels they would have surpassed "the proud Aryan."

While the article primarily condemned the immorality of whites, it concluded with a biting attack on Washington. "A negro [sic] of uncommon ability, the advocate of a new education for Negroes, has told them that in a thousand years they would be fitted to partake of the things the Aryan now enjoys." As a Negro, Wilson concluded, he could not be satisfied by these "negative pleasures."[49]

The sense that Washington, despite his constructive program, ignored the vital psychological basis for racial discrimination and could not overcome its effects upon Blacks appeared most clearly in the writings of Charles Chestnutt. Through his short stories and novels Chestnutt became the most respected Black literary figure by 1901, and he corresponded regularly and frankly with Washington, who apparently enjoyed his writing. Indeed his daughter, Ethel Perry Chestnutt, wished to teach at Tuskegee. As a lawyer and successful businessman Chestnutt believed that the most effective Black leaders had utilized practical methods, and he appreciated Washington's ability to work around racial prejudice by formulating diplomatic solutions to specific problems. In a brief biography of Frederick Douglass, published in 1899, Chestnutt emphasized how the Black spokesman had chosen expedient tactics to combat slavery, while William Lloyd Garrison and his supporters, "serene in the high altitude of their convictions," had sought the most ethically pure course. As he did with Douglass, Chestnutt praised Washington for his ability to coordinate the resources and good will of whites with the skills of Blacks.[50]

But Chestnutt, like Douglass, refused to ignore the lust for power, the moral ambiguities—even the sentimentality—which the transition from slavery to freedom had engendered in the South. Writing in a pamphlet in 1894, Douglass argued that southern mores had conditioned whites to brutalize Blacks. "We must remember that these people have not now and never have had any such respect for human life as is common to other men," Douglass concluded.[51] In his short stories and novels Chestnutt dramatized this dictum by showing how individual resolve could not overcome the force with which slavery had embedded stereotypes in the psyches of southern whites.

In a grim story published in 1899 entitled "The Web of Circumstance," Chestnutt commented that "human character is a compound of tendencies inherited and habits acquired." The hero, a freedman named Ben Davis—who as a hard-working black-smith accumulates land and articulates Washington's philosophy of self-help and political quiescence—is betrayed by his wife, his apprentice, and his own naiveté. At his trial for a theft he did not commit, his comment that Blacks should become land owners is twisted by fearful white witnesses and the judge to convey a demand for Black domination. After a lengthy jail sentence that transforms him into an embittered, brutal char-acter, his actions are again misinterpreted and he is killed by a white planter who had formerly respected him. In an equally pitiless story, the mulatto son of a white sheriff who had sold him away years before under slavery, returns quite unknown to his father and is accused of murdering a white man. Although his father saves him from a lynch mob and learns his identity, his escape attempt is thwarted when he is shot by his white half-sister. His father resolves to find the real killer, but the son gives way to despair. Trapped between the remorseless whites and the ignorant Blacks, he allows himself to bleed to death.[52]

Chestnutt's short stories were usually written around a single theme and did not require that he develop a character in depth or a plot in detail. The stories sustained interest because they could pivot on the moral choice a person must make, the knowledge a person gained from an experience, or the revela-tion of a past relationship that required a confession of respon-sibility. He was particularly concerned with the ambiguities of color and culture as experienced by fair-skinned Negroes, many of whom could "pass" for white. With a fine sense of irony and dramatic detail he satirized the pretensions of the urban elite and the discriminatory patterns of race relations. As Frances Keller has recently shown, however, Chestnutt's novels were designed not so much as literary constructs but as dramatic social history. He used the longer form not to develop subtle characters or to create intricate plot, but to explicate the causes of tragic events. If his Black and mulatto characters were more varied and intelligent than those of Albion Tourgee, he seemed to agree that moral resolve could not overcome the force of social tradition. The novel for Chestnutt became the format to demonstrate how individual tragedies were shaped by historical circumstances.[53]

Chestnutt's most compelling novel, *The Marrow of Tradition,* published in 1901, not only dramatized the moral ambiguities of southern race relations, but tested the validity of Booker T. Washington's social philosophy—and found it wanting. The plot followed the massacre of Blacks by whites at Wilmington, North Carolina, in 1898, but the theme was identical to those in many of his short stories. He traced the impact of white avarice, cynicism, fear of miscegenation, and irrationality—the marrow of "tendencies inherited"—on the hopes and ambitions of Blacks. Robert Bone has argued that Chestnutt's characters and subplots came from a stereotyped literary tradition, but Sylvia Render more appreciatively notes that he utilized folklore and folklife without distortion and he discussed serious subjects directly and candidly.[54] His choice of a horrifying historical event as the novel's climax suggests that he did not depart from realistic depiction to satisfy romantic or even naturalistic literary conventions. Each character was drafted as a social type and indicated how racial myths limited individual freedom. Southern traditions, Chestnutt asserted, required that individuals subordinate their ambitions to the social roles for which their race, sex, and age allegedly suited them. Chestnutt then created dramatic tension by describing how men dealing patiently and rationally with racial traditions were overwhelmed by those who exploited the anxieties, especially the sexual fantasies which such traditions had spawned. Beneath the prescribed social roles that kept the races apart lay deep-seated sexual taboos that had been repeatedly violated and could not be buried beneath self-effacing Negro achievements.[55] Chestnutt dramatized a point that DuBois, Johnson, and Grimke would state explicitly over the next decade: the repressed sexual behavior of southern whites, which originated under slavery, provided the source of anti-Black violence.[56]

Chestnutt, in part, wanted to know how freely people could live under the taboos of southern stereotypes. He created a young mulatto doctor who founded a hospital to improve health care for poor Negroes. Such an objective, Chestnutt assumed, had a place in any rational society. Yet the efforts to raise the economic and social status of Blacks clashed with the behavior that whites traditionally expected from the various Negro social types. Improvements in living conditions for Blacks, he suggested, would require careful manipulation as well as noble intentions. Compared to the disillusionment and suppressed rage of the educated mulattoes and the dishonesty of the ambitious whites, only Chestnutt's ignorant Black dock workers, in their resistance to the lynch mob, evoked the dignity of free men. The cataclysmic arson and murder with which Chestnutt closed his novel suggested that "self-help" by Blacks would not insure them respect, while violent resistance could lead to annihilation. As he wrote to Washington in early 1904, "I am profoundly convinced that a race without political influence is and will continue to become even more so a race without rights."[57]

Though Washington presented Blacks as a group conditioned by its ignorance of modern technology, the idea of a Black race remained far more complex to Chestnutt. He and other Black writers began to see more in the idea of the primitive person than simply incompetence. They began to interpret certain cultural traits of the freedmen not as a mark of stigma but as a heritage free of commercialism and adapted to survival. Not only did the dialect of southern Blacks demark them as an ethnic enclave, but their humor, their cuisine, their folklore, and their mutual good fellowship suggested a people with the full range of human intelligence and compassion.[58] The contrast between the mulatto doctor and the Black dock workers, furthermore, revealed a dilemma that went far beyond the choice of appropriate strategies for economic and political progress. Each symbolized a different Negro identity and pointed in a different cultural direction. The Black man represented the aggressive side of the primitive freedmen, who lacked modern skills but expressed an instinct for survival. The mulattoes symbolized American Negroes as a new race trapped between white and Black. They had assimilated the ideals of the white middle class, but remained socially ostracized. Indeed, Chestnutt ultimately suggested that full amalgamation over generations would provide the only solution to the race problem, but the choices available to his characters were more realistic and grim. He dramatized in literature what DuBois had shown sociologically: educated Blacks who understood the distance between the primitive world of the freedmen and the sophisticated world of urban whites still lacked the self-confidence to provide effective leadership. But they knew that to resist discrimination required a more refined sensitivity to tradition than Washington and his entrepreneurial followers seemed to possess.

While Chestnutt wondered how Negro social classes might understand one another, many Black artists began to question the propriety of Anglo-American cultural ideals as norms for Afro-American identity. Their sensibilities were thoroughly Westernized, but they saw as well a core of tradition that set them apart from their white fellow citizens—and one that would give them access to the masses. DuBois, for example, in a commencement address at Fisk in 1898 had spoken of one cultural ideal reigning supreme from Bombay to Rio, from Paris to New York. Here, though, he was simply reiterating the secularized teleology of late nineteenth-century liberalism that educated elites in the English-speaking world accepted. But before the Negro Academy in the same year he emphasized the unique aesthetic talents and spiritual resiliency of rural Blacks that enabled them to resist the venality of commercial civilization. Black artists went even further, however, and asserted that because educated Negroes failed to refine and nurture a Black cultural heritage, whites held the race in contempt. Negro performers complained of the stereotyped plantation roles they were forced to play in minstrel shows and on the stage. Such characterizations, they noted, did not allow Blacks to express how they actually felt about their heritage, their treatment, and their aspirations. They represented, rather, a caricature that whites wanted to see. If they hoped to nurture their professional creativity and improve the status of Negroes as a group, they must change the aesthetic ideals of their own social strata. They did not want urban Blacks to return to the social setting or the primitive behavior of the rural peasants. But like Mr. Ryder, the highly successful, light-skinned antagonist in Chestnutt's "The Wife of His Youth," they strove to make the middle class accept their relationship to Black cultural nurture. They wanted to utilize traditional singing styles, dance rhythms, and folk wisdom to dramatize how Blacks had resisted stigma.[59]

An incident in the early career of Paul L. Dunbar illustrated well the social stereotypes against which Black artists had to perform. Dunbar, like Will Marion Cook, J. Rosamond Johnson, and other Black performers, toured Britain and parts of Europe at the turn of the century to gain exposure and income. Because he arrived in London before the social season for the elite had begun, Dunbar could find bookings only at public clubs or smokers. With mortification he informed his literary sponsor, William Dean Howells, "I was put in upon programs between dancing girls from the vaudeville and clowns from the varieties. (At one place I went on after midnight when half the men were drunk.) Miss Bonds [his manager] cooly informed me that in such cases as this I was to *tell vulgar stories.* "[60] Dunbar, who understood too well the compromises Blacks had to make in the white world, hoped at least in his art to express himself freely.

From the theaters and vaudeville houses in New York after 1898 Black artists presented an alternative to the bland ideal of the Negro as imitator of the bourgeois ethic. Composers and performers like Will Marion Cook, Bert Williams, and Bob Cole found no more inspiration in the cheerful, self-effacing Black businessman than in the stereotyped buffoon of the minstrel show. If nothing else, the business ethic failed to appeal to their vitriolic personalities, which drove Cook to various romantic affairs and Cole to alcohol.[61] It stifled the artist who wished to depict the unique tensions, rhythms, and humors of Negro life as much as disfranchisement frustrated political activists like Trotter and Grimke.

No evidence indicates that Black composers, musicians, or entertainers openly critized Washington. Indeed, some performed to benefit Tuskegee, which they considered an invaluable example of race achievement.[62] But their heated debates over the aesthetic qualities and moral ironies of Black life clashed with Washington's efforts to impose an ethic of bourgeois striving over the Black imagination. Cook and Williams emphasized how the artist must dramatize what made the Negro unique from, not similar to, the white middle class. While Washington deplored any attention paid to the exotic character of rural Blacks that might distract them from modernization, the artists cultivated the rural tradition as the source of their own identity. As James Weldon Johnson—in whose hotel room in the New York theater district some of the intense debates occurred—recalled, Will Marion Cook especially "believed that the Negro in music and on the stage ought to be a Negro, a genuine Negro; he declared that the Negro should eschew white patterns and not employ his efforts in doing what the white artist could do as well, generally better."[63] Given the popularity of such artists as heroes among Black Americans, their influence helped shape a more culturally self-conscious public, many of whose young people were increasingly discontent with Washington's social ideal.

As the demand was growing for an independent Black politics, a frank assessment of race relations, and a new dignity for the Black personality, W. E. B. DuBois in 1903 published *The Souls of Black Folk.* Many of the essays had appeared previously as magazine articles or were reworked versions of DuBois's more technical sociological studies. This volume, though, was aimed at a general audience, and with it DuBois achieved two purposes. In a new essay entitled "Of Mr. Booker T. Washington and Others," he presented specific criticisms of Washington's educational philosophy and political strategy, thus indicating that temperate and impartial scholars saw severe limitations in the Tuskegee System. Second, the essays argued that Blacks need not defer to white philanthropy or cultural standards. Instead, they should see themselves as a people with a unique heritage that might yet rescue the nation from its materialistic binge. As DuBois pointedly reminded George Foster Peabody several years later, he headed each chapter with a line from a spiritual to emphasize the wisdom of the folk heritage.[64]

The Souls of Black Folk, like so much anthropology and history written at that time, including F. J. Turner's writings on the American frontier, represented an intellectual' romantic evocation of rustic traditions in the face of an expanding and impersonal industrial society. Like Turner and some of the even more romantic German writers of the late nineteenth century, DuBois saw moral strength in the folkways of the people with whom he identified. Particularly like the cultural Zionist, Asher Ginzburg (Ahad Ha'am), DuBois believed that a people could regain its sense of purpose despite intense persecution only through an examination of ethical strictures expressed in its traditions. Neither man conformed to a religious orthodoxy, though both utilized tradition as the symbol of a people's creative power. Despite DuBois's disavowal of sectarian interests, he stressed here, as in his sociology, how churches-from crossroads shacks to the elaborate tabernacles of the African Methodist Episcopal Church-created a humane orderliness in Black communities. He noted without regret that the rural preachers were losing their hold over the young, who sought opportunities in the cities. But the institution of the church demonstrated that Blacks had brought internal order to their communities and had trained leaders to withstand stigma.[65]

DuBois used this cultural heritage to deliver a broad political thrust. In a formulation that combined his "scientific" approach to social conflicts with his penchant for ambiguous metaphor, he announced that "the problem of the twentieth century is the problem of the color line . . ." He implied, first, with the practical formulation of the sociologist, that conflicts between groups could be perceived as problems, which honest men might resolve. Unlike the proponents of a "German Ideology," he neither succumbed to despair with modern society nor eschewed rational discourse, and unlike the political Zionists he condemned emigration to an ancestral homeland. Like Chestnutt, he emphasized that the conflict between Blacks and whites was as much internal as interracial and could grow more severe unless all of its consequences were honestly discussed. Second, DuBois saw that races would contend not only for wealth but much more broadly for the power to determine the moral and aesthetic standards for the new century's multiracial society. Like Cook and Dunbar, DuBois believed that Blacks could contest the white man's claim to moral superiority only by initiating their own cultural Renaissance. In a formulation that amply demonstrated the tragedy of several of Chestnutt's characters, DuBois noted that unless Blacks utilized the moral traditions expressed in their religion and music, they would face a "painful self-consciousness, an almost morbid sense of personality, and a moral hesitancy which is fatal to self-confidence."[66]

By demonstrating the psychological and aesthetic differences between Black and white Americans and by questioning the spiritual rewards of commercial civilization, DuBois became the first recognized Black scholar explicitly to challenge Washington's cultural premises. Of course, he also expressed the same reservations about Washington's political stance as did Trotter, Chestnutt, Grimke, and others. Only by exercising the suffrage, DuBois argued, could Blacks protect their property rights. As an educator, furthermore, he argued as persuasively as had Crummell that without a liberally educated elite, a group could not develop strategies to combat ignorance and poverty. In an essay entitled "The Talented Tenth," which appeared a few months after his book, he noted that "it is industrialism drunk with its own vision of success to imagine that its own work can be accomplished without providing for the training of broadly cultured men and women to teach the teachers of the public school."[67]

But DuBois explained more fully than any other Black writer how Washington's policies limited the ability of Blacks to withstand stigma. Unlike Kelly Miller, Archibald Grimke, and Charles Chestnutt, DuBois never fully accepted the thesis that the Anglo-Saxon middle class expressed the quintessence of civilized virtues. Negroes as a race had contributed uniquely to the nation's aesthetic and moral consciousness, he affirmed, and in studies of African families done shortly afterwards he argued that they honored the same ethical standards as did whites. For DuBois, therefore, Washington's version of the work ethic required Blacks to denigrate their history, deny their ancestors, and assimilate a culture that had serious moral defects. Using the legend of Atalanta to mythicize economic development in the South, DuBois—in a thinly veiled reference—likened Washington to the wily Hippomenes who tempted Blacks to reject their cultural heritage in return for the golden apples of material prosperity. In other essays, however, DuBois, precisely as had Chestnutt, argued that Black successes galled southern whites far more than Black stagnation. Washington, therefore, left his pupils not only without political sophistication, but psychologically unprepared to compensate for the suffering they would face as the descendants of despised African slaves.[68]

Because *The Souls of Black Folk* announced a cultural as much as a political challenge to Booker T. Washington, its importance lay in its cumulative influence upon the sensibilities of college-educated Blacks. Indeed, it had little immediate effect on the relationship between Washington and DuBois. A few months after the book appeared, DuBois delivered a well-attended lecture series at the Tuskegee summer institute for teachers. J. Frank Armstrong, manager of the institute, told Washington that both students and local people who attended had been pleased by the lectures. The book also appeared several months before the incident at the Zion Church in Boston, but after the fracas DuBois publicly denounced Trotter's tactics. He did not criticize Washington until William Lewis and others pressed charges against Trotter and continued to give notoriety to the incident. Washington, furthermore, continued to respect DuBois's scholarship, appreciated his enthusiasm for publicizing Black economic achievements, and referred students of Black social conditions to his work at Atlanta University.[69]

Gradually, however, Black intellectuals responded to DuBois's call for a candid expression of the psychological tensions under which they labored and a reassessment of their cultural history. While some Black audiences found DuBois pessimistic or brooding because he lacked Washington's enthusiasm for small gains, others were inspired by his frank exploration of their anxieties and hopes. Jessie Fauset, the literary editor of *Crisis* from the mid-1910s through the 1920s, felt that *The Souls of Black Folk* spoke expressly to her. "I am glad, glad you wrote it," she passionately informed DuBois. "We have needed someone to voice the intricacies of the blind maze of thought and action along which the modern, educated colored man and woman struggles." Shortly afterwards she noted how the book gave her confidence "to teach our colored men and women *race* pride, *self*-pride, self-sufficiency (the right kind) and the necessity of living our lives as nearly as possible absolutely, instead of comparing them always with white standards." Living almost exclusively among whites, Miss Fauset continued, she had to demonstrate the positive qualities of Negroes, "or else allow my personality to be submerged." While Hallie Queen might flinch at the anti-intellectualism of Tuskegee, Miss Fauset found a social purpose for intellectuality in DuBois. James Weldon Johnson, who became a close friend of DuBois after 1915, wrote anonymously in 1912, "every colored man in the United States . . . is forced to take his outlook on all things not from the viewpoint of a citizen, or a man, or a human being, but from the viewpoint of a *colored* man." Years later he wrote that his own novel, *The Autobiography of an Ex-Colored Man,* introduced psychological realism into Black fiction. But in it he referred to *The Souls of Black Folk* as the source for his own sensitivity to the veil of race through which his insights were almost unconsciously filtered.[70]

Racism and the Goad to Black Ethnicity

A more sophisticated image of Black Americans than that which Washington projected emerged after 1904 in several new institutions. Though all were shortlived, *The Voice of the Negro,* a journal edited in Atlanta by J. Max Barber and J. W. E. Bowen; the Niagara Movement, a loose coalition of political activists and academics forged by Trotter and DuBois; and

Horizon, a journal edited by DuBois for the Niagara Movement, all gave visibility and confidence to Black writers who could begin to think of themselves as a community. The negotiations that led to the creation of the Niagara Movement have been described by DuBois in several autobiographical works and in articles he published at the time and by Elliott Rudwick in his biography.[71] But the career of *The Voice of the Negro,* DuBois's priorities within the Niagara Movement and especially with *Horizon,* and even the disintegration of the Niagara Movement have not been related carefully to the emergence of a new image of Black Americans. Neither the journals nor the Niagara Movement were individually successful, but they encouraged the Black elite to see a common effort, national in scope, to deal more forcefully with Black political and cultural problems. Most men and women still praised Washington's work and offered him sporadic assistance. But by 1910 their collective achievements as educators, writers, and social workers gave them sufficient visibility and self-confidence to see themselves as persons who understood better than he the real needs of the race.[72]

The Niagara Movement provided the focus for opposition to Washington, but its actual operations and the reasons for its demise are shadowy. The idea for an independent Black political organization that might provide alternatives to Washington's strategies came from a number of men, including F. L. McGhee of Minneapolis, Charles C. Bentley of Chicago, and Trotter. With the demise of the Afro-American Council and the suffrage leagues as forums for serious debate, Trotter convened a meeting in his office on January 15, 1905, that included not only political activists like Grimke and Forbes, but academics like Miller and DuBois. The men drafted a petition to President Roosevelt asking the federal government to enforce laws protecting Negro voting and guaranteeing equal accommodations in interstate travel. DuBois by then seemed inclined to engage in political protest and direct criticism of Washington, but he was reluctant to join only with partisan politicians. He endorsed the petition but designed a permanent organization with far broader cultural as well as political objectives.[73]

Institutions like the suffrage leagues that Trotter had organized consisted largely of local political cliques and were open to those who felt inclined to join. DuBois, however, envisioned a permanent institution recruited and organized like a fraternal debate club that would combine the intellectuality of the Negro Academy and the political thrust of the Afro-American Council. He developed an elaborate organizational model, with state level bodies to recruit suitable new members and to determine the most pressing local problems. National officers and topical committees would coordinate local efforts. In addition, the organization would range well beyond political issues and emphasize the importance of Black ethnic identification. Much has been made of the elite character of DuBois's organizational model. Like most white reform-minded college graduates of his day, he believed that only the best informed persons had the capacity to lead—though they had the responsibility to understand the needs of the masses and to interpret alternatives clearly. While the culture of the Black peasantry might provide a sense of history and inspiration to the Black elite, they alone had the knowledge to refine that heritage so it might be used to assist the masses to adapt to the modern world. A Black reform movement, therefore, must begin with those who had expert knowledge and the widest vision.[74]

DuBois was most encouraged by events in Atlanta where a new journal, *The Voice of the Negro,* had not only completed its first year of publication, but had successfully withstood efforts by Washington to control its editorial policy. L. M. Hershaw, a Black journalist, writing for a national news magazine in 1905, called *The Voice of the Negro* one of only two Black magazines of real merit, and Mary Terrell later remembered it as an important chronicle of Black achievements. The exact relationship between the journal and the Niagara Movement is unclear. But its success until the horrible riot against Atlanta's Blacks by white mobs in late September, 1906, suggests how much local support DuBois had. It indicates further that Black opposition to Washington was not so much northern as urban—or at least urban professional. The more vocal Black professionals might reside in northern cities, but a contingent remained in the South and probably the largest group resided in Atlanta.[75]

DuBois must have worked rather closely with the editors of *The Voice,* J. W. E. Bowen and J. Max Barber, because he liked them personally and was interested in founding such a journal himself. Bowen was his senior colleague within the complex of Black colleges in Atlanta, while Barber was one of the few contemporary Black intellectuals who shared DuBois's more radical interests in Pan-Africanism and socialism. How closely DuBois worked with Barber is unclear, but he must have been informed of Washington's efforts to gain control of *The Voice* and had been encouraged by Barber's resistance. In January, 1905, as part of a symposium by prominent Blacks William Scarborough, Kelly Miller, and others on prospects for the coming year, *The Voice* published DuBois's article, "Debit and Credit." The essay was arranged like a balance sheet, in part to satirize the inconsistencies in Washington's philosophy of material accumulation as the basis of racial equality. DuBois listed as debits the spread of Jim Crow legislation, disfranchisement, lynching, and a specific charge that someone, obviously Washington, had paid $3,000 in "hush money" to Negro editors not to publicize the debits. He noted as credits the decline of Negro illiteracy, rise in land ownership, accumulation of property, and most important, an aroused "race consciousness" that made it impossible for "any Negro" (again obviously a reference to Washington), to advocate accommodation to white prejudice.[76]

"Debit and Credit" not only reiterated DuBois's criticism of Washington as stated in *The Souls of Black Folk,* but announced how effectively Barber and Bowen had resisted Washington's designs on their journal. Bowen, as senior editor, hoped that the journal would provide a forum where the best minds of the race could debate the issues of the day, while he and Barber developed an independent editorial policy. To further their objectives they invited Washington to contribute a brief essay to their first number. Washington, still cultivating Bowen as he had when inviting him to address the Negro Business League in 1902, sent an article emphasizing the importance of industrial education for Negro "uplift." Barber then invited Emmett Scott, who had been a journalist in Texas before becoming Washington's private secretary, to become an associate editor at a salary of $100 a year. Scott was to contribute four articles and an occasional editorial, which, Barber innocently added, should conform to the policy of the editors. Bowen also asked DuBois to contribute, and in March, 1904, his review of the Atlanta University conferences appeared. The most conspicuous political essays in the first few numbers were written by Kelly Miller, who emphasized the "progressive" distinction between politics as the "science of government" and as the process of winning elections. He balanced criticism of white racial attitudes with a condemnation of traditional Black politicians, and he noted that Blacks must be taught to cast their ballots for the best qualified candidate. But voting, Miller reiterated, was a vital function in a democratic society and must never be relinquished.[77]

Beneath the balanced collection of essays, however, occurred a conflict over policy which portended well for Washington's critics. Scott and Washington agreed to write for *The Voice* because they assumed it would avoid political controversy and publicize Negro achievements. They saw it as a minor literary venture, which, like all other cultural artifacts, would demonstrate to sophisticated whites how refined a handful of Blacks had become. Barber, however, saw it as the cultural equivalent of Trotter's nonpartisan political organization. As a survivor of the Wilmington riot described in Chestnutt's *Marrow of Tradition,* Barber wished to promote an aggressive Black political stance supported by a Pan-African sense of cultural identity. In his editorials he criticized individuals and institutions, commented regularly on current events, and accepted controversial essays on social topics. As he pointedly told Scott, Negroes could not afford to rely on whites for their political news or opinions. While accepting articles from sympathetic white social workers like Frances Kellor and Mary White Ovington, Barber especially sought to build a Black clientele. He published a candid exchange between Miss Ovington and William Pickens, then teaching at Talladega College, in which the latter noted that racial prejudice was as prevalent among northerners as southerners, but the race ratio in the North had not yet induced similar discrimination. It would occur, however, as immigration North increased, and Blacks must prepare to meet it.[78]

Such candid exchanges and criticisms of their own work soon led Washington and Scott to see *The Voice* as a threat to their diplomatic efforts to manipulate white public opinion. The break between Washington and the magazine occurred in the summer of 1904, when Barber, following his journalistic instincts, wished to move the magazine in a more political direction. During the summer Washington and Scott were deeply involved with Roosevelt's election campaign—which included, on Washington's advice, silence on southern race relations. In mid-July, however, Barber asked Scott for an introductory letter to interview George B. Cortelyou, chairman of the Republican National Committee. Although Barber supported Roosevelt, Scott feared that the interview might call attention to issues that neither Washington nor the president wished discussed in print. Scott refused to grant Barber's request, but the latter persisted. He had Bowen intercede directly with Washington, who reluctantly acquiesced in deference to Bowen's stature in the Atlanta Black community.[79]

Washington then became alarmed at Barber's persistence and at his blunt editorials. He asked the white publishers of *The Voice*, Hertel-Jenkins of Chicago, to remove Barber as editor. When they refused, he advised his friends to cancel their advertisements in the magazine. Barber learned of Washington's meetings with Hertel and Jenkins and complained to Scott of interference with his editorial freedom. Scott, however, denied that Washington had tried to influence the publishers. Bowen, working in good faith, continued to request articles from Tuskegee, but Barber edited them and criticized their implications on the editorial page. By December, 1904, Washington became exasperated with Barber. In a long letter he accused him of slandering the National Negro Business League and Tuskegee. Barber had repeated DuBois's general criticism of the moral limitations of business enterprise, but Washington said that he had received letters from "northern friends" who complained about the magazine's malignant editorial policies. Washington then reminded Barber that he had contributed $4,000 during the past two years to defend the civil and political rights of southern Blacks. "Do you know any other colored man," Washington angrily inquired, "who has stood up for the political rights of the Negro amid the abuses and curses of the Southern white people to the extent that I have during the past ten years?"[80]

Barber ignored Washington. He published "Debit and Credit," and in March 1905, when DuBois was contemplating the call for the Niagara Movement, he editorialized against the "soulless materialism" of Washington's program. In accord with America's democratic tradition, he concluded, one race should not emulate the other but should develop its own ideals. As if to illustrate the point, the March number also carried a brief sketch of the career of DuBois, whose idealistic and scholarly efforts in behalf of the race were presented to inspire Negro youth.[81] By 1906 DuBois and Barber made a major theme of the contrast between Washington's utilitarian educational philosophy and the moral imperatives of citizenship rights. Coverage of Tuskegee's twenty-fifth anniversary in May, for example, emphasized the vulgarity of speakers such as William Howard Taft and Andrew Carnegie, who praised material accumulation and denigrated political rights and higher education for Blacks. Washington himself was praised for criticizing the national neglect of Blacks, which suggested a new concern for moral questions on his part. But, the editors concluded, he lacked the depth to offer advice beyond Alabama's Black Belt. The cultural distinction between manual and liberal education became even more apparent in a somewhat sentimental essay by DuBois entitled "St. Francis of Assisi," which had been a commencement address to the colored high schools of Washington, D.C. Noting the recent destruction by earthquake of San Francisco, which had been named after St. Francis, he informed his youthful audience that the saint, like the city, had been "ruined" materially—but for a higher purpose. Like St. Francis, Blacks must renounce dreams of great wealth, which seemed so prevalent then, in favor of developing a more humane racial consciousness. In still another essay, DuBois noted that agitation alone could educate the world to the injustices and humiliation that Blacks faced. The great mistake of the years after 1895, he concluded, had been the pose of acquiescence, which had insidiously corroded Black race pride and self-confidence.[82]

The persistence of Barber and Bowen in Atlanta, the prodding of Trotter, and the encouragement of several others in northern states led DuBois to convene the men who organized the Niagara Movement. They met from July 11 to 13, 1905, at Niagara Falls, Canada, which they saw as a quiet retreat where they might escape American racial discrimination and discuss serious matters like gentlemen. DuBois wrote enthusiastically about the new organization in *The Voice* and attracted a cadre of men who served as secretaries for over twenty states. Active branches in Boston, New Haven, and Atlanta participated in local civil rights struggles. Annual meetings, between 1905 and 1908, buoyed the spirits of men who, like DuBois, believed in a nonpartisan organization to define objectives and strategies for the race.[83] But the Niagara Movement lacked ideological coherence and a consensus on leadership. DuBois provided much energy through his feverish work as secretary, but he undertook far too much. After his chores as teacher, researcher, and lecturer were completed, he would devote time to the movement. The Niagara Movement, like other major lobbying efforts, needed a full-time staff, a professional administrative head, and a set of specific objectives. DuBois and his colleagues, however, lacked the funds, the tactical flexibility, and to some extent the intellectual compatibility to organize a comprehensive agency. Many members had important political contacts, but none could devote full-time to gathering intelligence. In addition, DuBois at least resisted the notion of gathering mass support, without which the capacity to withstand internal discord and to mount appeals to white political and philanthropic figures would have been futile.[84]

Perhaps more important, the political and literary elements within the Niagara Movement never seemed to coalesce. DuBois, who had little time for the contacts with politicians that Trotter, J. Milton Waldron, and some other members enjoyed, could not convince them of the importance of cultivating a Black cultural heritage. Instead, Trotter, betraying his own intensely political nature, allowed his differences with Clement Morgan (a close friend of DuBois, a fellow Niagarite in Boston, and a Republican) to seep into the Movement. As a consequence, Trotter, Waldron, and the Freemen M. Murray family of Washington D.C. became estranged from DuBois, and the movement slowly collapsed from within. DuBois traced its decline to lack of funds, the hostility of its white enemies, and his own demanding personality. But men began to fall away for different reasons, and because the organization was designed to remain small, every defection became a major loss. In addition to Trotter, J. Max Barber was forced to disassociate himself from active journalism after the Atlanta riot in 1906. After surviving his second race riot in the South, he fled to Chicago. He edited *The Voice* for several more months, but Hertel and Jenkins finally sold it to T. Thomas Fortune, after which it seems to have ceased publication.[85]

The Atlanta race riot provided DuBois a unique opportunity to confront the ideology of southern racism and to confirm his faith in the importance of independent Black spokesman. The riot grew out of a bitter gubernatorial campaign in which all three candidates appealed to white supremacy and villified blacks as a degenerate and criminal race.[86] Washington had tried to calm public feelings a month before the election by meeting with white newspaper editors in Atlanta to have them modify the tone of their remarks and to publicize black achievements. The New York *Age* reported Washington's efforts and just before the riot claimed that conditions had improved. After the violence Washington returned to Atlanta and persuaded a group of black ministers and businessmen to meet with a similar group of whites in a "civic league" that might assuage race friction.[87] DuBois had been invited and attended the first meeting, but found whites like Charles T. Hopkins so overbearingly paternalistic that they would not accept the opinions of blacks as statements of serious grievances.[88]

In the wake of the riot, Ray Stannard Baker of the *American Magazine* toured the South to explore the sources of racial tension that led to events like lynching and riots. On the advice of Mary White Ovington, he planned to consult with DuBois and arranged to interview him with the Reverend C. B. Wilmer, a white minister known for his liberal spirit in dealing with blacks.[89] As the conversation proceeded, Baker asked DuBois and Wilmer whether black and white spokesmen conversed frequently and candidly, whether white complaints about blacks demonstrated class rather than race differences, and whether either race recognized the constructive acts of the other. DuBois noted that the interview was the first time in his ten years in Atlanta that he had had such a candid opportunity to exchange views with a white man.[90] Wilmer so cogently expressed prevalent white assumptions about black inferiority and so consistently ignored DuBois's suggestions that the impasse between races that necessitated a Niagara Movement was dramatically illustrated.

Black writers like DuBois and Chestnutt saw themselves as spokesmen for a diverse group whose masses had produced folk art and religious institutions that expressed their complex emotions and demonstrated their capacity for modern organization. They believed in a liberal cosmopolitan society that would become progressively more humane as ethnic groups, under the leadership of their own elite, came to sympathize with one another's values and customs. Wilmer, echoing the profoundly conservative social vision of writers like the historians Ulrich B. Phillips and Walter F. Flemming, the amateur sociologist Alfred Holt Stone, the scholarly minister Edgar Gardner Murphy, and many less prolific southern writers saw blacks as an inherently deficient "child race" that had descended from a barbarous African wilderness and lacked the cultural heritage to justify its self-direction. Blacks could be integrated into an organic southern social order, Wilmer argued, only by learning modern work habits under the tutelage of whites. Institutions like Hampton and Tuskegee could serve as useful cultural intermediaries, while colleges like Atlanta University seemed vestiges of an evil Reconstruction era when northern whites had interfered in southern development.[91]

In an essay in *The Sewanee Review* in July, 1904, Ulrich Phillips retreated beyond Booker T. Washington's call for independent black farmers by arguing that blacks could become modern workers only under the supervision of white managers on carefully organized plantations.[92] With somewhat greater circumspection, Wilmer claimed to sympathize with the social and political frustrations faced by the black elite. He saw them, however, as a "mulatto" minority that had grown up unnaturally in defiance of the inherent antipathies that races were presumed to feel for one another. Their demands for equal rights, he felt, did not reflect the normal "instincts" of blacks, but the frustrations of an anomolous and displaced stratum. Their claims to leadership seemed spurious to Wilmer, who suggested instead that DuBois and his group should convey to Blacks policies determined by a paternalistic white elite. With candor, however, DuBois responded that the demands by whites for obedience had and would continue to produce black spokesmen who in their obsequiousness would permit racial misunderstanding and bitterness to fester.[93]

Southern white spokesmen, as George Fredrickson has carefully documented, did disagree on the character and intensions of blacks. Politicians and propagandists like James K. Vardaman, Hoke Smith, Thomas Dixon, and Thomas Nelson Page campaigned for disfranchisement by playing on the image of the Negro as bestial criminal, while Murphy, Willis Weatherford of the southern YMCA movement, and others developed a counterimage of blacks as "childlike," with qualities of obedience, slothfulness, and good humor. Fredrickson is also correct to argue that such distinctions should not be minimized, because the child-race image implied that blacks were malleable and could be taught modern work habits through which they could contribute to a more efficient social order.[94] But neither image provided the black leadership stratum with the authority to offer alternatives to the social values and civic policies promoted by whites or to insist on alternatives to the pace of social change.

Furthermore, even the most humane white writers employed a pragmatism that, in emphasizing the innate racial antipathies that vitiated the enforcement of constitutional guarantees, justified the stewardship of their own social class.

Murphy, in attacking the campaign to enforce the Fourteenth Amendment in 1904, was almost gleeful in noting how many illiterate whites had been disfranchised under state constitutional amendments in Louisiana, Virginia, and Alabama.[95] The eradication of white illiteracy in the South would occur through the direction of the local elite, and once that had been accomplished blacks could hope for fairer treatment under the law. Murphy and Stone also emphasized that whites must understand black thinking on race relations, but to justify their own authority they cited only those passages from the writings of Washington, DuBois, and others that confirmed their own assessment of black deficiencies and justified black subordination for generations to come.[96]

The more humane southern writers, like blacks who discussed the topic, recognized the lack of scientific clarity in the discussion of race. Yet to protect their image of a stratified rural society, they reverted to an insistence on the immutability of certain race traits whenever their sense of the proper pace and direction for change was challenged. Stone, for example, believed race traits were immutable and race antipathies natural, yet relations between races depended on population ratios and the degree of modernization rather than a fixed distribution of skills or abilities. In speeches to college audiences at Cornell, Michigan, and Wisconsin (where he briefly replaced Ulrich Phillips in 1908) he cited examples from the Caribbean and South Africa to illustrate the diversity of black achievements. Yet he also noted that where a white elite had failed to direct the polity blacks had reverted to subsistence and barbarism. Murphy also referred to racial "instincts" and psychological traits that arose from genetic inheritance, but he also discussed "historic tradition" and "collective necessity" by which human agency had shaped and must reshape race relations. Murphy was even willing to admit that inferior races might have unique emotional and aesthetic sensibilities. But in the determination of public policy, he subordinated such qualities to the imperatives of social efficiency, which—providentially—only the "Anglo-Saxons" had mastered.[97]

Black writers, like whites, might criticize the premodern work habits of rural blacks, which led them to resist rigid schedules for completing tasks or even seeking continuous employment. But they could not tolerate the ridicule of Black behavioral traits by writers like Walter Flemming who, in "The Servant Problem in a Black Belt Village," argued that Blacks seemed incapable of rational thought.[98] When Ray S. Baker pointed out to Wilmer the class rather than genetic origins of premodern habits by describing similar behavior among peasant immigrants to northern cities, the latter reiterated his notion of race traits to defend his stewardship of race relations. Only by so insisting on residual and immutable difference between Blacks and whites could he continue to deny Black spokesmen a share in defining racial policy. Wilmer, for example, asserted that the manifesto of the Niagara Movement upset southern Blacks by raising their aspirations beyond their capacities. DuBois, with self-possession and irony, retorted that Wilmer must reverse his logic, because Black capacities, being mutable, had been suppressed by the limits placed on their aspirations. Indeed, because men like Wilmer and Edgar G. Murphy continued to defer to genetic rationales for discrimination, DuBois realized he must emphasize the economic and cultural achievements as well as the political rights of Blacks if he were to undermine the ideological base of discrimination.[99]

As DuBois struggled to edit *Horizon,* issue monthly fliers on Niagara activities, and recruit new secretaries in far-flung states, he felt the financial pressure and the lack of clerical, legal, and other technical assistance. The difficulties of keeping the movement together were brought home in his daily experience as editor of *Horizon* between 1907 and 1910. The journal featured literary and political essays by prominent Blacks, lengthy news columns, and a regular editorial statement by DuBois. Unable to obtain funding to hire Barber as managing editor, DuBois had to edit copy himself in Atlanta. The printing, however, was done in Washington, D.C., under the supervision of L. M. Hershaw and Freeman H. M. Murray. J. Milton Waldron, treasurer of the Niagara Movement, served also as business manager of *Horizon.* All three men were active politically, and Murray and Waldron especially were closely associated with Trotter. DuBois nurtured *Horizon* as his major literary outlet, but Hershaw, Murray, and Waldron failed to perform the publishing obligations with equal vigor. DuBois complained to Hershaw continuously about sloppy printing, failure to meet deadlines, and poor artwork. He chastized Waldron and Murray persistently for failing to solicit subscriptions and for refusing to make the guarantors of *Horizon* pay its small but pressing debts. Despite DuBois's harassment, Murray, Hershaw, and Waldron responded with indifference, and the prospects for the journal and the movement diminished.[100]

Within and beyond the Niagara Movement, between 1907 and 1910, DuBois worked primarily on literary ventures. Through James Weldon Johnson he seemed particularly interested in enlisting Black musicians and entertainers. He encouraged the librarian E. C. Williams of Cleveland to join the movement specifically to organize the inactive art department, which DuBois saw as a vital means to dramatize Black cultural achievements. "I should think," he wrote Williams, "by correspondence and library research we might begin to get together a group of men who would be interested in these things and who would begin to inspire each other and form a center of propaganda." He encouraged Barber to continue contacts with Black Africans like A. K. Saga of the Cape Colony, who had expressed an interest in creating a Pan-African League department, Benito Sylvain of Ethiopia, and Joseph Booth. Inspired by Franz Boas to study African history, he sought the help of Williams and many others to prepare over a ten-year span an *Encyclopedia Africana.* The project would gather historical and sociological data that would demonstrate conclusively the Negro's claim to equal recognition with other races.[101] When he moved to the new NAACP in 1910 as director of research and publicity, he took established intellectual interests, a set of incomplete plans, and a wide following with him.

While Black professionals did not create enduring institutions before 1910 to provide an independent political voice or to promote a cultural Renaissance, they did publicize a more complex set of Black needs and a more sophisticated Black personality than did Booker T. Washington. They clearly challenged his authority as an expert on the needs and mood of the race. As Oswald Garrison Villard, formerly a firm supporter, wrote to Washington in 1910, "It certainly cannot be unknown to you that a greater and greater percentage of the intellectual colored people are turning from you and becoming your opponents, and with them a number of white people as well." And Villard reminded him that these men and women were as successful in their careers as he was in his. "Certainly there is nobody more successful than Dr. DuBois," he insisted. After Washington had refused, Villard found among these "intellectuals" support for his own version of a permanent, nonpartisan lobbying agency that would undertake legal and demonstrative challenges to racial discrimination.[102] And within the context of protest, DuBois, Jessie Fauset, and others also began to develop a more articulate and varied sense of Black ethnicity.

4 | W. E. B. DuBois and the Consolidation of Cosmopolitan Leadership

Between 1910 and the first year of World War I, American Black writers were encouraged to reassess their relationship to white political parties and cultural conventions. The reevaluation was necessary in part because the Wilson administration in Washington in 1913 further undercut Black Republicans, and its policies humiliated its supporters among Black Democrats. But more important the growth of the NAACP as a modern lobbying agency, the appearance of a Black literature more critical of white behavior, and a new emphasis by DuBois and others on the prospect for a Pan-African awakening generated a more vigorous and cosmopolitan mood among the Black urban elite. The accelerated migration of Blacks to northern cities after 1916 provided a phenomenon around which to discuss the new Black mood, but a more assertive literature had already been produced. As a sign of the shift in assumptions about the character and needs of Black Americans, Booker T. Washington's sudden death in November, 1915, at the age of approximately fifty-nine, was not seen as a premature disaster. His passing was mourned, even by his critics, who saw in him a tireless worker who had brought a new recognition to the most commonplace Black achievements.[1] At the height of his power with white philanthropists, however, his intellectual limitations were increasingly emphasized among Black writers. As Horace

Mann Bond noted a decade later, his influence quickly receded "because the Tuskegee regime is fatal to creative genius . . . ."[2] Washington had been reduced from The Wizard to simply the president of an industrial school. His successor, the shrewd and affable Robert Russa Moton, the former commandant of cadets at Hampton, was viewed by many middle-class Blacks as "a white folks' nigger."[3]

The image of the Negro developed in *Crisis* and by writers like James Weldon Johnson and the enigmatic William Ferris between 1910 and 1915 made Washington's vision seem shallow and his strategies provincial. Despite some bitter disputation with several white officers of the NAACP, DuBois made *Crisis* not only its monthly bulletin, but the medium to promote Black achievements and the platform for his editorial views. Balancing a celebration of Black educational successes—even athletic heroics, art, and music—with a frank assessment of white prejudice, DuBois encouraged a more self-confident Black personality. The association developed the machinery to provide nonpartisan lobbying and a defense of Black citizenship rights, but Black authors in histories, novels, and short stories created a literary tradition to emphasize their cultural distinctiveness. Most writers did not yet question the social virtues of Victorian decorum. However, as they encountered discrimination despite their social polish and literary skills, they felt compelled to seek the basis for social loyalties in their traditions.[4] It was DuBois's singular achievement by 1915 to set Black humiliation into its international context and to suggest the means for a Black counterattack. In the cultural and political struggles of these years a new consensus on Black interests and tactics began to emerge.[5]

Heritage and Choice in Black Ethnicity

The new mood among Black writers was revealed in publications like William Ferris's *The African Abroad* and James Weldon Johnson's *The Autobiography of an Ex-Colored Man.* They differed in structure, content, tone, and even the meaning of racial identity. But both books emphasized the importance of racial distinctiveness rather than adherence to white cultural leadership for a rejuvenation of Black people. Their themes indicate the alternate approaches to a racial Renaissance that were then advocated, and their publication within a year of each other suggests the encouragement that DuBois and the NAACP perceived for their own work among the intelligentsia.

The full title of Ferris's tome was *The African Abroad, Or His Evolution in Western Civilization Tracing His Development Under Caucasian Milieu*. Its prolixity and its emphasis on the hegemony of European culture suggest both the archaic style of the author and his ambivalent racial feelings. While he lacked the social scientific training of Miller and DuBois and the political sophistication of Grimke, Trotter, and others, he nevertheless demonstrated how Washington's vocational ethos had unsettled a generation of writers who hoped for a more heroic Black future. Like DuBois, Ferris had been born and educated in New England and received bachelor and master of arts degrees from hometown Yale University in New Haven in the mid-1890s. He then earned a second master's degree in history and philosophy at Harvard.[6] The formal schooling, however, cluttered rather than liberated Ferris's imagination. He never developed an original thesis like Fortune or Durham—let alone a distinctive style and array of achievements like Washington and DuBois. In the late 1890s, he had met Alexander Crummell, who reinforced his penchant for philosophical rumination with a faith in a unique if indeterminate racial destiny. Ferris had been encouraged to speak before the Bethel Literary Society and to join the American Negro Academy.[7] Working steadily in the years between 1905 and 1913 while teaching and assuming pastoral duties in the African Methodist Episcopal Zion church, he compiled an enormous amount of historical data to demonstrate the wisdom of Crummell's racial philosophy. Because he mixed so much philosophical disputation with historical data and intensely personal reactions to men and events, he provides a useful guide to the social metaphors and psychological temper with which the Black college elite evaluated their experiences.

Although Ferris's objectives were often obscured by lengthy historical and autobiographical asides, the skein of his thought was consistent. As S. P. Fullinwider has noted, Ferris adhered to the evolutionary idealism of Emerson and the Transcendalists as conveyed through his teachers at Yale. He saw God, for example, as the ultimate idealist, who implanted in the minds of men virtues by which they must live. As each race evolved to express its ideals, individuals would be motivated by a sense of their own historic destiny. Ferris had learned that the mind functioned in response to a creative self rather than through the mechanical coordination of separate faculties. Nevertheless, he asserted that such selves were shaped by intrinsic racial predispositions. The Anglo-Saxon, he repeated from many sources, was aggressive and absorptive, taking ideas from the Hebrews, Greeks, and Germans, refining them for practical application, and spreading them to primitive locales like America and Africa to convert or even exterminate the heathen. The Negro, whether in America or Africa, had a psychology dominated by the passive virtues of love and artistry with which he would temper the West's industrialized and materialistic civilization.[8]

Crummell, Bruce, Miller, DuBois, and others expressed such views in their writings and speeches. Nevertheless, they acted on the assumption that the capacities of Blacks were constantly changing so they might readily adjust to modern life. Like them, Ferris emphasized how historical forces had disrupted pristine instincts and thrown races together to achieve a higher synthesis. Blacks, he noted, had been forced to live among Anglo-Saxons for so long and had been subject to so much miscegenation that they were neither genetically nor culturally pure. While they might retain certain African predispositions, they had also acquired an Anglo-Saxon will to proselytize. Either unfamiliar or uncomfortable with DuBois's model of the class composition of Black communities, which emphasized variations in behavior, Ferris assumed that a new race with its own intrinsic qualities had evolved. He coined the term *Negro-Saxon* to describe their mixed genetic and ideological condition, just as T. Thomas Fortune had coined the term *Afro-American* twenty years before to indicate their absorption of democratic political values in a manner similar to the European immigrants.[9]

Ferris's account of Anglo-Saxon achievements and Black absorption of some of the instincts upon which they rested suggests that he might have lauded Booker T. Washington as a racial leader who had correctly identified and accepted the materialistic premises of modern life. But Ferris clung to a teleological rationale for races and their interrelationships. Drawing primarily on Crummell, he argued that the unique psychological disposition of Negro-Saxons required them to shape, rather than merely reflect, historical trends and that Washington's program stifled the spiritual genius of the race. "I have rarely heard Dr. Washington speak," he wrote, "without having a chilled shiver go up and down my vertebrate column, without leaving the place with an oppressed or suppressed feeling, after having the truth hammered home that I am only a creature of the dust . . . ." Washington's chief mistake for Ferris lay not in his tactical dealings with whites, but in his attitude toward the meaning of the Black experience. Washington ridiculed Negro writers and artists not simply because he failed to appreciate their talents, but—far worse—because he failed to see that they alone expressed the unique qualities of the Negro-Saxon.[10]

As an antidote, Ferris relied not on a modern theory of personality formation to challenge Washington's techniques of inculcation nor on a sense of class consciousness that might reflect structural changes. Instead, he turned to the romantic and archaic notion of the hero in history, as proposed by Thomas Carlyle. Ferris argued that all races produced men who could articulate their ideals and combat slanders, and Blacks must recognize those who could play that destined role. His heroes were drawn from the long history of African contact with Europeans, and he assumed that Black people would determine their own future through international cooperation. He included capsule biographies of "the forty greatest Negroes in history," and sketches of numerous "men of color who are doing big things." These personages, he believed, provided precedents to show whites how well-prepared Black spokesmen were to lead a new racial Renaissance. The two most important contemporary leaders, Ferris believed, were clearly Washington and DuBois. Sorting them into categories of leadership, Ferris identified Washington, along with Toussaint L'Ouverture, as a hero who seized available opportunities, while DuBois, like Frederick Douglass, he asserted, had created a new vision. Washington might prepare the freedmen for positions made available by whites, but DuBois, true to his divine destiny, "transforms his environment after the pattern of his ideals."[11]

When published, *The African Abroad* was criticized for its pedantic style, disorganized content, and archaic themes. One learned from Ferris more about the content of a philosophy curriculum than the behavior of Black communities. In addition, Ferris did not become a political activist until he joined the Garvey Movement in 1919, and he has been ignored by scholars who have seen the primary conflict among Blacks to be over forms of accommodation or protest. Only in the last decade have students of cultural change begun to draw upon Ferris's work more thoroughly. Even they, though, have not suggested sufficiently how the confusion in his thinking illustrates the shifting temperament of the Black reading public. *Crisis,* for example, chided Ferris for his archaic philosophical speculations and his indifference to the practical problems Black people faced. Yet the reviewer added that many Blacks shared the anxieties Ferris held over the future of the race. In fact, Ferris had stumbled over the modern dilemma between individual choice and the compulsions of ethnic loyalty. S. P. Fullinwider and Wilson J. Moses have unnecessarily focused on his personality quirks (which must have been substantial) rather than the larger problem of individual choice within racial continuity with which he struggled. As Orlando Patterson has noted, all forms of ethnic identification limit the individual's choice of values and force the rational mind to accept an act of faith. Ferris assumed that genetic compulsions accounted for his incomplete identification with the African heritage or the Afro-American peasantry. He sought a resolution in philosophical ideals, which, he assumed, must arise from a new race, the Negro-Saxon.[12] Consequently, he pictured a changing, more confident Black temperament, and he realistically portrayed the conflict over values and tactics then being debated between Washington and the intellectuals. He chronicled Anglo-Saxon achievements within the context of an evolutionary social philosophy to which Crummell and DuBois both adhered because it legitimated Black efforts to modernize. As an expression of the Black search for purpose, even his ruminations reveal a growing capacity to defend a separate racial identity while recognizing the need for modernization. The African, for Ferris as for the men he most admired, was becoming more conscious of the reasons for his subordination, but once he had refined his racial ideals his role would be far greater.

If the longing for racial destiny was most fully expressed by Ferris, realistic anxieties over the meaning of race were the focus of James Weldon Johnson's novel, *The Autobiography of an Ex-Colored Man.* With the encouragement of Brander Matthews, a drama critic at Columbia University, it was published through a major New York house, Alfred Knopf, in late 1912.[13] Unlike *The African Abroad,* it created a major stir among Black readers, in part because it was published anonymously, but even more because it dealt frankly with the anxieties of racial identification, which Johnson saw as voluntary. Johnson was in so many ways the opposite of Ferris as a personality, a literary craftsman, and a social critic that his approach to the idea of race can be seen as the major alternative offered during the period. Ferris sought authority for the distinctiveness of the Negro-Saxon from without—in ponderous laws of social evolution and the transubstantiation of ideals. Johnson, however, gained authenticity from his candid internal probing of motives and his emphasis on the process of ethnic choice. As urbane and popular as Ferris was pedantic and insecure, Johnson had used contacts with Booker T. Washington and numerous Black politicians to obtain an appointment as a young consular official in Latin America between 1906 and 1912. The distance from the United States, he felt, helped him to determine how arbitrary were judgments about racial identity and individual merit and provided a solitude to weigh his observations.[14]

Johnson utilized a simple picaresque plot much like *Huckleberry Finn* to set off the complex meanings that race might have to different strata of Americans. He created a fair-skinned persona who might pass for white and who could thus gain candid views from persons on both sides of the color line. The character moved from childhood to middle age as alternately Caucasian, Negro, and finally Caucasian in various parts of the United States and Europe. Where Charles Chestnutt had made the choice of racial identity the focus of several short stories, Johnson used the longer novel form to demonstrate how a personality could grow only by successively rejecting traditional theories and stereotypes. Johnson's pensive central character was also given great musical talents but a very proper upbringing to personify an individual who deserved success by conventional standards. Thrust into many unusual situations because of his ancestry, he could explore the irrationality of white prejudice, refine the aesthetic creativity of Blacks, and reveal the varied tragedies of American race relations.[15]

If Ferris provided a set of intrinsic characteristics for the Negro-Saxon personality, Johnson dramatized the more modern and challenging notion that identity should legitimately be a creative act. By stigmatizing the Black heritage, however, white Americans had turned what should have been a source of pride into a series of desperate choices for people of African descent. Far from being dependent on paternalistic assistance, Johnson demonstrated that Blacks understood whites more profoundly than whites understood them.[16] But Blacks faced economic, political, and sexual exploitation, which robbed them of self-confidence, drew them occasionally to criminal behavior, and perverted what should have been stable and fulfilling relationships. The persona's mother was forced to live apart from his white father and was nourished by the myth rather than the substance of conjugal love. Black paramours were kept by wealthy white women to gratify their sexual fantasies; rather than developing mature relationships, they were often led to desperate acts. The persona himself was finally forced to reject his life's work with Black music in order to marry the white woman he loved and to find security for his family.[17]

The most striking feature of *The Autobiography* is the use of simple language to dissect candidly all sides of Black life and of race relations. In later years Johnson confided to Walter White that "I have had several very complimentary opinions about the prose of the book. This is more gratifying to me than a favorable criticism of the story itself."[18] For a man who placed so much importance on the value of free choice in identification, only a prose without academic diction or romantic conventions could reveal underlying motives. By avoiding academic jargon and utilizing personal details when presenting the views of educated persons, Johnson stripped them of authority and revealed in them the same self-interest as in the opinions of the uneducated. Utilizing also the persona's white appearance, Johnson exposed the hypocrisy and foolishness of conventional views of race and race relations. On a train ride through the South the persona encounters the full range of educated white opinions and psychological stances. A Jewish merchant, reluctant to antagonize Christians yet mindful of the prejudices against his own people that prevented him from condoning discrimination, "had the faculty of agreeing with everybody without losing allegiance to any side." A young Ohio-born college professor at an Alabama school stated pompously that after having lived in the South for a year he had come to believe that southern whites were handling race relations as well as possible. A GAR veteran quickly pointed to the professor's vulnerable position, which explained his change of views. The veteran, in turn, reiterated the ponderous philosophy of consecutive racial evolution, which in part allowed him to refrain from immediate protest. A Texas cotton planter, finally, simply defended the doctrine of inherent Negro inferiority, which the veteran quickly reduced to absurdity by citing examples of Black achievement. Each person defended stereotypes, and the persona concluded that the heart of the race problem lay not in the backwardness of Blacks or in any inherent racial characteristics but in the ignorance of whites.[19]

For Blacks to countervail, Johnson suggested, they must

develop a race pride based on the genuine appreciation of the skill of their ancestors.[20] Neither he nor any of his contemporaries among Black intellectuals yet appreciated the implications of the idea of cultural relativism, but in a way he moved beyond it. By emphasizing the Black origins of distinctively American music like the cakewalk and ragtime, he freed the evaluation of Black art from the patronizing air attached to the spirituals and the folk songs. His dramatic descriptions of New York "high life" no doubt opened a new window on Black society to the reading public. He had been raised without fear or awe of white men and felt completely at ease describing the Bohemia in which Blacks and whites mingled freely.[21] His emphasis on its destructive features, however, suggests that he regretted that only within its confines could individuals of both races be themselves with one another. The tragedy for Blacks, then, lay not in their inability to become white but in the wounds inflicted on them when they responded to the normal impulse to identify with their Afro-American heritage. Through a more honest appreciation of that heritage, he concluded, white Americans might no longer force persons of African descent to become "ex-colored men" in order to find some personal fulfillment. In his celebrated poem, "Fifty Years," which appeared in the *New York Times* on January 1, 1913, commemorating the emancipation, he reminded Blacks that they were full citizens not through the suffrance of whites, but because of their history of toil and sacrifice for the Republic.[22]

Ethnicity and Liberal Reform: The Origins of a Perpetual Struggle

Despite their differing definitions of race, both Ferris and Johnson saw in DuBois the most innovative Black writer of the era. As editor of *Crisis* he combined notices of Negro achievements so thoroughly with political protest that even Washington recommended it as a model to his journalistic supporters like Fred Moore and Lester Walton.[23] DuBois adhered more closely to Johnson's view of race loyalty as a conscious commitment than to Ferris's theory of primordial instincts that needed awakening. He hoped to extrude from the Black reading public a new pride in their achievements by setting their experience into as broad a context as possible. DuBois became the most articulate spokesman of Black political agitation during this period as he editorialized against discrimination, prepared publicity releases, and consulted with lawyers from the NAACP. But his primary concern lay with developing a deeper psychological and broader international perspective on the Black experience. Politics and culture were for him intimately related, but the latter required more careful nurture and promised greater rewards.

In the summer of 1911, for example, DuBois saw an opportunity to strike at the exploitation of Black Americans and to promote their image as an articulate people by describing their circumstances to an international conference. For several years the Ethical Culture Society had hoped to promote international peace by convening prominent members of the various "races." By the spring of 1911 Gustave Spiller, a representative of the society, invited prominent spokesmen from Asia, the West Indies, Africa, and from some racial minorities, as well as several anthropologists and missionaries, to the First Universal Races Congress to meet in London from July 26 to 29. Through his contact with John Milholland, a white founder of the NAACP, and a member of the Ethical Culture Society, DuBois was invited to represent the American Negro. Although he could not convince the editor of *The Century* to employ him as a correspondent to ensure coverage in the national press, he did publicize it extensively in *Crisis.* [24]

Some scholars, and DuBois himself, have noted how the conference avoided the complex political problems arising from imperialism. But DuBois considered London the center of world politics and culture, and he and many speakers used the occasion to air their local problems before a new international audience. In fact, as Michael D. Biddis has noted, several London papers *did* criticize colonial policies. A correspondent from the *Times* stressed the incongruity between the scholarly papers that emphasized racial or economic conflict and those of philanthropists that called for good will. In his own talk DuBois captured his ambivalence well. With Black spokesmen from

South Africa, Nigeria, Egypt, and Haiti present, he set the narrow topic of Black progress in America since Emancipation into a wider political context. Like the other hundred-odd speakers, DuBois was limited to seven minutes, during which he balanced the achievements of Blacks against a widening pattern of discrimination. In a summary of his talk prepared as part of a general review of the conference for *Crisis,* DuBois concluded with a direct but polite criticism of Washington. "One theory proposes that [American Negroes] should emancipate themselves by acquiring wealth, but it would seem that the intellectual emancipation should proceed hand in hand with economic independence," he suggested. The full text, published in the proceedings, indicated that DuBois had been more critical than the *Crisis* summary implied. He had argued that Washington misunderstood both the structure of American society and the means for combating discrimination. The American labor force consisted not of competitive individuals, DuBois countered, but contending racial groups. To impart skills to Black workers without training a leadership to defend their collective interests would simply expose naive laborers to the attacks of their more aggressive white counterparts.[25]

The cooperation of nonwhite peoples, rather than the content of individual speeches, encouraged DuBois to see in the conference a new context for analyzing the plight of Black Americans. They shared cultural stigmatization, economic exploitation, and political suppression with most of nonwhite humanity, but colored peoples were finally protesting against their conditions. The conference on several occasions called not simply for philanthropic assistance to the unfortunate but for a recognition of the moral equality of all civilizations. A ranking of peoples, several speakers argued, had become inappropriate, because different cultures represented equally legitimate efforts to adjust to different environments. Individual physical differences, speakers insisted, bore no relationship to mental capacities. While DuBois played a small role in the conference, he felt himself for the first time part of an international movement to legitimize the equality of colored peoples. For that reason he gave it more advance publicity and fuller coverage in *Crisis* than any event until the race riots of 1919.[26]

Elliott Rudwick has emphasized how DuBois's desire for recognition led him to publicize his speeches in London and to exaggerate the consequences of the conference before various scholarly and elite gatherings. The penchant for international meetings and a romantic fascination with racial leadership no doubt led DuBois to see in the conference a greater lever for change than it could possibly have provided. His participation did indicate that after years of exile in Atlanta, he had finally joined the intellectual avante garde that promoted Ethical Culture, Women's Suffrage, the Peace Movement, and more exotic causes like Esperanto.[27] But the significance DuBois attributed to the Races Conference did not grow primarily from personal needs. He could, of course, become so absorbed in conferences that to promote their key issues he might romanticize the setting and overstate the consequences.[28] But, as a propagandist after the London Conference, he shrewdly focused on the issue of cultural equality. Until Black spokesmen could discard the mask and appear as the advocates of a distinct people, he argued, whites would see no reason to discuss social equality with them.

The mask, as DuBois understood and as Louis Harlan has again emphasized, was the refuge of the enslaved, which, while deflecting overt attack, sapped them steadily of their psychological independence. It had been the major tool of Booker T. Washington. Despite his puffery over his London connections, DuBois understood very well how the conference, if properly promoted, might liberate its participants. Such inner security, he had insisted for many years, must precede assertions of economic and political equality.[29]

The institution through which DuBois hoped to achieve Black liberation, the NAACP, had to be honed to its task because of its dual focus. Most of its white officers and its Black membership identified Blacks primarily as citizens deprived of their rights. DuBois in part agreed with this view and as publicity director he wrote strong public statements defending the claim of Blacks to equal treatment. He further agreed that the association should become the nonpartisan lobbying agency needed to monitor government action and to develop an agenda for Black political advancement. But DuBois and the Black staff he gathered to him at *Crisis* also saw the association as the proper vehicle to promote a cultural Renaissance. His comments on the biracial conference from which the association developed were only guardedly enthusiastic because he sensed the condescension of many white members. Even after he had become editor of *Crisis* he continued as secretary of the exclusive Niagara Movement. A small contingent met at Sea Isle City, New Jersey, in the summer of 1910, and as late as September, 1911, he sent a circular to members urging them to join the NAACP but to retain their autonomy as a separate group. In 1916 he suggested to James Weldon Johnson, the new field secretary, that in addition to organizing NAACP chapters, he gauge prospects for a more exclusive and secret order of Black men.[30]

The need to protect the cultural autonomy of Blacks within the organization preoccupied DuBois from its founding until he left in 1934. While some persons believed that his emphasis in the early 1930s on the formation of separate Negro cooperatives represented a rejection of the Association's objectives, they rested on his earliest observations of rural communities.[31] Seeing himself the sophisticated interpreter of genuine folk communities, DuBois, as the white civil libertarian Roger Baldwin remembered, " never let you forget he was colored. Dignified, Harvard educated, a self-conscious gentleman, he played the aristocrat among Negroes." George S. Schuyler, the vitriolic Black journalist, reminded an interviewer in 1962 that the early Black leadership that DuBois attracted to the NAACP had far broader cultural interests than did their successors. DuBois in particular gave *Crisis* its intensive preoccupation with racial pride. Carl Van Vechten remembered that under DuBois *Crisis* was not as accessible to young white writers as was *Opportunity,* the journal of the Urban League edited by Charles S. Johnson. DuBois, Van Vechten noted, "was more interested in violent articles about what should and should not be done for and by the Negro."[32]

DuBois's decision to become a salaried employee of the NAACP constituted at least a tactical compromise of his racial ideals. His subsequent relationship with its white officers, at least one of their fair-complected Negro successors (Walter White), and the biracial board of directors remained ambiguous because they felt uneasy with a separate Black cultural perspective within the organization. Most members agreed with Mary Ovington that DuBois brought a unique genius to the organization. But like another founder, Oswald Garrison Villard, publisher of the New York *Evening Post,* they saw Negroes primarily as persons in need of rehabilitation and integration into the body politic. The interracial composition of the association placed whites like Villard in the vanguard of American social reform, and DuBois as much as any of the female officers appreciated its affinity to the woman's suffrage movement. But some of the white officers never perceived how their strength threatened the autonomy of their Black associates. Villard in particular assumed the association would speak with one voice for civil rights, but DuBois saw it as a loose coalition in which Blacks must retain an autonomous role.[33] The dual objectives of nonpartisan lobbying and of cultural Renaissance were not inherently incompatible. Indeed, the NAACP and *Crisis* were more successful in balancing the two components of Black identity than was the contemporary Zionist movement in reconciling the dual loyalty of the American Jew.[34] But DuBois's effort to retain an independent voice within the association created more turmoil than any event until its officers disagreed on the entry of the United States into World War I. Even that moral dilemma, however, was resolved more amicably.

From the beginning, as Elliott Rudwick has described in great detail, DuBois clashed with equally strong-willed officers over the appropriate focus of the association. On the surface the conflict seemed to be over administration, with the board assuming that salaried employees like DuBois, officially the director of publicity and research, would simply reflect their policy.[35] No sooner had DuBois arrived in New York, however, than he and twenty-two other Black members of the association separately issued a pamphlet from 20 Vessey Street, the office of the association in Villard's *Evening Post* building, attacking statements about American race relations that Washington had made in Europe that summer. Although DuBois and the others listed "The National Negro Committee" rather than the NAACP as the official sponsor of the pamphlet, their signatures and the place of publication implied that it either expressed association policy or had its approval. The pamphlet argued that Washington had become so financially dependent upon white support for Tuskegee Institute that he deliberately ignored aspects of discrimination that "certain powerful interests in America" wished to conceal. Washington had been misrepresenting conditions, DuBois concluded, and his committee could not allow such statements to go unchallenged. Though agreeing with the pamphlet's contents, Villard apologized to Washington for the apparent subterfuge, and his animosity toward DuBois festered.[36]

At the heart of DuBois's controversy with the NAACP board lay his desire to make *Crisis* a journal primarily for Black readers. In format, name of editorial and feature colums, editorial tone, and wide coverage of international events affecting nonwhite peoples, *Crisis* closely resembled *The Voice of the Negro* and *Horizon*. Its editorial bias was evident from the first number, in which DuBois argued that "constructive work" as preached by the "Black Leader" (obviously Washington) would not allow Blacks to gain full equality. They needed instead a group consciousness and an independent voice. To young Black artists *Crisis* became a mecca, in part because the staff, aside from volunteer assistance from Mary Dunlop Maclean and Mary Ovington, consisted entirely of Blacks. DuBois attracted real literary talent, like Jessie Fauset. The addition of James Weldon Johnson to the NAACP staff in 1916 and his close association with DuBois indicated the willingness of musical and literary artists to devote their talent to political protest in a way that had not been true of the smaller, semi-secret, and scattered Niagara Movement.[37]

The move to Harlem, the development of Black businesses on Chicago's South Side and Detroit's Near East Side, and the founding of building and loan associations and banks in Philadelphia between 1910 and 1920 signified the emergence of a new entrepreneurial leadership within Black communities. The

founding of the National Urban League in New York in 1910 to
assist southern migrants with immediate housing and employment problems announced that modern forms of social work
would be directed for the first time towards Blacks. While the
Urban League promoted social scientific research that DuBois
willingly endorsed, it remained deeply wedded to Washington's
view of Black disabilities. The appearance of *Crisis* announced a
new intellectual contingent who replaced both the politicians of
Washington and the southern educators as the innovative
spokesmen for Black America. Many of the new northern Black
business leaders like Jesse Bingha, Robert Abbott, and the
Wrights of Philadelphia were southern-born and accepted Washington's emphasis on capital accumulation and institutional
separation from whites. But in an urban setting they insisted
also on the civil and political rights for which the NAACP
stood. The Wrights in particular found DuBois's intellectual
achievements an inspiration and in subscribing to *Crisis* sup—
ported his forum for outspoken political and cultural views.[38]

With circulation of *Crisis* steadily growing, DuBois encouraged Fauset, Williams S. Braithwaite, Benjamin Brawley, Johnson, and others to write about urbane, articulate Blacks, as well
as about uneducated rural people. Their stories and poems won
the respect of new literary figures like George Jean Nathan and
H. L. Mencken and they appealed to critics like Horace M.
Kallen, Randolph Bourne, and John Dewey, who saw America
as culturally diverse rather than an Anglo-Saxon society. By
1915 *Crisis* had already emerged as the focus for a Black cultural revival and its staff had developed a distinct fraternal feeling.[39]

If, as many scholars have argued, the image of the Negro
presented in *Crisis* was decidedly middle class, within the
political context of that era such an image represented a new
Black assertiveness. To present Blacks as decorous, pensive, even
fastidious was not a capitulation to white values, but was part
of the same battle against the ideology of racial hierarchies that
had been dramatized at the Universal Races Congress. Still
wedded to the notion of universal brotherhood achieved through
common standards of civility, DuBois and his associates were

not embarrassed nor did they feel compromised promoting middle-class decorum. (One need only examine the dress of the urban working class of that era to realize how pervasive were concerns over proper decorum.) Despite the emphasis on respectability that pervaded the numerous articles on Black educational achievements, family life, and the meetings of the association, white readers were upset by the image of Black institutional separation. As early as 1914 even Mary Ovington complained that *Crisis* had become boring to white readers. In the same vein, DuBois criticized several of Vachel Lindsay's technically innovative poems, "Congo" and "Booker T. Washington Trilogy," because they depicted Blacks as primitives. Lindsay replied that he had merely wished to depict the extraordinarily sensuous character and aesthetic skills of Blacks and that DuBois had apparently misinterpreted his motives. Joel Spingarn, however, explained that Black writers like DuBois felt that to combat racial stereotypes whites must be shown sophisticated Blacks dealing with modern problems. Only through a similar literary treatment of people of both races would the public believe that all human beings shared intellectual capacities. For the same reason James Weldon Johnson had refrained from depicting rural Blacks in *The Autobiography of an Ex-Colored Man.*[40]

To keep *Crisis* free to depict a unique perspective, DuBois strove to make it financially independent of the Association. By late 1915 he announced that his salary would be drawn entirely from the "Crisis Fund" rather than from the association treasury, though apparently he could never become completely self-sustaining.[41] To further encourage wider Black promotion of their cultural heritage he devoted much of his time during 1915 to directing an all-Black cast in a musical pageant entitled "The Star of Ethiopia." The pageant was produced at a time when white authors like Ridgley Torrance were beginning to present plays on Broadway on Black themes but were still disallowed from using Black performers. In part to countervail against such discrimination, DuBois gave elaborate coverage to his all-Black extravaganza in *Crisis.* Indeed, for him it became the domestic equivalent to the Races Congress of 1911. If the

Congress presented a cosmopolitan image of nonwhite peoples, the pageant displayed highly refined Afro-American artistic achievement. DuBois and others had orchestrated traditional melodies, embellished dances, and mythesized themes from Black history to demonstrate the continual evolution of Black artistic talents. Though Villard complained about the amount of time DuBois devoted to the pageant while still an employee of the association, DuBois defended his work in lyrical terms. He wrote in *Crisis,* "The Pageant is the thing. This is what the people want and long for. This is the gown and paraphernalia in which the message of education and reasonable race pride can deck itself." With almost a thousand persons in a chorus and dance troupe, the pageant was staged in Washington, D.C., and Philadelphia. Although DuBois was disappointed with his inability to raise more capital and with the indifference of the white American Pageant Association, the enthusiasm of the participants and the founding of numerous Black dramatic companies especially in Harlem led him to hope that a new theater to dramatize Black history and folk art would soon emerge.[42]

With characteristic energy DuBois formed the "Horizon Guild," a group that he hoped to incorporate to sponsor a series of pageants on Negro history over the next decade. Harold Cruse has argued that the development of such a distinctive Black theater failed because Black dramatists lacked the imagination and courage to project a distinctive Black vision and because the middle class would not support them. But for DuBois, pageants that displayed the singular musical achievements of the race and involved masses of participants would dramatize the cultural basis of the Black demand for social as well as political equality. Undiscouraged, he continued to bring in musical artists to direct large-scale entertainments in New York.[43]

Tensions between the tenets of liberal reform and assertions of Black ethnicity were expressed in a variety of ways in the early years of the association. They were more pointedly dramatized perhaps because of Villard's inflexible personality, which was often exacerbated by his class pretensions and ethnocentrism. He refused, for example, to capitalize the word *Negro* in the *Evening Post* when requested to do so several times by Booker T. Washington, in part because he believed that Blacks, unlike Indians or Jews, had no distinctive national identity. Nor did he publicize the refusal by the Harvard Club of New York City of his request to allow the Black Harvard graduate Leslie Pinckney Hill to address them on behalf of the Manassas Industrial School, of which Villard was a major benefactor. Villard also refused to entertain Blacks or Jews at his home, probably, DuBois believed, in deference to his southern-born wife.[44] In addition to harboring a general sense of Black incapacities, Villard began to accuse DuBois of failing to meet the primary ethical standard of progressivism, efficient administration. DuBois, for example, kept his books at *Crisis* loosely, and Villard felt the association was denied a fair accounting. More important, DuBois refused to clear his editorial opinions with the board of directors. At many bitter meetings in 1913 and 1914, Villard objected to continuing editorial criticism of Booker T. Washington and others that might discourage them from supporting the association. When editorials drew letters of protest from Wilberforce president, William S. Scarborough, and the Baltimore branch president, Dr. Francis Cardoza, and when DuBois prepared to condemn racial bias in admissions at Oberlin and Johns Hopkins, Villard threatened to resign. Mary White Ovington clarified the source of tension, when she noted that "Villard has always been opposed to [DuBois] being here. He did not want him at the beginning and he has never been convinced that our choice for Director of Publicity and Research has been wise."[45]

Because Villard could not accept the legitimacy of both a liberal and an ethnic evaluation of events, he developed doubts about DuBois's intellectual integrity. The conflict was sharpened by the coincidence that each man published a biography of John Brown on the fiftieth anniversary of his execution. DuBois had been commissioned by the editor of the American Crisis Biography Series, the historian Ellis P. Oberholtzer, to write an "interpretive" study rather than an exhaustive account based on archival research. Villard, working independently, prepared what he felt would become the definitive study. Although DuBois had informed Villard of his limited intention, the latter's review in *The Nation* failed to consider how DuBois had accomplished his purpose. Villard considered a biography honoring Brown "from the point of view of the Negro" long overdue. But he dwelt exclusively on DuBois's alleged factual errors and his reliance on memoirs praising Brown rather than determining what a "Negro point of view" might be. Albert Bushnell Hart, the mentor of both men at Harvard, admonished Villard for his narrow review and reminded him that DuBois's "reputation as a careful scholar is not much disturbed by the weight which he attaches to one kind of evidence over another."[46]

Villard's review, like his later criticism of DuBois's editorial policy with *Crisis,* seemed to rest on sound professional criteria. Nevertheless, it betrayed an unwillingness to recognize that a Black author might legitimately see a different meaning in a controversial subject than might a liberal white. Villard, for example, believed that Blacks should primarily be grateful to Brown, while DuBois explained how different racial vantage points might lead to honest differences of opinion. As Hart intimated, Villard confused the need for a uniform canon of internal evidence with the discretion allowed a scholar to draw his own moral conclusions. Both authors agreed that Brown's puritanical character led him to ignore alternate of political action. But where Villard criticized Brown's use of violence compared with other forms of abolitionist protest, [47] DuBois set Brown's vision of revolution into the context of ante-bellum race relations.

As Herbert Aptheker informs us, at one point in the negotiations with Oberholtzer, DuBois suggested as his subject Nat Turner, around whom he hoped to weave the history of slave rebellions in the Americas. Unconvinced that Turner had sufficient historic stature to serve as the focus for a volume, Oberholtzer suggested John Brown. Forced to use a white man to develop an interpretation of Black history, DuBois at least made race relations into a major theme of the book.[48] Technical-

ly, as Arnold Rampersad suggests, DuBois followed the intellectual guidelines for assessing historical personages that had
been suggested by Hippolyte Taine. He extracted from the life
of a heroic figure a "master thought," in the case of Brown that
the repression of truth always cost a society more dearly than
its pursuit.[49] He had reached the same conclusions, however, in
his historical monograph on the suppression of the slave trade
and in his study of Philadelphia's Negroes. He adopted for *John
Brown* the ethical imperative he saw in all of American race
relations. As a contribution to historiography, however, DuBois
demonstrated how unusual Brown was, even among abolitionists, in cultivating close relations with Blacks. Indeed according
to DuBois, Brown's faith in his revolutionary mission rested on
his unique friendships with so many of them.[50]

By gathering more evidence on political events and economic and social conditions in Kansas and elsewhere, Villard
felt he could distinguish more accurately than had DuBois
between Brown's apocalyptic fantasy and the prospects for a
less violent resolution of the slavery issue. Assessing the relation
of means to ends in appropriate liberal fashion, he concluded
that Brown's violence had thoughtlessly drained the abolitionist
movement of the moral stature that Villard's own grandfather,
William Lloyd Garrison, had striven to build. DuBois, however,
criticized Brown not for his defection from liberal standards but
for failing to fulfill his commitment to Black opinions.[51]
Rampersad has argued that DuBois figuratively identified with
Shields Green, the fugitive slave who joined whites in the
struggle for Black liberation and followed Brown to martyr-
dom.[52] More likely, however, DuBois identified with Douglass
and Delany, whose confidence in their own judgment led them
to develop an independent view of tactics. DuBois likewise felt
justified in resisting white reformers. As Felix Frankfurter, after
praising Villard's *John Brown*, noted, "He is a self-righteous
person and self-righteous people are usually as unwise as he is.
He erects public characters into heroes and then, when they are
not as saint-like as he thinks he is, he reviles them."[53] DuBois
consistently felt this side of Villard's temperament, and in his

conduct as well as in his literary judgments he resisted the demands for deference.

In his relationship to the NAACP DuBois also sought to publicize the activities of Blacks rather than measuring his judgment against a Progressive code. Perhaps unjustifiably, at least until it became self-supporting, he saw *Crisis* as his personal medium to counter the white man's pejorative image of the Negro. He resisted all efforts by the board to make it a "house organ" that simply reported the policies of an institution, as he alleged the New York *Age* and other Black newspapers did for Washington.[54] In retrospect, *Crisis* was dominated by a celebration of Black creative writing and educational and artistic attainments not by a strident editorial policy. Far better than prior Black journalists, DuBois separated editorial comment from news coverage while maintaining a consistent emphasis on civil and social equality. As he explained to Mary White Ovington, he had to retain editorial autonomy so that Black readers could expect from him a personalized view of events. By trying to mute his criticism of Washington and other Black persons or institutions, DuBois contended, the association would impede the emergence of Black self-confidence.[55]

To gain financial and political support from people whose talents he respected, DuBois maintained his uneasy alliance with the association for twenty-four years. It provided him initially with and office, a staff, and the capital to launch an independent journal. DuBois, however, soon moved the office of *Crisis* to other quarters specifically to escape Villard's scrutiny, and he saw *Crisis* as the center of an expanding Black cultural revival quite distinct from the association. In 1914 he proposed the Crisis Publishing Company, which would be incorporated independently of the association and would publish, buy, and sell books. By 1915 he suggested that the relationship between himself, *Crisis,* and the association be reorganized. Under each of three plans he devised, he would retain responsibility for the journal and its autonomy would be assured. As Mary Ovington noted, the creation by DuBois of *Crisis* as a successful "colored magazine" had created a tension between the political purposes of the association and the cultural interests of its editor. The association might have access to *Crisis* "as an independent magazine," but the interests of the two seemed no longer to be synonymous.[56]

His work as *Crisis* editor, furthermore, allowed DuBois to consolidate his position as chief proponent of a more cosmopolitan and therefore a more self-confident and aggressive Black image. During the first years of the association, when its form as either an elite or a broad-based organization remained unclear, DuBois helped screen prospective new Black members. When the drive to organize branches and draw a wider membership began, he saw his role in wider terms. Like the white officers, he believed the New York headquarters should provide expertise, but he lectured widely at Black churches throughout the east and traveled even to California to build a wide following for the association. With the growth of branches that reported regularly to the New York office, DuBois had better access than any other Black spokesman to events and sentiments throughout the country. His information was more varied and complete, and his ability to draw more authoritative conclusions was greater than any other Black writer, even Booker T. Washington. Gaining wider exposure himself and providing coverage in *Crisis* of events in hundreds of Black communities, DuBois eclipsed people like Trotter and Grimke, whose reputations for vigor and articulateness had until then equaled his own.[57]

As the association gained wider allegiance among the Black elite and middle class, potential leaders who did not reside in New York lost the opportunity to hold office and set policy. By 1915, for example, many white board members came to believe, in part because of the precedent set by the Urban League and in part because of DuBois's struggles with Villard, that a Black man should become chairman of the board of directors. Archibald Grimke seemed the best candidate, but his residence in Washington precluded his daily supervision of the association's business. Mary Ovington, who had broached the idea of a Black chairman, and several others vetoed Grimke's nomination. When James Weldon Johnson became the first Black executive secretary in 1920, he was promoted from within the New York office, and his combination of literary and organizational interests coincided with that of DuBois.[58]

The Resolution of the Non-partisan Strategy

The staff at *Crisis* led a cultural revival that, like movements in American and other literatures, sought to elevate local color into serious commentary on the values of ordinary people. The majority of Black professionals, business people, and even urban migrants, however, were initially more concerned with the defense of their rights as citizens. DuBois understood and accepted this priority, although he strove to keep the two in tandem. Like so many of his friends he had learned that Blacks could not defend their citizenship rights without allies. When rumors that Villard or even Joel Spingarn (with whom DuBois was highly compatible) had threatened to resign from the association leaked beyond New York, Black professionals like Reverdy Ransom, William Pickens, John Hope (DuBois's closest personal friend), and Butler Wilson pleaded with them to stay. DuBois also conciliated the white officers—even Villard—because he appreciated their influence in philanthropic and political circles.[59]

From the headquarters in New York, therefore, the white officers, with DuBois's assistance, sought finally to consolidate a modern, nonpartisan lobbying agency for Black Americans. Unlike prior efforts with Fortune's Afro-American League, Trotter's National Independent Political League, or the Niagara Movement, the officers of the NAACP sought to bring legal and promotional expertise to bear on a narrow set of issues divorced from patronage or community development. As individuals, DuBois (through *Crisis*) or Villard might endorse presidential candidates or recommend a friend like James Weldon Johnson for a consular post, but the association did not. Like the farmers who formed the Farm Bureau Federation and the labor unions in the American Federation of Labor, the professionals organizing the NAACP narrowed their focus to deal with legal and promotional issues while creating local cells for intelligence and support. The association thereby hoped to deal effectively with peonage, lynching, segregation, and to increase Black civic participation.[60]

The major strategic deficiencies of the association by 1913 lay in the small number of branches and the lack of a reliable agency in the nation's Capital to monitor the actions of the federal government. The need and opportunity for both agencies became more striking in 1913, when Woodrow Wilson became the first southerner since the Civil War to be elected president. Wilson, of course, had been nominated by the Democrats not on his heritage as a southerner but on his reputation as a reform governor of New Jersey. His political slogan, "The New Freedom," connoted a new respect for local institutions like small businesses and family farms, and he had the endorsement of Louis Brandeis, whose national reputation rested on a defense of working people, including women and children, and consumers. DuBois, after rejecting Taft and Roosevelt as hopeless perpetrators of racial discrimination, supported Wilson, who in an interview with Black politicians like Bishop Walters of Jersey City, had promised to treat Negroes fairly.[61] But Wilson's peculiar conception of fair treatment, plus the influence in his administration of southern politicians, led to a crisis for the NAACP shortly after his inauguration.

Villard, as owner of the *Evening Post* and *The Nation*, had access to Wilson, and as chairman of the board of the NAACP he suggested before Wilson's inauguration the appointment of a national commission to investigate race relations.[62] While Wilson agreed that such a commission might clarify conditions, he and members of his cabinet had their own opinions about how to improve relations between the races. Wilson, much like Villard, believed that Blacks constituted a backward but improving race, who needed controlled opportunities to demonstrate their abilities, and followed the doctrine of "separate but equal" announced by the Supreme Court in the case of *Plessy* v. *Ferguson* in 1896. If Blacks were separated from whites and entrusted with the complete administration of a federal bureau, Wilson believed, they might demonstrate their executive as well as their clerical skills and prove themselves worthy of advancement through the civil service. To further this experiment in racial engineering, he nominated Adam Patterson of Oklahoma as registrar of the U.S. Treasury to head an all-Black bureau. Members of his cabinet, however, offered opposition. Postmaster General Albert S. Burleson of Texas believed that Blacks should simply be kept in subordinate roles. Secretary of the Treasury William Gibbs McAdoo, who was originally from Georgia, argued that any "experiments" to provide unique opportunities for Blacks would not be supported by a Senate controlled by southern Democrats.[63]

By summer 1913, prospects for a Black role in the New Freedom had faded. In August Wilson abandoned the suggestion for a commission of inquiry on race relations because, he told Villard, it suggested to southern white politicians an indictment of their racial mores. "It would be hard to make anyone understand the delicacy and difficulty of the situation I find existing here with regard to the colored people. . . . I never realized before the complexity and difficulty of this matter in respect to every step taken here."[64] When the nomination of Patterson was defeated in the Senate, Wilson did not try to nominate another Black, and rumors flew that a white man would be nominated as minister to Haiti. At the same time a pattern of segregating Black federal employees from whites began to appear in workrooms, lunchrooms, and toilets of various government agencies. The incidence of segregation during the Wilson administration has been well-documented by several scholars, but its implications for modern forms of public administration and of protest have not been clarified.[65] As a policy, for example, segregation did not occur uniformly, because it was neither imposed by legislation nor by presidential directive. It emerged, rather, from the collaboration of middle-level bureaucrats who sought to impress their superiors with their prescience and efficiency in reflecting "public opinion."[66] Likewise, the fight against segregation did not originate with a central agency like the NAACP but began with protests from local Blacks who then looked for stronger support. The importance of the fight against segregation for the NAACP lay not in its ability to end the practice but in its use of the issue to develop a permanent nonpartisan agency to monitor Congress and the civil service.

Black employees had faced various forms of discrimination in agencies of the federal government for many years, and the Taft administration had curtailed Black appointments in post offices and custom houses. However, a visit in March, 1913, by Mrs. Woodrow Wilson to the U.S. Bureau of Engraving and Printing (which employed more Blacks than any other bureau in Washington) led to more formal efforts to segregate the bureaucracy. Mrs. Wilson became upset to see so many white women and Black men working in close proximity and apparently complained to Assistant Secretary of the Treasury, John Skelton Williams, who, like her, was a Virginian with intense racial biases. Williams inspected the bureau, where he insulted Black clerks, taunted whites for working alongside them, and implied that formal patterns of segregation would be imposed. In a city where even the barbers in Capitol Hill shops received appointments through congressmen, lesser bureaucrats responded quickly to the bruited desires of cabinet officers. In May Mrs. Charlotte Hopkins, a white social worker who relied on Congress for funding, visited the bureau to discuss segregation with its superintendent, John Ralph. She assumed that if Black federal employees accepted segregated facilities, the president and Congress would renew funds for Black welfare recipients. While convening a meeting of bureau employees, she learned that Ralph had already segregated lunchrooms. To avoid the appearance of initiating policy, however, Ralph noted that he had merely *extended* a pattern of racially separated dressing rooms to eating areas. When questioned by NAACP officers, Miss Hopkins replied that among the Black employees only "two girls" objected. They, she added, were "almost white and a bad type—open work stockings, jewelry, high heels—that kind . . . ."[67]

From July through September Wilson issued no policy statement, but reports of extended segregation reached NAACP headquarters from Black federal employees. The employees feared that open protest would cost them their jobs, and the association had little recourse but to send letters of complaint to Wilson and McAdoo. Local protest by the association was further stymied because the new branch in Washington was headed by men dabbling in Democratic party politics. The struggle to replace these men and to organize a branch to carry out non-partisan lobbying preoccupied the association for the latter half of 1913.[68] It led, however, to the formation of an agency for which both Villard and DuBois had been working almost a decade.

Reorganizing the District of Columbia branch was part of a three-pronged effort to free the association from all vestiges of factional partisanship. In addition to endorsement by DuBois, Wilson had received support from several prominent Blacks who had turned to the Democrats several years previously when the Republicans had curtailed patronage.[69] Three of the most prominent, Bishop Alexander Walters, Trotter, and the Reverend J. Milton Waldron of Washington, were also associated with the NAACP, though each had a somewhat different attitude toward patronage. The failure of the Wilson administration between 1913 and 1915 to respect Black opinion and to take any of the three men into its confidence undermined their credibility and allowed the association to assume their role as spokesmen on civic issues for the race. By the time the Republicans returned to power in 1921, the older Black officeholder elite like Pinchback, George White, Judson Lyons, John Dancy had lost their influence. The association was then recognized by both major parties and Progressive insurgents as the race's spokesman on public questions.

Bishop Alexander Walters, though a member of the executive board of the NAACP and not himself a candidate for office, demonstrated how a sponsor of officeseekers could undermine the association's ability to defend civil rights. DuBois, like Booker T. Washington, had little respect for Walter's intellectual or administrative abilities. The officers of the association, however, recognized his wide contacts and had consulted him early in 1909 for suggestions on prospective members. Even though Mary Ovington knew he rarely came to New York City, she thought he would make a useful vice-chairman of the Association's New York City local when it was organized in 1911. Walters also became a member of the national executive board, though between May, 1911, and October, 1912, he attended only four of the monthly board meetings and none subsequently. Villard, however, believed that as an arbiter of patronage Walters might open contacts for the

Association that would be useful. However, when Secretary McAdoo justified segregation in part because it had had the support of several "prominent" Negroes, Villard learned that Walters had been among them.[70] The NAACP board did not then openly chastise Walters, but it cut him off by failing to elicit his advice. In September, 1913, Villard sarcastically wrote to him, "You have so many influential friends that we are counting on you to help us in the fight" [against segregation.] When Walters could offer no assistance and realized the Association would not aid him in his quest for Negro appointments, he quietly resigned in October, 1913. He was replaced on the board by Archibald Grimke, for whom the national officers planned a much larger role.[71]

Like Walters, Trotter actively petitioned the Wilson administration for his associates in the National Independent Political League who sought appointive office. True to his commitment to remain free to criticize officeholders, however, Trotter did not seek an appointment for himself. Trotter's militant style, however, must have been known to the Wilson administration, which never consulted him on policy. He had to learn of segregation through a public announcement by the NAACP. Seriously chagrined, he duly protested on behalf of the Political League. Although he never joined the NAACP ostensibly because he felt it would be dominated by whites, he agreed with its political objectives and distributed its circular protesting segregation in Boston.[72]

The tension between Trotter and the Association no doubt arose from personal antagonism with Villard and DuBois at Harvard in the 1890s, Villard's support of Washington through 1908, and encounters with DuBois in the Niagara Movement. DuBois refused to speak in Boston, and Villard condemned Trotter's tactics.[73] In addition to personality clashes, however, Trotter still associated with a political clique, even though his views on nonpartisanship were fairly close to that of the Association. He criticized F. H. M. Murray's response to the NAACP circular letter against segregation, for example, in terms similar to those of DuBois and Villard. Murray had noted that segregation had begun under the Republicans and that the Political

League had also protested. But Trotter reminded him that "the jimcrowism is so bad we cannot afford to be explaining where it originated. Such looks like an extenuation of the offense."[74] DuBois, however, claiming a publishing deadline for the oversight, failed to report Trotter's protest visit to Wilson on behalf of the league in November, 1913. Trotter was not appeased by the explanation and complained to Joel Spingarn that DuBois lacked the magnanimity to credit others for their actions. Villard, he added, had exacerbated the condition of Blacks by supporting Washington for so many years.[75] The Association, therefore, did not inform Trotter of its subsequent lobbying activities, and he remained isolated from it. During the Association's campaign in early 1914 to defeat bills designed to segregate the civil service, *Crisis* gave its new lobbyist, Archibald Grimke, full credit.[76]

The least publicized but most important conflict between the officers of the NAACP and Black Democrats occured with J. Milton Waldron, who served as president of the District of Columbia branches of both the National Independent Political League and the NAACP. Waldron could not choose between a factional nonpartisanship that rallied an electorate and administrative nonpartisanship that lobbied permanently on all issues of interest to the race. As he informed McAdoo, the Political League would not enter the Democratic party "en masse," but would "support national and states candidates who were known to be in favor of justice and fair play for all people" For his support of Wilson, though, Waldron expected an appointment. As soon as the officers of the Association in New York learned that he applied for a position through McAdoo, they sought to remove him as president of the Washington, D.C., branch. Mary Ovington explained to May Nerney that the officers respected Waldron's record as a defender of Black civil rights, "but since he . . . was an applicant for office he would unduly antagonize many Washington people whose help we need."[77] Waldron felt the antagonism against him in New York grew from personal quarrels, especially with DuBois over *Horizon* matters. But the great majority of the District of Columbia branch members supported the Association. Neval Thomas assured Joel Spingarn, "the two hundred who will remain in the Association, after the withdrawal of Dr. Waldron and the sixteen he controls, will do enough cooperative work to encourage you."[78]

As information about segregation filtered to New York from federal employees like Henry Baker, Mrs. Carrie Clifford, and Neval Thomas rather than from Waldron, the officers concluded they must remove him. After some election manipulations in Washington and a futile trip by Waldron to New York during which he promised to renounce his desire for appointive office, the board recognized the Neval Thomas-Carrie Clifford faction. Archibald Grimke was appointed temporary chairman until elections could be held in January, 1914.[79] As May C. Nerney told him, "Washington is at present the strategic point and no one knows better than you the difficult situation we have to meet there just now. If you would step in and help us be assuming the Presidency of the branch, it would mean more for our association and for the colored people than I have the eloquence to put into words."[80] Grimke was subsequently elected president, and a group loyal to him and to Neval Thomas continued to control the branch into the 1930s.

As part of his presidency of the Washington, D. C., branch, Grimke became the permanent lobbyist for the association. To become the key spokesman for the Negro before government commitees was a fitting climax to the career of a man with such wide political contacts and so much experience in dignified dissent. With his prestige he also solidified support for the New York office among the intensely factionalized Black middle class in Washington. While his persuasive powers could not alter the policy of segregation, he—along with Neval Thomas—created an image of efficient administrative nonpartisanship. With lawyers preparing court cases, some of which were immediately successful, the growth of branches in several northern and midwestern cities, and the work in Washington, the NAACP could feel that by disassociating from the Black appointive officeholders it had finally formed the modern lobbying agency to defend Black citizenship rights.[81]

Pan-Africanism and American Pluralism: The Origins of a Cultural Reconstruction

With the initial years of institutional organization completed, the Universal Races Congress an apparent success, and various cultural ventures under way, DuBois especially found the national focus for Black development too confining. Arthur Schomburg in New York and Carter Woodson and Kelly Miller in Washington were organizing archives and encouraging the study of Pan-African life, and DuBois felt encouraged to take a broader view of both political and cultural activism.[82] An invitation to write a brief volume on the history of the Negro for the Home University Library of Modern Knowledge, plus the outbreak of war in Europe in August, 1914, allowed him to set Afro-American history into the widest possible context. The publication of *The Negro* and an essay, "The African Roots of War," in the *Atlantic Monthly* in 1915, allowed DuBois to seize the moment of Europe's internal collapse to present a radical reinterpretation of Black history. He did not know when he agreed to write *The Negro* that Europe would plunge into civil war. But the basic themes he developed in the book were so consistent with his essay and so thoroughly a part of his thinking by then that the war merely provided a sardonic backdrop to his vision.[83]

For DuBois the history and destiny of Black Americans now had to be understood as an extension of their identity as Africans. In his prior studies like *The Negro American Family,* he referred to African customs as background. In *The Negro* only the next-to-last, though the longest, chapter dealt with the United States. The bulk of the book reiterated material marshaled by George Washington Williams and even William Ferris, as brought up to date by numerous explorers and scholars, to demonstrate the saga of complex civilizations in Africa. But DuBois advanced an argument that had not yet been stated by an American Black writer. He added that Africa had played an integral role in the rise of modern industrial society and would contribute to the resolution of its injustices. The slave trade had not simply been an immoral and exploitative use of people, but had been the opening phase in the modern organization of capital. Its final era had come with the conquest of Africa and the capture of its resources by the European powers. However, as Europe's men were devoured in the trenches, Africa, assisted by a dispersed Black intelligentsia, stood on the threshold of independence and revitalization.[84]

In both the book and the essay DuBois for the first time utilized a theory of political economy that explained racism not simply as an aspect of white American class privilege but as a necessary component in the grand sweep of imperial expansion. He followed the arguments of Europeans like J. A. Hobson and E. T. Morel, who had described how cartels, to obtain cheap raw materials, had induced their governments to conquer Africa rather than merely protecting trade. DuBois's essays were published a year prior to V. I. Lenin's *Imperialism, The Highest Stage of Capitalism,* and did not reflect the sophisticated explanation of the various phases through which the accumulation and investment of capital passed. Nevertheless, far better than Lenin and the other European Leftists, DuBois described the special problems faced by the colored victims of colonization because the industrialists had marshaled racist doctrine to gain support for imperial ventures from American and European working classes.[85]

An even more telling comparison, however, should be made between DuBois's new work and that of Fortune in *Black and White.* Perhaps it is more than coincidence that both were written shortly after each man had arrived in New York City, where each encountered radical theorists while embarking on new journalistic careers. But more important, and as a mark of his effort to move beyond Fortune, DuBois fused race consciousness with, rather than opposing it to, class analysis. He saw continuity rather than simply analogy in international comparisons. Blacks were not simply in a situation similar to Russian serfs but were victimized by the same historical agents. By the early twentieth century, though, Black peoples had a vanguard in America and the West Indies to lead in their revitalization as they moved in larger numbers into the working class. Where Fortune retreated to race institutions as an expedient in lieu of class organization, DuBois saw a Pan-African alliance across class and national boundaries as a necessary psychological and political step. He recognized the theoretical benefits of class, as opposed to race, alliances against exploitation by capitalists. But with the outbreak of the Great War he saw the prospect for a more immediate and successful race movement to abolish colonialism while educating white workers. In the concept of a "Pan-African" history, he took the subordinate Negro out of his American minority context, and elevated him to an ally of all opponents of international imperialism.[86]

By using the war to build a broad racial consciousness rather than anti-militarism among American Blacks, DuBois was more akin to his American Jewish contemporary and fellow Harvard Ph.D. Horace M. Kallen than to Marxist theorists of economic imperialism. Kallen, promoting the Zionist movement—especially its cultural wing—among Jewish college students, envisioned America in modified European terms as a land of ethnic nationalities; within America's liberal framework, however, each nationality would become more prosperous and more tolerant of one another. DuBois, envisioning America as a segment of a Western world that had prospered through exploitation of Black labor, linked race consciousness to political protest. But again within an American context he envisioned a negotiated and gradual accrual of "rights" not a revolutionary upheaval. The war for Kallen provided the peoples of Europe the opportunity to reorganize under the moral influence of liberalism, where national minorities would have equal civil rights and equal opportunities to develop their cultural institutions. For DuBois the war provided Black peoples the opportunity to develop the political means to resist imperialism while undergoing modernization.[87]

Kallen's "Cultural Pluralism" and DuBois's Pan-Africanism both embodied a hope for social reconciliation, but they also reflected the difference between the experience of European ethnic minorities and Africans in the Americas. Jews in particular, as well as Blacks, experienced forms of cultural deracination and denigration of their traditions by the dominant Anglo-Saxons. Both Kallen and DuBois wished to restore psychological equilibrium to their respective peoples by buttressing strategies for political reorganization with a cultural reawakening. Kallen's pluralistic theories, in addition, were more than simply aesthetic. He observed the coincidence of ethnic and economic stratification in America's cities, and he had also faced academic anti-Semitism. But, he argued, each European group underwent some social mobility, with those who were last to arrive being quite naturally the least favored for the moment. When dealing with Blacks, however, Kallen, like so many cultural liberals from Randolph Bourne and John Dewey to the enigmatic Mencken, faced an anomaly. To counter racial theorists like E. A. Ross who insisted that new immigrants conform to middle class social norms, they cited the cultural achievements of European peoples and the vitality that all cultures experience from cross-fertilization. Blacks, though among the earliest Americans, seemed to Kallen unsuited to such comparisons. He noted rather blandly, that "there seems to be some difference of opinion as to whether the negroes (sic) also should constitute an element in this blend." Of course, Kallen believed that Blacks had contributed to American culture, though he told Alain Locke several years later that he did not know precisely what or how.[88]

DuBois, however, argued that Blacks were not simply an ethnic nationality awakening to its achievements, but a stigmatized caste most of whose members were subject to exploitation generation after generation. Black freedom, and the psychological release of Blacks for cultural creativity, would require a coordinated ideological and political effort that must redistribute to some extent the ownership of the factors of production. The Vardamans were more powerful enemies than the Rosses, and the counterattacks must also be more comprehensive. DuBois recognized that Jeffersonian liberalism, which Kallen venerated as America's basic social philosophy, had reached its limit at the free Negro. He sought instead a reversal of American history, which he believed, had used racial exploitation as a means to bring prosperity to the European immigrants and their descendants.[89]

DuBois and Kallen differed not only in temperament and in their perception of relations between America's various cultural groups, as John Higham properly notes,[90] but in their sense of the dynamic forces in history. Their respective explanations for the origins of the war, for example, provide a classic theoretical confrontation between the benefactors of liberal pluralism and the victims of racial exploitation. Kallen, contrasting the freedom of minorities in America with their subordination in Europe, attributed the war to the expression of primordial nationalism. He explicitly rejected the imperialist explanation because he found many bankers and traders who opposed the war. DuBois, however, saw the hidden origins of the war not in humanity's impulsive desire for traditional loyalties, but in the highly rational machinations of international cartels. "The Balkans are convenient for occasions," he wrote, "but the ownership of materials and men in the darker world is the real prize that is setting the nations of Europe at each other's throats today." By careful manipulation of governments, bankers and industrialists allowed their international rivalries for raw materials to push their nations into war. Blacks, therefore, faced not simply a struggle for a more equitable place in American society but the more demanding task of helping to liberate a continent.[91]

DuBois must surely have read some of Kallen's essays, at least those that appeared in *The Nation,* but he seems never to have commented on the concept of cultural pluralism. It certainly lacked the imperatives of conflict to combat the exploitation he observed, and it presupposed a cultural consciousness he and his associates at *Crisis* were trying to generate. Kallen did know of DuBois, but considered him a foolishly angry man who could not transpose his "feelings of injustice and undeserved degradation" into constructive policy proposals.[92] DuBois, however, faced centuries of exploitation intensified by racist propaganda rather than a generation of uprootedness modulated by growing cultural consciousness and political influence. He needed a more radical theory to encourage a more strident self-defense. In the wake of the war only a Pan-Africanism calling for an independent Africa with Black

Americans as a militant vanguard seemed capable of seizing the historic moment for Black people. And DuBois's book and essay, widely read by Black intellectuals in America, the West Indies, and even parts of Africa, provided the theoretical explanation for their mission.[93] If Ferris had called attention to the continuing relationship between "Africans Abroad," DuBois provided the rationale for a spiritual return and a modernization of the homeland. As the Great War proceeded, the prospects for DuBois's vision seemed increasingly bright.

5 | The Promise of Cultural Reconstruction

World War I, as many scholars have noted, marked the end of the moral hegemony that Western civilization held over nonwhite peoples. The images of Black Americans, West Indians, and even Africans that emerged from the war ended an era when Black skin and barbarism were synonmous. As Richard Wright recognized, "that war provided the first real break in this continuity of hopelessness."[1] In an age of increased Black mobility and literary self-consciousness, writers in various ways resolved the conflicting images of the Negro proposed in the late nineteenth century by Alexander Crummell and T. Thomas Fortune. As the war began most writers focused on specific problems like lynching, peonage, or disfranchisement. But as they discussed social rehabilitation and self-defense in northern cities, the growth of Black theater and pageantry, the use of Senegalese troops by the French and Black officers in the U.S. Army, and the prospects for more liberal policies in postwar African colonies, they set Black Americans into a wider cultural and political focus. No longer depicted as America's depressed freedmen, they were seen as an urban people who might assist in the modernization of their African brothers and even in the education of white men.

Furthermore, the claim by Booker T. Washington, Kelly Miller, and others that Blacks, unlike European immigrants, did not have "hyphenated" loyalties, became obsolete as President Wilson and Prime Minister Lloyd George, in competition with the Bolsheviks, interpreted the war as a mandate to extend self-determination to the oppressed peoples of the world.[2] If Blacks, like other Americans, had legitimate hyphenated loyalties, they must also have respectable cultural roots. In the literature of the war and its aftermath, Blacks were depicted as a complex people with diverse branches capable of determining their own direction.

The means by which Black writers developed a new synthetic image of Black Americans were both diffuse and fragmented, but a sense of new Black creativity prevailed. Even Booker T. Washington took greater account of Black cultural developments and spoke more aggressively on race relations. At first, however, Black writers who supported the war and those who opposed it failed to deduce from it portents of dramatic change. At a conference at Joel Spingarn's family estate shortly after Washington's death, for example, neither Washington's former supporters nor his critics suggested that the war might alter either the consciousness or public image of Blacks. Even the extensive if muted Black opposition to the war largely emphasized how it distracted public attention from the struggle for civil rights at home.[3] However as Blacks began to move North and as others were drafted, those intellectuals who failed to reconsider the war's implications became isolated from those on the move and, ultimately, from the shaping of a Black response to peace.

To denigrate the moral basis of white power, Black writers turned to theories of imperialism, and to support Black claims to moral parity they pointed to numerous examples of Black productivity, and especially creative artistry, in Africa as well as in America. As the machinations of white capitalists were exposed and the achievements of Black scholars, artists, and soldiers were cataloged, a vanguard of Blacks appeared to right the white man's wrongs. The phenomenon of young Walter White explaining to Norman Angell and H. G. Wells in London in 1922 how lynching in America had serious implications for the British West Indies typified the new confidence and sophistication of Black leadership. While Black socialists like Philip Randolph and Chandler Owen and more exotic Marxists like Cyril Briggs and W. A. Domingo might stress class solidarity, their very presence as Black agitators reinforced the growth of race pride.[4]

Ethnicity and the Reeducation of Booker T. Washington

To appreciate how deeply felt was the "mass movement in America and elsewhere among Negroes . . . to esteem things Negroid and to pursue ends racial and African,"[5] one might begin by examining some subtle changes in the thought of Booker T. Washington between 1910 and his death in November, 1915. Washington had become so committed to his role as mediator between southern Blacks, southern white educators, and northern philanthropists that he could not sanction a rapprochement with his critics without undermining his own position. He even declined to attend a conference in New York on Negro industrial education, in which several of his former pupils participated, because it was held in Villard's office.[6] Yet he began to appreciate how an oppressed people must seek inner strength in its traditions. His rudimentary appreciation of the psychological and political functions of culture led him also to question whether nonwhite people must turn for social ideals exclusively to the white middle class. The outbreak of World War I led him further to criticize the acquisitive behavior promoted by white Americans, and he finally seemed to understand why DuBois might believe that a people could regain its self-confidence only by cultivating its traditions.[7]

Like so many Afro-American writers, Washington first appreciated the complexity of his heritage by traveling abroad. At the urging of his associates he sought a hiatus from his frenetic pace in the summer of 1910 by touring Europe. Typically, he was accompanied by a research assistant, the white sociologist Robert E. Park, and he turned his vacation into an educational expedition. Washington was received abroad as a celebrity. He met royalty and addressed prominent gatherings. By publicizing contacts with eminent persons he hoped to demonstrate the universal respect for his ideas. But the published accounts of his travel, which appeared first as a series of magazine articles in the *Outlook* and then in much extended form as a book written by Park under Washington's intensive supervision, emphasized social conditions among the working classes and the peasantry. Unlike most American tourists, he said, he intended to measure change rather than worship tradition. "I have never been greatly interested in the past," he noted, "for the past is something you cannot change. I like the new, the unfinished and the problematic. My experience is that the man who is interested in living things must seek them in the grime and dirt of everyday living." In particular he wished to compare the plight of the American Negro with that of "the man farthest down" in Europe.[8]

European social conditions affected Washington as they did so many self-made Americans whose struggles had been nurtured by a faith in democratic ideals. The upper classes were contemptuous of the poor and the working classes seemed so ignorant that their prospects for economic progress seemed far less than for American Negroes. Urging Robert Park to emphasize the differences between American Blacks and Europe's slum dwellers, he wrote that "the condition of the Negro in the cities of this country is many per cent better than it is in the crowded cities of Europe that we saw."[9] The poverty and filth of the London slums, begging in the streets everywhere, and blatant discrimination against persons because of their class or ethnic origins reinforced Washington's disdain for European patterns of deference. Racial animosities, clashes between nationality groups, and the enforced debasement of women subverted even the minimal efforts at reform, he reported. In Austria-Hungary, for example, the state had tried to educate only a few farmers while assuming that the majority would remain satisfied with a subservient economic and political status. Most farmers were members of ethnic minorities, Washington noted, and according to the traditions of the empire should not have expected equal status with Austrians and Magyars. When farmers from minority groups responded to educational opportunities by demanding economic and political rights, they had been suppressed more cruelly than had any similar group in America. In Poland, he added, the nobility and landlords continued to terrorize the peasants, while in Italy women were treated like beasts of burden.[10]

Washington presented a more candid and critical assessment of European conditions than did college-educated Blacks like DuBois and Mary Church Terrell, who had found in France, Germany, and England relief from the tensions of American racial discrimination. Indeed, Washington, in a style reminiscent of Andrew Carnegie's *Triumphant Democracy,* used every opportunity to demonstrate the advantages American Negroes enjoyed in health, education, and economic opportunities compared to the poor in Europe. *Crisis,* however, severely criticized Washington's basis for comparison. DuBois interpreted the travel accounts as they appeared in the *Outlook* in 1911 as a continuation of the optimistic statements that Washington had made while in Europe and to which he and his Black associates had so vehemently protested. Washington, DuBois stated, seemed deliberately to select egregious examples of exploitation and class discrimination in Europe, while understating the disabilities of southern Blacks. According to reviews republished in *Crisis,* several British journals, including the *Manchester Guardian,* agreed that Washington had overstated the retrogressive features of European life.[11]

When the essays appeared as a book entitled *The Man Farthest Down* and when much previously unused material was included in a second volume entitled *My Larger Education* in 1911, they conveyed a different impression. Washington never renounced his dislike for pomp and tradition and never explicitly changed his political views. But he found in Europe some institutions that provided lessons for Black and other Americans, and he became increasingly critical of some American institutions that seemed deliberately to exploit Blacks. Even labor unions, he found, might under the proper guidance enhance rather than impede productive social change. In Italy and Hungary members of the Socialist party had organized farm workers into unions that bargained with landlords for higher proportions of the crop in payment for their labor. "Through this party for the first time," he asserted, "millions of human beings who had no voice in and no definite ideas in respect to the government under which they lived are learning to think and to give expression to their wants."[12]

The Danish Socialists and philanthropists had developed a comprehensive educational system, which Washington found the most impressive innovation on his trip because through it the agricultural classes had gained control of the government. The rural schools, he reported, allowed sons of the peasants to study whatever they chose, thus encouraging and meeting a demand rather than imposing aristocratic standards upon rural people. The country high schools stressed scientific courses and training in advanced agricultural techniques that provided models for rural education elsewhere. Moreover, the curriculum stressed "folk history" to create "class consciousness" among the youth, and through that consciousness Danish farmers had developed the cohesiveness to become a political power. In an expression of some of his most deeply held prejudices, Washington wrote that he had believed that the study of "culture" had been a device utilized by a college elite "to glorify its own achievements and to convince itself of its right to rule the masses." The use of Danish folk culture, however, had created self-esteem in rural children and had encouraged them to attempt agricultural innovation in the heroic spirit of their ancestors.[13]

Washington traveled through Denmark without Robert Park and on his own came to appreciate more fully how cultural artifacts might inspire ordinary people.[14] In Denmark Washington's understanding of the psychological value of Black dolls for Black children was reinforced and he reflected that the spirituals might not simply entertain whites but revitalize Blacks. Like the Danish peasants, Washington stated, Negro farmers also had a folk history with which they could identify and from which they could derive pride in racial accomplishments. Such feelings, he now seemed to realize, could provide a wider meaning for the regimen of personal self-control and self-denial he had consistently preached. Art, for Washington, was still not a realm with standards and objectives of its own, nor did he see it as the spontaneous expression of the people, which it seemed to be in peasant Africa. For him it had become a vital "property" of the group from which the artist came and for which he should be laboring.[15]

Although the European trip hardly turned Washington into an economic or political radical, he felt sufficiently self-conscious about his praise for the Socialists to disclaim any political ties with them. In addition, at Park's suggestion, he carefully avoided endorsing women's suffrage while prescribing greater respect for work traditionally done by women. But if his political courage failed him, he did encourage a more sophisticated understanding of Black people. He congratulated scholars like DuBois, Kelly Miller, and Carter Woodson for collecting historical material that demonstrated the talents of Blacks. He allowed his director of research at Tuskegee, Monroe Work, to assist DuBois with a program honoring the fiftieth anniversary of the Emancipation Proclamation, though for political reasons he encouraged the National Negro Business League to sponsor its own celebration.[16] Washington, though, did try to broaden the vision of the league, in part by having local branches protest instances of discrimination and in part by introducing it to Negro artists. In 1914 he invited James Weldon Johnson, whose work was then appearing in the New York *Age* and who was doing theatrical work with his brother Rosamond and Will Marion Cook, to address the league's annual convention in Boston. Emmett Scott told Johnson in December, 1915, how much Washington before his death had regretted that he could not introduce Johnson to the students at Tuskegee as well.[17]

In his private correspondence and in several public statements Washington also became increasingly critical of the pretensions of Anglo-Saxons to cultural superiority. In *Up From Slavery* he had remarked laconically, referring to Indians, that white men haughtily expected all other races to adopt their standards. By the outbreak of World War I, he became a bit skeptical of the wisdom of white civilization. Influenced by Andrew Carnegie's pacifist views, he doubted that the fighting would continue, and he planned a return trip to the Continent for the summer of 1915. As the violence intensified, the American economy entered a recession, contributions to Tuskegee declined, and Washington cancelled his trip. His plan for expanding Tuskegee publicity through a new magazine on scientific agriculture to be edited by Isaac Fisher was curtailed, but his faith in the qualities of the Black personality seemed to grow.[18] European political leaders seemed to him irrational, and he wrote sardonically to Robert Park, "I see nothing to do but just lay the European trip aside for the present; that is until white people get a little more civilized. I really think it would be worth while to consider sending a group of black missionaries to Europe to see if something can be done for the white heathen."[19]

Unlike DuBois, Washington never developed a theoretical analysis of Black exploitation that saw the freedmen, like West Indians and Africans, the victims of imperialism. Nevertheless, he began to protest the abuse of Blacks by business and government and to see patterns of exploitation. In a letter to President Wilson in mid-1915, Washington condemned the use of American marines to pacify Haiti. Though only a few years before he had argued that Haitians needed Western tutelage, he now noted sarcastically that "shooting civilization into the Haitians on their own soil will be an amazing spectacle."[20] Indeed, that Emmett Scott chose to publish this letter in an official biography of Washington only a year after it went to the President suggests the rising sense of aggressiveness among some of Washington's closest followers. In a speech given under the auspices of the Urban League in Harlem in 1915 and published posthumously in the liberal journal *New Republic,* he argued that segregation had become a tool through which white businessmen gained unfair advantage over Blacks. Segregation kept Negroes systematically out of white areas, but it did not prevent white businessmen from trading with Blacks. When demanding segregation, whites stood not on the constitutional ground, however dubious, of separate but equal. They simply retreated to crude opportunism. At the same time Washington quietly intervened to prevent Birmingham city commissioners from segregating residential sections of the city by ordinance and expressed intense displeasure at rumors of such moves in cities like Baltimore and Louisville.[21]

Washington, finally, became conscious of the new medium of motion pictures, which could influence in important ways the public image of the Negro. When D. W. Griffith produced the epic "The Birth of a Nation" in 1915, President Hollis Frissell of Hampton, learning that it could not be suppressed, hoped to modify its degrading image of the Negro by allowing footage of students at his school to be included. But Washington correctly concluded that the inclusion of the Hampton scene suggested that the school endorsed the film, and he moved to denounce it. When two officers of the Boston Negro Business League also endorsed it, he demanded they retract. The film, he wrote, was "stirring up useless race prejudice wherever it plays" and should be suppressed. When Washington was subsequently solicited to become president of a film company designed to promote a positive image of Blacks, he suggested that James Weldon Johnson take the post. Emmett Scott and Johnson had previously discussed the possibility in New York, and in the wake of "The Birth of a Nation" a venture under Johnson's supervision seemed a valuable counterattack. Washington's death and Johnson's new interest in the NAACP no doubt ended the project.[22]

In seeking to cast off the inner dread implanted in Blacks by American racism, Washington never fully realized the power of cultural traditions. Although he gradually developed an appreciation of Black aesthetic qualities, for him culture remained an adjunct of rather than a means for shaping economic and social modernization. In a moving yet terse epitaph in *Crisis*, DuBois carefully weighed Washington's failure to promote a distinctive sense of Black personality. Washington, he noted had provided a program to inculcate habits upon which individual self-esteem might rest, and he had made southern whites accept Blacks as potential partners in modernizing the region. But, DuBois concluded, Washington had never acknowledged how whites around the world utilized the Tuskegee program to reinforce Black subordination.[23] Yet DuBois failed

o appreciate how events like the European trip and his obser-
ations of the war and of segregation allowed Washington,
however, modestly, to encourage new standards for assessing
Black achievements.

Amenia: The Obsolescence of A World View

Washington was hardly alone in being slow to recognize
how the war would change Black communities and alter the
perceptions of Black writers. The intellectual and political
limitations of his generation are best illustrated by the Amenia
Conference of 1916, which was designed by DuBois and Joel
Spingarn to reconcile Washington's successors like Robert
Moton and Fred Moore with his critics. So flagrant had discrim-
nation become that DuBois hoped a meeting in the relaxed
setting of the Spingarn family estate in Dutches County, New
York, would enable the Tuskegee group, the NAACP, and other
organizations to develop an effective division of labor. To
emphasize its importance, Spingarn invited Woodrow Wilson
to address the gathering, but the president, for unstated reasons,
had to decline.[24] Yet the issues discussed, the resolutions, the
subsequent memories, and the historical treatment of the
conference suggest that it represented the politics of nostalgia
rather than the reconciliation and springboard to innovative
action that DuBois anticipated. In a pamphlet published nine
years later, DuBois called it "an historic Negro gathering," and
asserted that it had been a landmark in the development of
Black self-confidence. But DuBois's great admirer Benjamin
Brawley, writing the first major social history of Black Americans only five years later, failed to mention Amenia, and neither
has Florette Henri in the most recent comprehensive survey of
the period. Eugene Levy notes that the resolutions Amenia
produced reflected neither policy commitments nor innovative
perspectives on old issues, and Elliott Rudwick has observed
that the tensions between the old antagonists were not resolved.[25]

No doubt the Amenia Conference had different meanings
for its various participants. James Weldon Johnson saw it as his

reintroduction to the tensions of institutional leadership after having been out of the country for many years, and shortly afterwards he agreed to become field secretary for the NAACP. John C. Napier and Mary Church Terrell remembered Amenia as a pleasant social gathering demonstrating that persons of differing opinions could speak reasonably together. Several years later Roy Nash congratulated Joel Spingarn for conciliating opponents. "It must be a very nice feeling to know that you once made Fred Moore and DuBois lie down on the same cot," he jokingly reminisced. John Hope and Neval Thomas both felt Amenia had strengthened the civil rights movements, though neither could explain how.[26] Emmett Scott, Robert R. Moton, and Kelly Miller, perhaps ruminating on their own diminished stature subsequent to the conference, never commented on it; William Monroe Trotter chose not to attend, ostensibly because he felt the meeting, by emphasizing reconciliation, would vitiate autonomous Black organizations like his Political League.[27] Perhaps unintentionally, DuBois revealed how the meeting simply celebrated the successes of a contingent of middle-aged reformers secure in their own opinions. His only specific measure of its achievements came in comparison with a prior event rather than subsequent activities. Compared with a conference called in 1904 in New York by Booker T. Washington under the auspices of Andrew Carnegie, Amenia provided Black participants full freedom of speech. They did not have to listen to a set speech by a designated "leader," nor did they feel constrained by affluent whites. Instead, as at the London Races Congress of 1911, colored persons dominated the discussion.[28]

The topics discussed and the resolutions, however, reveal that the elite of a generation had rehashed issues that events would soon eclipse. The sessions focused on topics Washington and DuBois had debated over the past dozen years, including "Industry and Education," "The Negro in Politics," "Civil and Legal Discrimination," and "Social Discrimination." The two concluding sessions on "Practical Paths" and "Working Programs for the Future" were presided over by William Pickens (then dean at Morgan State College) and Robert Jones (soon to become a bishop in the Methodist Church), and by James Weldon Johnson and L. M. Hershaw, respectively. Although the sessions were informal and all participants would speak freely, not a single new topic was broached nor a single young person allowed to lead a discussion.[29]

The resolutions failed to anticipate the key issues of migration, urban self-defense, independent Black politics, or Pan-Africanism, which would emerge in conjunction with the war. Of the seven resolutions, one called for an end to "the antiquated subjects of controversy," and two others attempted to do so by endorsing "all forms of education" and the need for full political rights. The special problems of southern race relations, which presumably precluded militant agitation, were acknowledged, and the participants agreed that they should meet annually to reconsider issues. The participants, however, returned to their institutions, failed to meet again, and carried their personal antagonisms into the war. In addition, the resolutions emphasizing the peculiar stringencies of southern life and the value of varied educational formats seemed quickly to lose their force. The NAACP sent Johnson on an organizing tour of southern cities, and by 1917 he had, to the astonishment of everyone, presided over the establishment of over a dozen locals from Richmond through Jacksonville. By 1919 the branch in Atlanta had over seventeen-hundred members and sponsored a voter registration drive. Southern Blacks reported improved wages and working conditions as local employers competed with northern industrialists for Black labor. By 1917, furthermore, a report (however numerous its biases) by Thomas Jesse Jones for the Anson Phelps Stokes Fund recommended many progressive changes in southern Black schools, including modernized curricula and state support.[30]

Like the Universal Races Conference and "The Star of Ethiopia," the Amenia Conference remains significant not for specific achievements but for what it symbolized about the psychological stance of a generation. Elliott Rudwick is not incorrect to conclude that as a political event it was "overrated."[31] But it should be seen rather as a ceremony of maturity for the men and women who defined their problems around Booker T.

Washington. Although he had passed from the scene as a focus for discontent or for defense, his cohorts remained fixed, at least temporarily, on his definition of alternatives. Men and women bred to believe in the evolution of a humane civilization and to perceive of themselves as the vanguard of a newly freed race now believed they had achieved consensus on key issues and on principles of leadership. Ralph Bunche, writing a generation later, however, felt the persons represented at Amenia had misunderstood the class composition of Black America and unjustifiably elevated themselves to leadership for a mythic "race."[32] Writing after the "great migration," Bunche could not only see a more complex urban people but had himself borrowed from the more radical literature produced by the war. The Amenia groups still saw Blacks as a rural people for whom the small urban elite must function as tutors. Indeed, Neval Thomas confessed that at the time he was most discouraged by the indifference of the masses to the leadership of the NAACP.[33] Both the domestic and international changes wrought by the war, however, gave currency to a more complex and aggressive image of Black Americans, and greater opportunities to men like Thomas.

Migration: The Search for a Radical Meaning

The central event in Afro-American history in the twentieth century has been the great migration from the rural South to the urban North. It began in earnest in 1916, abated during the depression of the 1930s, and reached even larger dimensions between 1940 and 1966.[34] Migration provided new economic, social, and political opprotunities for the newcomers and their children, altered the ethnic composition of the northern city, upset southern agricultural patterns, and challenged stereotypes about Black people, The initial large migration was spurred by the outbreak of World War I, which curtailed European immigration to the United States and created a demand for new sources of unskilled labor in Connecticut tobacco fields, Cleveland foundries, Chicago stockyards, Pittsburgh steel plants, and on railroad section gangs throughout the North.[35] As workers responded to the unprecedented demand for their labor, intellectuals gradually percieved that fundamental change was under way. Initially, Black writers reiterated an aggressive defense of Black civil rights and a fresh catalog of the disabilities that attended relocation. The difference between the "southern" and "northern" atmosphere, which had been stressed at Amenia, seemed less marked. Robert Moton, George Haynes, Kelly Miller, and even Emmett Scott openly criticized white lawlessness and the exploitation of Black labor, while DuBois and his colleagues balanced the benefits and dislocations of Black settlement in the cities.[36]

Although most Black writers agreed that the migration opened new options to Blacks, they did not immediately draw from it a new image of Black Americans, The most engaging irony of the migration was that as a fundamental change in Black life, it was initially studied amd interpreted by men who supported Booker T. Washington. The most prolific student of the migration, George E. Haynes, had obtained philanthropic support for the Urban League and directed its work with migrants by arguing that they must be systematically socialized to northern conditions. In the years before World War I, he saw the migrants as a steady stream of unskilled workers that should be grateful for employment but skillfully prepared for occupational upgrading. With the increase in black migration, the drastic reduction of European immigration and the expansion of the American economy to meet the supply needs of the war, the U. S. Bureau of Labor hired Haynes to head its new Division of Negro Economics to keep the government fully informed of the effects of the migration on mobilization. As the government moved to monitor the morale of the labor force, it sanctioned a conservative view of the migration and its consequences by providing Haynes the opportunity to become its official chronicler.[37]

Haynes, Scott, and Moton did not try to emphasize the continuing wisdom of Washington's program, which rested in part on the assumption that Blacks would remain in the rural South. But they did imply strongly that the tactics of his opponents, particularly political agitation, would be far too simple a means to utilize in understanding and mastering the varied opportunities the migrants were seeking. They did not seek to explain the causes of the migration in a general theory of exploitation such as DuBois emphasized in *The Negro*. Instead, they emphasized the individual problems Blacks faced with land tenure, credit, law enforcement, and racial caste, and in the immediate dislocations in southern agriculture between 1914 and 1916.[38]

If the approach to the migration was hardly radical, the writers did use it as a vehicle for further attacking the racial mythology surrounding the freedmen and their children. Within the context of a guarded support, Haynes, Scott Moton, and others abandoned a view of migration as a mechanistic response of peasants to "natural laws." Kelly Miller, for example, had written in 1906 that Blacks still preferred migration to rural areas in the southwest, in part because people "normally" moved from areas of higher to lower population density.[39] By 1913, and certainly after 1916, Haynes and others say the move North not as part of the "natural history" of a primitive type, but as the response of suppressed individuals to an unprecedented demand for their labor, a demand that heightened their self-esteem. As opposed to the exodus of 1879, the migration of World War I provided evidence of the complexity rather than the simplicity of Black people. Its participants were depicted neither as folk heroes nor peasants but as men and women awakening to the options of modern life.[40] Their letters and interviews, expressed in homely and ungrammatical prose, revealed the wonder, hope, disappointment, and determination of all poor newcomers to the industrial city. As Emmett Scott noted, "the great hordes of restless migrants swung loose from their acknowledged leaders" and now made their own decisions.[41]

The image of the migrant, however, still resembled that of Booker T. Washington's rural dependents, now living in northern cities with a great deal more self-assurance but a continuing need for social rehabilitation. Carter Woodson, though criticizing southern Black spokesmen for discouraging the migration, characterized the newcomers as "the men far down" who "must increase their industrial efficiency; improve their opportunities to make a living; develop the home, church, and school; and contribute to art, literature, science and philosophy to clear the way to the political freedom of which they cannot be deprived."[42] Presumably in an effort to demonstrate that the migration should no more be seen as a panacea than had been suffrage during Reconstruction or the exodus to Kansas, Haynes and the others publicized problems of housing, seasonal unemployment, de facto segregation, discrimination by labor unions, and the high cost of living. While the limits on opportunities in the North were noted, race relations in the South were depicted as having steadily improved because southern mill owners, farmers, and other employers were frightened by the loss of their workers. After efforts forcibly to prevent the Blacks from emigrating had failed, the white employers in many southern towns had agreed to discuss labor conditions with Black spokesmen. In a fashion reminiscent of the meetings arranged by Booker T. Washington, representatives of white and Black churches, the employers, and local government officials met to exchange views. Often advisory committees were organized through the auspices of the Division of Negro Economics. In the northern cities, however, the migrants appeared to need the assistance of a bevy of social workers, church groups, the YMCA, and other intermediaries to regain their equilibrium.[43]

Writers like Miller, Woodson, and Scott agreed that the mood of the Black masses had been altered by the migration. They attributed this change, perhaps correctly, to the patriotic fervor aroused by the war and to the maturity of a new generation of southern Blacks who had never known enslavement and who rejected the deference that had constrained their parents. But because the writers assumed that Blacks were victims fleeing their circumstances, they could not locate within the culture of the migrants the basis of their new militancy. Scott, explicitly invoking the new vogue of Freudian psychology, attributed new Black militancy, which the Chicago *Denfender* especially promoted, to the release in the North of "suppressed wishes." Haynes, drawing on contemporary studies in social psychology, argued that Blacks North and South would respond best to indigenous leadership, which must, however, "be learned in the American ways of thinking and doing things." Kelly Miller at least mentioned the aesthetic interests of rural Blacks, but with a condescension quite different from James Weldon Johnson's genuine appreciation. The "primitive" music, according to Miller, expressed "blind, half-conscious poetry, breaking through the aperture of sound before the intellect had time to formulate a definite cast of statement."[44] But the list of dislocations was stated more fully and concretely than were the inner sources mustered by the migrants. A decade later, when musing on his own rural upbringing, Woodson could see nothing but ignorance in the South and degeneration in the storefront churches.[45] The tone of the migration studies remained what it had been in 1913, when Haynes had referred to the migrants as among the socially handicapped. The migrants, of course, had created their own institutions to adjust to the city, but the attitude of their chroniclers remained that of Booker T. Washington, as he asked white people to help his race "get well."

In the hands of a man with a more theoretical bent, however, the migration became part of a larger struggle and the migrants a more assertive social force. Asked to assess the meaning of the migration just as the United States entered World War I, DuBois turned the conventional analysis on its head by making Blacks rather than whites the progressive economic and social force. In an essay for *The Independent,* he argued that the migration again demonstrated how little white men understood Blacks. Blacks, he argued, responded to the same interests and impulses as other people, and since emancipation they had been seeking alternatives to the oppressive conditions in the South. "Fast as the white South has moved," he wrote, "the modern world and the Negro have moved faster." Black aspirations had simply outstripped southern opportunities. The main obstacles to their northern migration had been European immigration, northern prejudice, and fear by northern Blacks that a southern influx would impair the opportunities that did exist. With the curtailment of European immigration in 1915, however, and the recruitment of Black labor, they had streamed North. The challenge, DuBois continued, now lay not with Blacks, who could support themselves if necessary, but with northern whites. With the limitation of European immigration after the war, he said, Black workers and merchants might open vast new markets for American industry in the nonwhite world. But if immigration were again opened and discrimination against Blacks resumed, "then the Negro will more and more be thrown back to the peculiar inner economic cooperation which he has been organizing on a rapidly growing scale for years in the South and which is now moving North."[46]

The migration brought in its wake fearful riots in East Saint Louis, Illinois, in 1917, and in Washington D.C., Chicago, and elsewhere in 1919.[47] The violence claimed over one-hundred Black lives in East Saint Louis and dozens in Chicago, but in the interval Black spokesmen could see improvement in the economic position and especially the psychological stance of Blacks that even the bloodshed could not diminish. DuBois and Martha Gruening visited East Saint Louis and produced for *Crisis* a twenty-page spread dominated by gruesome pictures and dramatic testimony from witnesses and victims. So shaken were they by their observations of charred houses and pictures of mutilated victims that they allowed the evidence to speak for itself. They were equally angered by the role of the trade union leaders, who, instead of promoting class solidarity, had urged their white membership to view Negroes as aliens who should be driven from the city. While admitting that Blacks had served as strikebreakers, they could only condemn the pitiful competition that led union leaders to resort to racial epithets.[48] Nevertheless, DuBois noted in a separate editorial, higher paying jobs and the promise of police protection would continue to lure Black workers to industrial cities, and a more imaginative leadership would have to resolve racial tensions.[49]

By 1919, Black investigators like James Weldon Johnson, Walter White, and even George Haynes could see in the Black response to violence more confident individuals and better organized communities. White in Chicago enumerated a complex set of causes based on the new niche Blacks had secured in the stockyards and packing houses, in the political coalition supporting Mayor William Hale Thompson, and in residential districts on the South Side. So crucial a role did Blacks now play in the economy and polity that local newspapers had to resort to the same tactics as had the southern press prior to the riots at Wilmington and Atlanta years before. Blacks, however, had adjusted to the villificatory propaganda. Instead of running from the mob, as they had in East Saint Louis, they now defended their homes and jobs.[50] In Washington, James Weldon Johnson encountered the same spirit of Black self-confidence and group cohesiveness, led by the local branch of the NAACP. Its officers had protested to the newspapers against their inflamatory editorials on Negro criminality and, after the riot, had developed support for a congressional investigation. In contrast to the shocked tone of DuBois's reporting on East Saint Louis, Johnson noted that the Black response to Chicago and Washington had saved the nation from further wanton bloodshed and "marked the turning point in the psychology of the whole nation regarding the Negro problem."[51]

In conjunction with the migration DuBois saw in the Black role in World War I another sign of the Black man's capacity to determine his own fate. While his political views were challenged by more conservative writers like Kelly Miller and more theoretical radicals like Philip Randolph, his assessment of the historical meaning of the war was quickly adopted by most Black writers. In April, 1917, he called a conference of delegates from NAACP branches to meet in Washington to determine the association's stance toward American entry into the war. Pacifists like Mary White Ovington and Frazier Miller opposed American participation, but DuBois urged the delegates to endorse the Allied side. The resolution, however, avoided patriotic rhetoric and the assumption that the choice represented a moral imperative. Instead, the delegates simply asserted that the Allies seemed the lesser of two evils because the Germans had treated Blacks more cruelly, while the British and Americans promised to improve in the future. No doubt the majority of delegates agreed with Kelly Miller and Robert R. Moton that Blacks as Americans would prove as patriotic as they had been in other wars. But even those conservatives balanced assertions of Black loyalty with condemnation of continuing discrimination. Mixed with their assurances that Blacks would volunteer for the army, work in war industries without striking, and buy liberty bonds came the reminder that "the social problems of America will never be solved by mobbing or segregating black men in the North, nor burning or lynching in the South." The war, in fact, became another new Black opportunity for choice.[52]

Carrying this argument to its extreme, DuBois developed a fundamentally racial interpretation of the war. For him it offered not merely opportunities to improve Black economic or social conditions or to bring more candor to race relations. Nor did it merely display the greed of capitalists seeking profits nor the savagery of warriors like Theodore Roosevelt glorifying military discipline at the expense of reason. Instead, the war provided a moral and cultural turning point in which history no longer revealed an inexorable Progress but a contradiction in Western culture that only Black persons could resolve. With the emergence of a Black vanguard in America, the West Indies, and Africa to tap the resources of the Dark Continent for mankind, a more humane world order could be brought into being. Those who stood aloof, like the Socialists, or who, like Moton and Miller, shrank from the racial interpretation of the war could not act intelligently for Blacks at the peace table. Moving well beyond Crummell's vision of a racial reunion, DuBois felt that if Africans, West Indians, and Afro-Americans were to further their independence, their spokesmen had to build an interpretation of the war and of modern history around their distinctive roles.

The difference between the assumptions of DuBois and the more conservative Black writers was well illustrated in two talks given before the Mu-So-Lit Club of Washington, D.C., in the fall of 1915, when the war still seemed to most persons a distant European embroglio. DuBois, who had already published "The African Roots of War," gave one talk and Kelly Miller, who had just published a pamphlet denouncing President Wilson's segregation policy in the federal bureaucracy,[53] gave the other. Miller's brief comments—perhaps condensed for purposes of discussion—when combined with pamphlets he published during and just after the war, revealed a mind confused rather than inspired by the portents of social upheaval. Miller, as August Meier has noted, had for a generation vacillated between support for and criticism of Booker T. Washington's gradualist approach stressing the social rehabilitation of Black Americans.[54] Miller's shifting positions may in part have arisen from his flexible temperament, but throughout he also maintained a rigid image of the Negro. For him Blacks were natural subordinates, capable of absorbing the white man's work habits and guarding his wayward conscience but incapable of initiating a new course of action. He could condemn the irrationality of specific acts of discrimination, but he could not reassess standards of authority. His emphasis on the need to weigh all sides of an issue also concealed a rigid faith in the exclusive virtues of gradual change. He placed so much faith in the vision of a unified Christendom where Blacks would play a distinct role of suffering servant that he could not comprehend a world marching to race or class conflict and assenting to varied standards of beauty and order.

The war for Miller might upset the political balance of power, but it would restore a traditional moral order in which the weaker would keep the conscience of the stronger. "This is essentially a white man's war," Miller wrote, and the "American Negro is so far removed from the intimate issues of the European struggle that its effects upon him must be secondary and indirect."[55] He assumed that the war would somehow bring the lower classes into the conduct of public affairs. But he could neither counsel Blacks to seek allies among white radicals nor to repudiate their roles as suffering victims to assume worldly responsibility. Even after the war he asserted that the psychological characteristics of people were eternally set and that Blacks must support a conservative social order. In his call for a "Negro Sanhedrin" or a meeting of the heads of various Black organizations, in 1923, he wrote, "Meekness, forgiveness, long suffering and non-resentfulness of spirit, the essential Christian virtues, are embedded in the soul stuff of the Negro race."[56] Miller simply refused to take responsibility for reassessing the character of Black America and promoting the prospects for new strategies. Cyril Briggs, serving in 1923 as executive head of the radical African Blood Brotherhood, considered Miller's view of the Negro almost amusing. "One wonders," he confided to James Weldon Johnson, "whether the dean and his 'advisors' have mentally abolished such questions as lynching, peonage, economic exploitation, relation to world movements, relation to liberation movements in Africa, industrial betterment, etc., etc.,"[57]

DuBois, however, told the Mu-So-Lit Club that Black people were at the heart of the war, which had been precipitated by European capitalists quarreling over the land and labor of "the darker races." From the "breathing space" created by war, therefore, nonwhite peoples must escape the image of the suffering victim, assert their own interests, and win the respect of their former white masters, who were now weakened by the slaughter in the European trenches. Black Americans, who had been freed when whites slaughtered one another during the Civil War, could now play the unique role of providing the technical expertise, and even investment capital, for more recently freed dark peoples.[58] The outbreak of war in Europe for DuBois no doubt fulfilled the terrible warning of reckless imperialist rivalries and the bright promise of colonial assertiveness that he had seen in London in 1911. When he went to Paris in 1919 to represent the NAACP at the Peace Conference, *Crisis* listed as one of his major credentials his experience at the Universal Races Congress.[59] DuBois to some extent shared Kelly Miller's image of Black Americans as uniquely virtuous because of their suffering, and he agreed that Africans could not gain immediate independence because of their lack of sophistication in international politics. But he insisted that Blacks had the moral authority to help reconstruct the political order.

War: The Occasion for Cultural Reconstruction

The promise of Black political initiative that DuBois presented to the Mu-So-Lit Club gained substance in *Crisis* reportage and essays as the war dragged on. Diligently the staff chronicled the achievements from which should accrue Black leverage for helping to define the terms of the peace. Reports of Blaise-Diagne and the Senegalese in the French Army, Rabindranath Tagore's Nobel Prize and the Indians fighting with the British, and finally American Negro soldiers with their own officers became staple items in *Crisis.* While DuBois took no overt satisfaction in the slaughter of Europeans, he could see in it one of the inexorable conflicts from which a new freedom for the oppressed must come. As he noted in *Crisis* in September, 1916, "Brothers, the war has shown us the cruelty of the civilization of the West, History has taught us the futility of the civilization of the East." Something new, he wrote, constantly emerged from the traditions of Africa, and the moment had come—at home and abroad—to assume a protagonistic role on the world stage.[60]

The new spirit of race pride leading to at least a tentative Pan-African identification for younger Black writers appeared in several volumes during the war. In 1918, for example, James Weldon Johnson's friend, the young historian Benjamin Brawley, published a brief volume entitled Africa and the War. While hardly an original contribution to scholarship after DuBois's essay and book, it marked an important ideological shift in Brawley's own work and suggested the turn that Afro-American historical writing would take in the 1920's. Brawley in 1913 had published *A Short History of the American Negro,* a conventional account of enslavement, emancipation, and Reconstruction, with additional brief chapters cataloging Negro achievements as church builders, soldiers, writers, artists, and inventors. Following in condensed form the outline of George Washington Williams's work of the 1880's, it assumed that Africans had been barbarians before the Europeans arrived, that slavery had "destroyed completely almost every spontaneous social movement among the Africans," and that Black music, to express serious emotions, must be refined rather than "debased" by ragtime and similar spontaneous sentiments.[61]

Africa and the War, leaning heavily on *The Negro,* interpreted Black history not simply as an escape from primitivism but as a struggle for the knowledge to throw off imperialism.

Africa, Brawley now agreed, had been at the heart of the war, and some of its more important battles had been fought there. The defeat of the German drive to control central Africa, he explained, had rendered their struggle to control central Europe nugatory because they now lacked the African raw materials to employ European workers. "Africa then," Brawley concluded, "is the great prize of the war . . . [and] the disposition of this continent then becomes the greatest economic and political question to arise out of the present war and even in the twentieth century."[62] While the politicians at Versailles did not find the disposition of the colonies the most perplexing issue, out of this view of Africa's importance came for Brawley a much broader interpretation of Afro-American history. In his major publication, *A Social History of the American Negro,* in 1921, he reiterated DuBois's emphasis on the reciprocal relationship between Black Americans and Africans. Like the Irish and Greek immigrants, who on gaining some economic and political security revitalized their traditions rather than succumbing to the melting pot, Blacks were now also able to assert their ethnic pride. This new assertiveness had grown from the recognition that their problem and their culture crossed national boundaries in which they existed merely as minorities. While Brawley, like so many of his contemporaries who wrote on Africa, retained a missionary paternalism, he now promoted rather than shrank from a cultural reunion because, he wrote, "a whole people had been reborn, a whole race has found its soul."[63] The vision of Crummell had taken root in the writings of the young.

The young Black socialists A. Philip Randolph and Chandler Owen presented a similar interpretation of the war in their pamphlet, *Terms of Peace and the Darker Races.* Despite their youthful discontent with DuBois, the *Crisis* staff, and academics like Brawley, their points of agreement indicate how a new consensus was emerging on the interpretation of Black history and destiny. Published two years after "The African Roots of War," *Terms of Peace* utilized knowledge of subsequent military and political events and emphasized class rather than race loyalties. Randolph and Owen, for example, noted how the ruthless trench warfare on the Western front, the military superiority of the German army, and the events of the Russian Revolution had converged to require a negotiated rather than a dictated peace. They argued also that a permanent and lasting peace depended not on events in Africa, but on a democratic revolution in Europe and America, where Blacks must receive full civil rights.[64] They presented a modest agenda of progressive reforms, including women's suffrage, regulation of child labor, and referenda on declarations of war and on international treaties, though they hoped ultimately for a redistribution of wealth and working-class solidarity with the Russian Revolution. To avoid future wars they called for an International Peace Commission to adjudicate disputes between nations and to enforce decisions. Nevertheless, in their explanation of the war's origin and in their proposals for Africa's future they accepted the premises stated by DuBois. Like him they dismissed the tensions in the Balkans as merely precipitates of violence and argued that "the real bone of contention" lay in the exploitation of "darker people for cheap labor and darker people's rich lands."[65] They assumed also that Africa required modernization, and they recommended a Council on the Conditions of the Darker Races, composed of representatives of the colonial powers, the colonized peoples, and, as a vanguard of educational and social reform, representatives of Black America.

Randolph and Owens assumed that Black Americans would enter the urban proletariat and that Africa would undergo a secular revival. Ingeniously they suggested that businesses investing in the various African colonies be taxed to support secular schools, many of which could be staffed by Black Americans. Within twenty years, they said, young Africans trained in political science as well as in engineering, mining, and economics might direct the development of their new nations.[66] Their vision differed from that of DuBois, however, in their indifference to Afro-American or African cultures. As college-bred intellectuals like DuBois and his circle, they appreciated the value of literature in expanding one's theoretical grasp of social problems. But like their contemporaries E. Franklin Frazier and Abram Harris, they found identity in avant-garde radicalism rather than in racial visions. Like T. Thomas Fortune over a generation earlier, they sought explanations in theories of class conflict rather than in the revitalization of race loyalties and saw simple tutorial, rather than reciprocal, relationships between Black Americans and Africa. Where DuBois saw virtue in indigenous village and tribal institutions, a local democracy that romantically evoked his own Great Barrington town meeting, Owen and Randolph never discussed the structure of colonial administration. Where DuBois gained great spiritual release on his trip to Liberia in 1923, they called for an end to the hold of religion, indigenous as well as Christian, over African education. Where they assumed a Western-educated elite would bring Africa quickly into the modern world, DuBois believed that native peoples would insist on substantial cultural continuity.[67]

While Owens and Randolph might find the cultural high life of wartime Harlem bourgeois, to DuBois, Johnson, and others they were an integral part of a revitalization of the Black personality that accompanied the repudiation of imperialism. *Crisis* carried extensive notices of the founding of several Black theatrical companies in Harlem and the successes of Black entertainers and musicians like Bert Williams, Will Marion Cook, Harry Burleigh, Roland Hayes, and Marian Anderson. Their concert tours and entertainments portended a new Black influence on the general public. At the same time Brander Matthews, in a collection of essays on the contemporary theater, noted the disappearance of minstrelsy with the closing of all but one of the New York houses. He considered the "fall" of minstrelsy an important milestone in American culture because it suggested a new public image of the Negro. Minstrelsy by 1915 failed "to provide a more accurate presentation of Negro characteristics," he wrote, because it failed to reflect changes in the thoughts and behavior of Black people. Compared to the band of James Reese Europe, which celebrated the virtuosity of Black musicians through the new forms of ragtime and jazz, white minstrels and their set routines were monotonous and artificial. They were the stage equivalents of the old-time darkies, whose passing even southern planters—not to mention students of the contemporary northern migration—clearly recognized. As Robert Russa Moton noted shortly thereafter, "White minstrels with black faces have done more than any other single agency to lower the tone of Negro music and cause the Negro to despise his own songs."[68]

In conjunction with the impressive growth of formal Black theatrical and musical companies, DuBois, in addition to founding Horizon Guild, became vicepresident of the Music School Settlement for Colored People in New York, where J. Rosamond Johnson was music director. With Franz Boas, and probably at the request of George Foster Peabody, he also sponsored the research of the white folklorist Natalie Curtis Burlin on "plantation" music of southern Blacks and gave wide coverage to the more sophisticated compositions of Nathaniel Dett music director at Hampton Institute.[69] Many notices also appeared about the folk song extravaganzas staged by Black concert singer Azalia Hackley. Though hardly as large or imaginative as "The Star of Ethiopia," they involved hundreds of Black performers in dozens of major cities. By 1918 she informed Peabody, she had for over ten years curtailed her own concert appearances to "educate a music hungry people beginning with Folk songs . . ." Several Black musicians in New York City accused her of toadying to whites by suggesting that folk songs expressed the limit of Black musical artistry, but she angrily denied the charges. For her the folk songs were the root of Black cultural consciousness, and the scene of hundreds of people singing them was the source of immense racial pride.[70]

George Foster Peabody, Robert Moton, and Natalie Burlin even asked Secretary of War Newton Baker to allow Black instructors to use spirituals to boost the morale of Black recruits, and Baker enthusiastically agreed. *Crisis* felt Baker displayed a special interest in meeting the needs of Black troops, even though the secretary believed Black demands for equal treatment were relatively minor matters in the conduct of the war. Nevertheless, along with Mrs. Woodrow Wilson, Baker found Negro spirituals particularly moving and believed that the recognition afforded the songs by the army would heighten the patriotism of Black troops. As Mrs. Wilson condescendingly told Peabody, "I do think the feeling that they get into their singing when they sing their own music is one of the greatest importance to their happiness and their usefulness." Joseph E. Blanton, Moton's half brother who taught at the Penn School on St. Helena Island, was then employed to tour over a dozen army camps to teach versions of the spirituals, some with lyrics adapted for the war by Mrs. Burlin. Blanton convinced drill instructors that the singing would improve the marching precision of the men, and the companies were then assigned to regular instruction in music. "I have found the officers and men very responsive to the idea of using Negro plantation songs to inspire the fellows to greater deeds of heroism and courage," Blanton informed William A. Aery, Hampton's publicity director. Blanton persuaded the Black recruits of the importance of the songs by arguing that they had helped their ancestors endure slavery. He inspired the men to "love their own songs," he said, rather than seeing them merely as a means to an end defined by the war department.[71]

The revival of Black folk music by Azalia Hackley and Natalie Burlin aroused conflicting views as to its proper form and ultimate meaning. Miss Hackley and James Weldon Johnson, for example, believed that the spirituals needed extensive "development" through vocal arrangements, more articulate lyrics, and orchestration to demonstrate that Blacks could reach similar levels of artistic sophistication with whites.[72] Mrs. Burlin observed that northern Blacks felt reluctant to sing the spirituals, especially before whites, because they were ashamed of the slavery from which the songs had come. When people like Rosamond Johnson tried to organize choral performances, she informed Peabody, the singers would rarely attend rehearsals regularly. Northern Blacks, unlike southerners, never "spontaneously" took up a song to express group cohesiveness. According to Mrs. Burlin, Will Marion Cook and Rosamond Johnson had "begged" her to utilize her research skills to obtain the same "serious recognition" for Negro music as her work had already brought to the music of the Indians of the Southwest. She believed, however, that the spirituals should be recorded in their original form because they expressed the uninhibited core of the human psyche with which industrial America had lost touch. She, like Vachel Lindsay, courted a romantic racialism that artists like Mrs. Hackley and the Johnsons shunned. Yet, Mrs. Burlin added, folk music could provide the basis for more complex compositions if Black artists, who alone had developed subconscious empathy with the rhythms and mood of their people, attempted the task. Indeed, in Nathaniel Dett she saw a potential Black Franz Liszt or Mussorgsky who might, through Black folk traditions, bring new life to the music of the entire nation. The accuracy of Mrs. Burlin's research drew favorable reviews in *Crisis,* where DuBois simply saw it as complementary to the work of Mrs. Hackely. He too praised Dett's compositions and was delighted when the latter received a fellowship to study composition in Boston.[73]

More important than the revival of the spirituals to DuBois and James Weldon Johnson, however, was the beginning of the serious presentation of Black characters and themes in Broadway plays. By 1917, Ridgley Torrance, a southern white playwright, produced *The Rider of Dreams, Simon the Cyrene,* and *Granny Maumee* on Broadway with Negro casts. Two of the actresses, Opal Cooper and Inez Clough, Johnson found especially effective—an opinion he shared with drama critic George Jean Nathan of the avant-garde magazine, *The Smart Set.* The success of the plays, however, raised a perplexing problem, the opposite of that raised by efforts to revive the spirituals. Where the spirituals represented authentic folk art that might need "embellishment" to meet sophisticated white standards, the plays expressed the imaginings of sophisticated whites about Black sensibilities. In a lament that has more recently been repeated by Harold Cruse, Johnson told Benjamin Brawley that Black actors operated under the severe handicap of "playing plays written essentially for white characters." In 1932, after commenting on *Glory,* a play about Black life by Nan Bagy Stephens, he told Brawley, "It is strange how southern white writers can dig down into Negro life, often a good deal deeper than Negro writers themselves. I don't know whether it is that they have the advantage of objectivity or whether they work harder on a book." In addition to the lack of sophistication exhibited by Black writers, Johnson noted, Black audiences would not support their work.[74]

Torn between the new interest in Black themes with its attendant opportunities for Black performers and the limited amount of serious writing by Black playwrights, Johnson and his colleagues soon turned their attention to the new musicals, like *Shuffle Along* written by Noble Sissle and Eubie Blake. What it lacked in serious theme, it seemed to make up for with technical originality and spirited performance. By 1917 Johnson, Brawley, and Braithwaite formed a literary triumvirate that paralleled that of Rosamond Johnson, Will Marion Cook, and James Reese Europe in music. Their camaraderie indicated a very self-confident enclave intent on interpreting Black achievements to appreciative white critics.[75] The intense debates that had begun in a rooming house on Fifty-fourth Street in the late 1890s were now the staple fare of a generation of artists, musicians, and poets.

The élan of racial Renaissance, promoted during the war by *Crisis* and expressed by Black writers of many persuasions, was carried over to the making of the peace. The story of Black participation in postwar deliberations has usually been confined to a discussion of the Pan-African congresses initiated primarily by DuBois in early 1919—and more recently to the sporadic activities of the Garveyites in West Africa. The leading scholarly biographer of DuBois, Elliott Rudwick, has judged the Pan-African movement "one of DuBois' biggest failures," while George Padmore, the leading propagandist for a socialist Pan-Africanism between the world wars, argued that DuBois "gave body and soul to Sylvester-Williams's original idea of the Pan-African congresses and broadened its perspectives." A final assessment of the importance of the Pan-African congresses and of the Garveyites must await a scholarly history of the African and West Indian elite who organized and led liberation movements between the Versailles Conference and the Nigerian and Ugandan civil wars.[76] Judged solely as an event in Afro-American history, however, DuBois's Pan-African activities have been misunderstood because they have been judged as political rather than as cultural ventures—and as an aberration from his allegedly "integrationist" philosophy.

The Pan-African activity, however, should be seen as part of DuBois's effort to educate Black persons to a wider sense of their history. DuBois went to Paris not primarily to organize a Pan-African movement but to gather data for a history of Black participation in the war and to present the opinions of the NAACP on colonial Africa to influential persons in President Wilson's party. As DuBois explained in *Crisis,* he went to Paris because heads of state were reorganizing world politics. European minorities were sending delegations and American Blacks also needed representation.[77] The Pan-African Congress, while certainly a venture he hoped to organize, became a logical extension of his other propaganda work, and it probably lasted longer than he anticipated.[78] Both the proposed history and the Pan-African movement, whatever other meanings one might see in them, depicted Blacks as independent actors on the world stage and emphasized especially the importance of contact between the American, West Indian, and African intelligentsia and middle classes. By November, 1920, DuBois concluded that the greatest achievement of the past five years had been the emergence of a "New Spirit" based on a "feeling of power." "The mass of black folk have made the Great Discovery," he wrote. "They have found each other."[79]

DuBois went to Paris largely at the request of the board of directors of the NAACP, who wanted direct reportage on the peace conference and who hoped he might, in however limited a capacity, influence colonial policy. DuBois himself had hoped to assemble data for a history of Black participation in the war with the help of Blacks like Emmett Scott, who held official positions and had access to government documents and confidential information. Scott, however, had contracted with a New York publisher to prepare a volume for popular consumption, which became a semiofficial history. Carter Woodson, whose work at *The Journal of Negro History* since 1916 DuBois had enthusiastically endorsed, wanted the NAACP to sponsor the journal and his other work and to appoint him editor of the proposed history. The association could not assume such a financial burden, and DuBois felt that a history under his own supervision would finally allow him to fulfill the research role for which he had initially been hired.[80] Because he could not gather data from key persons in the United States, the association decided to merge their desire for representation at the peace conference with DuBois's interest in the history. Acting officially as correspondent for *Crisis,* he obtained a passport and sailed in December, 1918, on the *Orizaba,* the ship reserved for American journalists accompanying President Wilson to the peace conference.[81]

Because of his belief in the political importance of cultural activities, DuBois had generated immense enthusiasm for undertakings such as the *Encyclopedia Africana* and the pageant, "The Star of Ethiopia." His commitment to the history was equally strong. In a lengthy report from Paris to the NAACP board in early January, he described his difficulties in gathering information because of the continuing censorship and the opposition of several U.S. Army officers. Nevertheless, he had made some valuable contacts, especially through Robert R. Moton, who had been sent by the war department to pacify Black troops but who still wanted the truth to be known "even when he cannot tell it." DuBois was further encouraged by contacts with the seven Black deputies in the French parliament, who were to obtain permission from Premier Clemenceau for a Pan-African Congress. He saw a place for all of these struggles in his history. But the same constraints that had impeded a truthful accounting of discrimination against Blacks during the war persisted. He could not distribute propaganda for civil rights or African independence, he reported, because France was still technically at war and government censorship was severe. "If I should attempt an anti-lynching meeting here I would be kicked out incontinently; but it is quite possible that by bringing up the whole question of Africa the question of the treatment of Negroes throughout the world may come in for the attention it deserves."[82]

A few days later he sent to the chairman of the NAACP board detailed instructions for using the branches as a means for gathering data on the participation of Blacks in the war. In major cities like New York, Philadelphia, Baltimore, and Washington especially, experienced researchers were to be selected to gather documents, letters, maps, stories of personal experiences, and all other information that would help recreate the conditions under which Black troops were made to wage war. "I say solemnly and without hesitation," DuBois wrote after learning how Emmett Scott and others had failed to report discrimination against Black troops, "the greatest and most pressing and important work for the NAACP is the collection and writing and publication of the history of Negro troops in France . . . You have not the faintest conception of what these men have been through."[83]

DuBois remained in France to organize the Pan-African Congress. While there he prepared two interpretive sketches of Black participation in the war, which appeared in *Crisis* in March and June, 1919. These articles, in addition to continuing the Pan-African theme by discussing all Black participants rather than just the Americans, had as their central focus the political education of Black troops. American Blacks in particular had learned that white Americans intended to use them in such a way as to leave domestic race relations unchanged. But more important, out of the humiliation had come mutual support, and Black Americans had come to see themselves as "a nation within a nation." They had sufficient confidence to perform their duties despite harassment and to demand improvement in their status at home and in conditions in the African colonies. "A new radical Negro spirit has been born in France," DuBois concluded, "which leaves us older radicals far behind."[84] The major events in DuBois's history were political rather than military: the struggle to open a camp to train Black officers, to prevent intense segregation by the Army in France, to obtain equal recognition for the achievements of Black troops, to counter German propaganda leaflets that publicized race discrimination in the United States, and to encourage French sympathy for the Black troops who were helping liberate their homeland. The villains were white officers like General C. C. Ballou of the ninety-second Regiment, who refused to insist on equal treatment for his men, and the victims were men like

Colonel Charles Young who were deprived of command on flimsy evidence. The heroes were the Black troops, who had seen intense fighting and had been decorated for bravery—but by the French rather than the American army.[85] To substantiate his allegations, DuBois sent documentary evidence to NAACP headquarters and had soldiers and others leave more material for him in New York. He hoped to prepare a three-volume study with the cooperation of E. C. Williams (his former collaborator on the abortive *Encyclopedia Africana*), Benjamin Brawley, Charles Young, John Hope, George Haynes, and the officers of various Black units.[86]

This history was apparently never completed, possibly because those who hoped to participate lacked the time or because insufficient evidence was available.[87] But the material that did appear provided an interpretation that countered Scott's bland recitation of government encouragement, Black achievements, and reconciliation of differences through his own mediations.[88] DuBois's emphasis on the political interpretation of military events also indicated the role that Blacks should play in helping to shape the peace. The war for DuBois had not simply provided opportunities—as Scott suggested—but had been a symptom of imperialism, and it should be celebrated not for heroic achievements but for its ability to have weakened the international exploitation of Black peoples. Nonwhite participants, who had chosen to align with the victors, had to press their advantages and demand recognition. As DuBois noted in a collection of essays entitled *Darkwater,* which was published later in the year, the war had required the white race to recognize "for the first time in the history of the modern world that black men are human."[89] The war may have ended, but the political struggle continued at the peace conference where Blacks must press the psychological advantage their valor had won for them on the battlefield.

The Pan-African Congress, as an adjunct to the peace conference, had to fit the interests of unrepresented Africans to a sense of what the Allied Powers were willing to hear. The NAACP board, convinced by DuBois's propaganda during the war that the fate of American Blacks was tied to the fate of

Africa and believing that no nation at Versailles would speak for the Africans, consented to pay part of his expenses. They could hope to receive a hearing because of the contacts Villard and Spingarn had with Ray S. Baker, Walter Lippmann, and Colonel House, and in part because of the influence of Black delegates in the French Assembly. In New York on January 6, 1919, the NAACP held a public meeting to support the Pan-African movement. Speeches were delivered by John Shillady, the association's executive secretary; James Weldon Johnson; Horace M. Kallen, who was introduced as an associate of Norman Angell of the League of the Free Nations; Black veterans; and even a few missionaries. Johnson announced the association's view of the origins and meaning of the war by referring to "The African Roots of War" and to numerous letters he had received asking the association to influence world opinion on the disposition of the German colonies.[90]

Kallen also reiterated DuBois's condemnation of the European bankers and traders in Africa and added that those natives who had opposed colonialism had been slaughtered. The report of Kallen's speech noted only that he had discussed "theoretical issues," but he had recently argued in *The Structure of Lasting Peace* that the African territories, as undeveloped land, occupied the same position for European states as had the western territories for the thirteen American colonies in 1787. Central Africa, he concluded much as had Chandler Owen and Philip Randolph, should be unified into a territory that should be held as a trust by a League of the Free Nations. Its mutual development, he argued, could substitute harmony for conflict in Europe and prosperity for exploitation in Africa. The audience must have responded favorably, because Kallen was more impressed by the meeting than by any of his other quite extensive work for the peace conference.[91]

In Paris DuBois could not hope to influence governmental relations between the European powers, but he did work for specific freedoms for the African colonies. Through official contacts made by Blaise Diagne, he arranged a meeting at the Grand Hotel in Paris on February 19 to 21 of fifty-seven influential Blacks as informal delegates. The largest contingent, sixteen men and women, was from the United States, but thirteen came from the French West Indies, seven from Haiti, smaller groups from the British and French colonies, and others from Liberia, Egypt, and the Portugese, Spanish, and Belgian colonies. The delegates understood that the colonies would not be granted self-government and agreed that the natives lacked the political acumen to make decisions that extended much beyond their own villages. Instead, the congress hoped to devise a plan by which modernization could be brought to Africa by minimizing exploitation and emphasizing education and local self-government. Three weeks earlier the British and French had presented a detailed plan for annexing the German colonies. But President Wilson held out for a mandate system, under which each of the Allied powers would present annual reports on its trustee territories to the proposed League of Nations. Wilson had transferred to the colonies the vision of a tutored and gradual self-development by Blacks that he had suggested for the federal bureaucracy. When applied to American Blacks it was denounced by the NAACP as reactionary. When substituted for unfettered imperialism on the international stage, it seemed to Ray S. Baker "the machinery for a new and liberal policy in world colonial administration."[92]

Against this background, the Pan-African Congress supported Wilson's principles but proposed a more radical strategy. To emphasize the capacity of Africans for self-government, they balanced requests for individual instruction in Western skills with respect for the integrity and civility of village traditions. *Crisis* might lament that the West inevitably viewed other cultures as barbarous simply because of their differences, and James Weldon Johnson might decry how Africans were denied credit for their contributions to Western civilization.[93] But the Pan-African conferees had to designate signs of modernization as achievements so that natives mastering those skills would have a legitimate claim to share in governance. Somewhat as Horace Kallen had suggested, then, the congress requested that the former colonies of Germany and those of weaker states like Belgium and Portugal be unified into a Central African Territory directly under a bureau of the League of Nations. As part of the integrity of the Pan-African idea, they also demanded recognition of the independence of the Black countries of Liberia, Abyssinia, and Haiti, which was then occupied by the U.S. Marines. At the peace conference, the Allies, preoccupied with internal dissension and frightened by the Bolshevik threat to capitalism, distributed the former German colonies among themselves. But they were forced to accept Wilson's ideas of trusteeship territories. Though little movement was made toward self-government in Africa, DuBois noted by the mid-1920s that in the French and British colonies the native intelligentsia had initiated moves toward local assemblies to which the colonial powers had assented.[94]

In retrospect, DuBois felt the Pan-African congresses fell victim to the opposition of the European governments and in part to the provinciality of American Blacks, most of whom could see little reason for continuing contributions to Africa while discrimination remained rampant in the United States. James Weldon Johnson warned of this problem in 1919 and acceded to American public opinion when he said that "the National Association realizes that our fight is here at home . . ."[95] Yet in the wake of the war and as part of a more cosmopolitan view of the destiny of Black people interest in the Pan-African connection continued. When DuBois proposed a second Pan-African Congress because, as Ida Gibbs Hunt noted, the League of Nations had failed to protect Africans from exploitation, the most prominent members of the NAACP provided support. DuBois was able to raise a special fund to finance his trip to England, France, and Belguim, where the sessions were held. The contributors included George Crawford, Harry E. Davis, Charles Bentley, and other Niagara veterans, who joined J. Max Barber in showing a new interest in West Indian and African problems. Far less prominent people like M. C. Slaughter, secretary of the Bowling Green branch of the association, seemed to catch the popular mood. He was proud to contribute ten dollars for his branch, he said, because it was invested in an "effort to prove to the nations of the world that *The Negro Race* is *one* of the many nations of the world, and that as such demands of other nations such recognition as is given the most superior nation among them all." Only Butler Wilson of Boston explicitly refused to contribute on the grounds that the NAACP's legitimate work lay in the United States, though others sharing that view may simply not have replied to the request for funds.[96] Most gratifying to DuBois were contributions from student contingents from the Sudan and the Gold Coast.[97]

The Pan-African vision to some extent expressed the war-borne sentiment personified by Black mobility, military service, and contact with West Indians and Africans in France and even in Harlem. The movement led by Marcus Garvey, though shunned by most of the intelligentsia, gave it further currency. Certainly the psychological liberation from the provincial imagery of the American Negro and his perennial "problems" had wide appeal to intellectuals. Indeed, the cynicism of imperialism, like that of segregation, was exposed now even by men with rather conservative political views. As part of its new international interest, Moorefield Storey of the NAACP financed a scathing exposé by James Weldon Johnson of the American exploitation of Haiti. Johnson debunked American efforts to bring education and better health standards to the republic. He emphasized instead the fortitude and courage of both the local elite and the peasants in resisting the incursion by the marines, who were sent at the request of the City Bank of New York. Warming to his subject, Johnson concluded that "inferiority always was the excuse of ruthless imperialism until the Germans invaded Belgium, when it became 'military necessity.'"[98]

The new sense of spiritual amplitude was perhaps best expressed by Walter White, who in 1921 accompanied DuBois to the second Pan-African Congress. White, as a protégé of James Weldon Johnson and an extremely fair-skinned individual, exemplified the person choosing Black cultural identification. His racial identity shocked people like H. G. Wells and Norman Angell, who showed great interest as he explained to them the consequences for the British West Indies of lynching and other crimes against Blacks in the United States. As he, in turn, observed DuBois criticize the officers of the prestigious

Aborigines Protection Society for their condescension towards colored peoples, his racial identity took on a deeper meaning. Writing home to Mary White Ovington and James Weldon Johnson, he emphasized that "the realization has come of how provincial I was two months ago . . . I am now able to see old problems in a way that is much broader than before."[99] Unlike Paul Dunbar at the turn of the century, who was viewed as an exotic, White was respected for his ability to instruct rather than to entertain Englishmen. Comparing DuBois's frank lecture to the Anti-Slavery Society members with H. G. Wells's comment that most Englishmen did not appreciate the social sophistication of American Blacks, White felt a new pride in his ethnic identification. Such a sense of relief from the pressure to become rehabilitated, to be able instead to see how white men needed enlightenment, gave the postwar intelligentsia a stronger sense of purpose than that possessed by any prior generation of racial spokesmen.

Conclusion:
A Cultured Race

By the early 1920s, young Black writers self-confidently saw themselves as part of an ethnic people that had produced a rich and varied culture. In the diverse social world of Harlem especially, the old debate over Black identity and dignity waged by T. Thomas Fortune and Alexander Crummell; Booker T. Washington, Charles Chestnutt, and W. E. B. DuBois; Kelly Miller, William Ferris, and James Weldon Johnson continued, but with more sophisticated premises. The analysts of racial ideologies and leadership still identified opposing camps largely according to tactics. They measured achievements, however, according to a person's ability to explore the distinctive traditions and promote the civic interests of the race. Followers of Booker T. Washington were still placed on the right because of their willingness to accommodate white political pressures, but they were criticized even more for lacking a distinct racial vision. The judicious young academic Horace Mann Bond observed that while the migration North and increased education made Blacks less receptive to Washington's ideology, his successors also lacked the imagination to lead. "One is almost tempted to conclude," he wrote, "that the Tuskegee regime is fatal to creative genius, for in no field, save that in which the eminent chemist Carver holds sway,

213

does a Tuskegee man present himself in the guise of leader of Negro opinion or culture."[1]

On the left a strange mixture of Marxists and Garveyites gave Fortune's vision of Black Populism broader and more daring, though not necessarily more realistic, reinterpretations. Marxists like Cyril V. Briggs of the African Blood Brotherhood and Philip Randolph of the Socialists transformed the vision of Black proprietorship into the urban context of proletarian struggle or at least biracial working-class agitation.[2] Garvey and his followers, who included Fortune as contributing editor of *The Negro World,* mobilized a new stratum of West Indian immigrants and southern migrants for cooperative business ventures, self-defense and dreams of international racial empire.[3]

Observers of Black America now agreed that the center of the political spectrum was occupied by W. E. B. DuBois, as editor of *Crisis* and the focus of a coterie of civil rights activists, writers, and Pan-African intellectuals. Not a single major analyst of Black leadership mentioned partisan politicians or emphasized the continuing importance of the ideology of social rehabilitation. As Bond shrewdly observed, the center obtained its vitality and authority because it made cultural endeavors through diverse media the basis for an independent Black voice. "With the spectacular literary preeminence which almost inevitably insures preeminence in things of the spirit," he wrote, "there can be no doubt but that the leadership of DuBois is a thing of the present which is as powerful as it is helpful."[4] By the decade's midpoint, DuBois was nominated for a Harmon Foundation Award, which would recognize his contribution to literature. In support of his nomination Joel Spingarn informed George Haynes, administrator of the Harmon Foundation's Negro Awards, that DuBois "has had the greatest influence of any individual on the growth of Negro culture, including literature in the United States." Albert Bushnell Hart, though still acknowledging Booker T. Washington as the most forceful Black personality he had ever met, believed that DuBois, through his literary skill, had forced white Americans to recognize that the intellectual potential of Blacks equaled that of whites.[5] The young economist Abram Harris, who would become one of DuBois's leading critics, also recognized his great power in forwarding the Black struggle for dignity. Through literature, Harris saw, DuBois had expressed the inner needs of Black Americans and had defended their citizenship rights more effectively than any other twentieth-century figure.[6] George Haynes, though the leading spokesman in the 1920s for Washington's philosophy of rehabilitation and inter-racial reconciliation, agreed that the new generation of Blacks who had never been enslaved believed that Black cultural achievements provided the basis for an "authentic race pride."[7] He too argued that Black leadership had become divided into three camps, though he felt that the right and the center had the same objectives. He could think so, however, only because men like Robert R. Moton and he himself had come to accept the premise of DuBois, that "the new world problems are problems of the color line."[8] They could be resolved because Black cultural achievements demonstrated the social and intellectual potential of the race. In the latter part of the decade in his administrative work for the Harmon Foundation, Haynes contacted an impressive array of proposers, referees as well as nominees, to convince the foundation of Black achievements. The foundation made awards in eighteen different areas of social service, including homes for the elderly, playgrounds, Boy and Girl Scout troops, and student loans. The director, Miss Mary Brady, complained, however, that Haynes felt the Negro awards should receive the most attention. The major Negro awards were for achievements in literature, music, art, and race relations, which both Haynes and the director believed would "develop creative work and pride of race among the negro (sic) group." After attending a presentation ceremony at the Abys-sinian Baptist Church in Harlem in 1928, Miss Brady was impressed by the large attendance and the enthusiastic response that the awards seemed to generate among the audience.[9]

The most emphatic and influential statement of the new cultural interpretation of Black needs and achievements was made by the young academic Alain Locke. In magazine articles and as editor of the volume, *The New Negro* in 1926, he re-capitulated all of the major themes that had emerged from the migration and the war. Recognizing the significance of DuBois's work for the prior twenty years in probing the spiritual needs of Black peoples, he noted that "the Negro . . . seems to be shaking off the psychology of imitation and implied inferiority."[10] Under the influence of *The Souls of Black Folk,* a new literature by Blacks had superseded the stereotypes of the past. Migration and immigration had brought together, in Harlem especially, diverse Black peoples who were learning from one another of the achievements of Africans, West Indians, and Blacks scattered across the American continent. The war, furthermore, had taught Black Americans about the exploitation of Africa and created a sense of mission among some intellectuals to free that continent. When Locke, for example, interviewed Ras Taffari (the future Haile Selassie) in 1924, DuBois enthusiastically solicited the story for *Crisis.*[11] Cross-cultural relations by then had already produced a trilingual Black newspaper in Harlem and a Garvey Movement that filled the streets with an outpouring of race pride. It had created a "consensus of feeling" that "resents being spoken of as a social ward or minor."[12]

Locke, like most Black intellectuals, was not a political ideologue, however much he may have sympathized with the Marxism of Claude McKay or carefully noted the support for Blacks being offered by the Soviet Union and the Communist party. Instead, he and others saw in the efforts by Black Americans to promote their own cultural achievements the means to liberate themselves from the syndrome of dependence. As he noted in his report on Kelly Miller's abortive effort to organize a Negro Sanhedrin in 1924, Blacks had developed a consensus for cooperation based on "the spiritual assets of the race in all forms of the cultural arts."[13] By doing so they were paralleling the examples of the various immigrant groups that had congregated in American cities and were promoting cultural revivals to support political independence in Europe. Indeed, Locke likened Harlem to the Irishman's Dublin or the Czechoslovakian's Prague.[14]

The desire to see the major changes in Black communities as a growing cultural consciousness may have been spurred by similar ethnic awakenings among immigrant groups. George Haynes certainly appreciated the social cohesiveness among Italians, Greeks, and Jews, and Locke noted that a knowledge of persecution was developing international loyalties among Negroes as it had among the Jews.[15] In calling Harlem the Negro's "cultural capital" and "Zion," Locke consciously copied the cultural variety of Zionism that appealed to his friend Horace Kallen and to most other college-educated Jewish intellectuals of that era.[16] Furthermore, as Harlem grew to be the largest Black community in the country, Blacks could see further parallels with their Jewish and Italian neighbors. New York by 1920 contained far more Jews than any other city in the world and more Italians than Rome. Similarly, Chicago, the new symbol of Black capitalism, contained almost as many Poles as Warsaw and more Slovaks than Prague. Ethnic groups, in addition were more culturally and politically assertive than ever before. The new nations created after the Versailles Conference provided the basis for ethnic demands on American foreign policy. Such demands became rallying points for political careers for the new American-born generation of Italian and Polish lawyers.[17] Similarly, race pride provided the veneer for the careers of people like Oscar dePriest and Jesse Bingha and similar businessmen and politicians in New York, Philadelphia, and elsewhere.[18] Nevertheless, the preeminence in the Black press of literary figures like W. E. B. DuBois and James Weldon Johnson and young writers like Claude McKay, Countee Cullen, and Langston Hughes indicates clearly that race consciousness among Blacks derived not from a desire to emulate the immigrant groups but from an indigenous search for dignity.

Many white commentators, furthermore, also emphasized that only a cultural awakening could demonstrate that Blacks did not suffer from inherent mental limitations. At the most sophisticated level, Franz Boas noted in an article in the *Yale Review* in 1921 not only that psychological tests failed to show any inherent mental differences between Blacks and whites, but also that the achievements of African civilizations clearly demonstrated that Blacks had always been capable of the highest forms of abstract reasoning.[19] Literary critics like H. L.

Mencken urged DuBois, Locke, and Johnson to ignore white standards and develop arts in which Blacks surpassed whites.[20] Mencken and Carl Van Vechten verged very closely on romantic racialism by emphasizing the psychological and emotional differences between Blacks and whites in a manner to suggest a uniform Black character.[21] Nevertheless, they encouraged Black writers to develop moral and aesthetic standards that would accurately reflect Black life and reveal as much about human nature as would any that might be proposed by whites. Indeed, as early as 1920, Frederick L. Hoffman, the author of *Race Traits and Tendencies of the American Negro,* contrasted "false theories of so-called economic progress" with "genuine race pride." Commending Carter Woodson for the high standards of *The Journal of Negro History,* Hoffman noted that Blacks must be "a race proud of its own people, of its own achievements, and for that matter of its own color, which God gave it, and which no argument or sophistry can set aside."[22]

Perhaps the ultimate admission that Black culture had become a powerful social weapon came from Lothrop Stoddard, the arch racist. His book, *The Rising Tide of Color,* had rallied the "Nordic" reading public behind the immigration restriction and Jim Crow legislation just after World War I. By the mid-1920s even he had retreated somewhat from sweeping denigrations of all "colored races." He expressed instead confusion over the relationship between heredity, social loyalties, and cultural achievements. On the basis of historical achievements and political assertiveness, for example, he conceded that the Chinese and Japanese were neither culturally nor genetically inferior to *Anglo-Saxons,* though he admitted a repulsion toward them as a race. While apologizing at intervals for seeming to rank races, he nevertheless stated that Blacks were "probably" inferior. Invoking the name and philosophy of Booker T. Washington in defense of racial "integrity," he proposed an elaborate system of intensive segregation that he called *bi-racialism,*—a system that closely resembles contemporary South African apartheid. His plans, however, seemed frustrated by mulattoes, who appeared to him the intellectual if not the genetic equals of Anglo-Saxons and who seemed above all to demand the legal right to intermarriage. With substantial bitterness he conceded that a mulatto like DuBois and a radical like Claude McKay then held the center of attention in the Black press, and he lashed out at the Black "insurgent intelligentsia who are today seeking to use their art as a battering ram to smash the color line."[23]

DuBois, who with some amusement debated Stoddard on the question, "Shall the Negro be Encouraged to Seek Cultural Equality?" at the Chicago Forum on March 17, 1929, easily dissected the confusion in his thinking and also summarized the significance of the Renaissance that had swept over the Black world. Deploring the defensive tone of Stoddard's arguments, DuBois noted that arrogant Anglo-Saxon patricians refused to respect the rights of Black citizens or to understand their interests. Blacks, he asserted, neither coveted intermarriage nor were they willing to accept a pace and direction for change dictated by a white elite. Instead, supported by scientific research that had disproved the genetic immutability or hierarchy of races, Blacks had developed new cultural forms so they might explain their unique experiences to a wider world civilization.[24] Seeking refuge from the deterioration of his patrician class in discredited theories of race, Stoddard understood only too well that the Renaissance of Black culture symbolized a social revolution.

Recent critics of Harlem's intellectuals have argued that the poets and novelists turned too eagerly to white literary arbiters rather than seeking the meaning of their art in Black communities.[25] To explore this assertion fully would require another volume. Yet it is sufficient here to note that the debate over the meaning and purpose of Black life conducted in the years between Reconstruction and the Renaissance allowed Black writers to cut free of the paternalistic ethic of rehabilitation. In a world whose political leaders and cultural arbiters still recognized race—however vaguely· defined—as a means for categorizing people and who only slowly accepted the moral consequences of cultural relativism, Black spokesmen were compelled to face a continuing dilemma over standards. As they began to explore more honestly and confidently the Black psyche that DuBois had initially exposed, they found equally intense pressure placed upon them. Alain Locke, James Weldon Johnson, Langston Hughes, and others recognized the special problems of Black artists, who faced both stereotyping by whites and the fear expressed by Blacks that the exposure of idiosyncrasies might reinforce white theories of racial deficiencies. Late in the decade Johnson, writing for the *American Mercury,* noted that "a psychoanalysis of the Negro author of the defensive and exculpatory literature, written in strict conformity to the taboos of Black America, would reveal that they were unconsciously addressing themselves mainly to white America."[26]

In a commencement address at Howard University in 1930, DuBois recapitulated the intense debates among Black educators over how to encourage indigenous standards while coping with modernization and the imposition of white economic and political power. "Ours," he said, "is the double and dynamic function of tuning in with a machine in action so as neither to wreck the machine nor be crushed or maimed by it."[27] Despite the metaphor, which reflected the new employment of Blacks in factory jobs, DuBois reiterated the struggle of Black intellectuals since Reconstruction: to create a social cohesion through which Blacks might shape their own future. The masses, replenished by the continuing migration of wary southerners, still lacked the confidence to demand their rights.[28] But the elite, through a continuing debate over the focus and purpose of Black life, had finally come to believe in the cultured race within.

| Notes

INTRODUCTION

1. Ali A. Mazrui, *World Culture and the Black Experience* (Seattle and London, 1974), 36.

2. James Weldon Johnson to Walter White, October 19, 1927, NAACP Papers, Library of Congress.

3. Ralph Bunche, "Conceptions and Ideologies of the Negro Problem," (1940), 103-05; Bunche, "The Programs, Ideologies, Tactics and Achievements of Negro Betterment and Interracial Organizations," (1940), 767-68, both manuscripts part of the Carnegie-Myrdal Study, Schomburg Collection, New York Public Library.

4. August Meier, *Negro Thought in America, 1880-1915, Racial Ideologies in the Age of Booker T. Washington* (Ann Arbor, 1964); Elliot Rudwick, *W. E. B. DuBois: A Study in Minority Group Leadership* (Philadelphia, 1960); Louis R. Harlan, *Booker T. Washington: The Making of a Black Leader,* 1856-1901 (New York, 1972). Emma Lou Thornbrough, *T. Thomas Fortune Militant Journalist* (Chicago, 1972); Stephen R. Fox *The Guardian of Boston, William Monroe Trotter,* (New York, 1971).

5. Ralph Bunche, *A World View of Race* (Port Washington, NY, 1968 ed.) 82-83.

6. Edwin Redkey, *Black Exodus, Black Nationalism and Back-to-Africa Movements, 1890-1910* (New Haven, 1969); Nell I. Painter, *Exodusters: Black Migration to Kansas After Reconstruction* (New York, 1977).

7. Hubert Harrison to James Weldon Johnson, May 12, 1925, James Weldon Johnson Papers, Beineke Library, Yale University; William Toll, "W. E. B. DuBois and Frederick Jackson Turner: The Unveiling and

Preemption of America's 'Inner History,' *Pacific Northwest Quarterly,* LXV, 2 (April 1974), 66-78.

8.   Harold Cruse, *The Crisis of the Negro Intellectual* (New York, 1967), 32,39,42-43; Cruse, *Rebellion or Revolution?* (New York, 1969), 80-85.

9.   See especially Arnold Rampersad, *The Art and Imagination of W. E. B. DuBois* (Cambridge, Mass. and London, 1976); Frances R. Keller, *An American Crusade: The Life of Charles Waddell Chestnutt* (Provo, Utah, 1978): Eugene Levy, *James Weldon Johnson: Black Leader, Black Voice* (Chicago, 1973).

CHAPTER 1

1.   The story of Black participation in the Civil War and Reconstruction has been told in Dudley Cornish, *The Sable Arm: Negro Troops in the Union Army, 1861-1865* (New York, 1956): Robert Cruden, *The Negro in Reconstruction* (Englewood Cliffs, N.J., 1969); W. E. B. DuBois, *Black Reconstruction in America, 1860-1880* (New York, 1964) and in numerous monographs on individual states, especially South Carolina, Mississippi, and Louisiana where Blacks played their largest roles. The story has been summarized in John Hope Franklin, *From Slavery to Freedom: A History of Negro Americans,* 4th ed. (New York, 1974), 214-59.

2.   Nell I. Painter, *Exodusters: Black Migration to Kansas After Reconstruction,* (New York, 1977), 55-68, 106, 132; William W. Rogers and Robert D. Ward, *August Reckoning: Jack Turner and Racism in Post-Civil War Alabama* (Baton Rouge, 1973), 24-38, 84-102; William W. Rogers, *The One-Gallused Rebellion: Agrarianism in Alabama, 1865-1896* (Baton Rouge, 1970), 11-13; William Cohen, "Negro Involuntary Servitude in the South, 1865-1940: A Preliminary Analysis," *Journal of Southern History,* XLII, 1 (February 1976), 31-60.

3.   C. Peter Ripley, *Slaves and Freedmen in Civil War Louisiana* (Baton Rouge, 1976), 92; Joel Williamson, *After Slavery: The Negro in South Carolina During Reconstruction, 1861-1880* (Chapel Hill, N.C., 1965), 316-17.

4.   John G. Sprout, *"The Best Men": Liberal Reformers in the Gilded Age* (New York, 1968), 29-44; John Blassingame, *Black New Orleans, 1860-1880* (Chicago, 1973), 154; John M. Langston, *From the Virginia Plantation to the National Capital* (Hartford, 1894), 263, 283, 288-91;[Frederick Douglass], *Life and Times of Frederick Douglass Written by Himself* (New York, 1971), 283; "Letter to Major Delany," reprinted in Philip Foner, ed., *The Life and Writings of Frederick Douglass,* IV (New York, 1955), 276-78; Painter, *Exodusters,* 26-27.

5.   Albion Tourgee, *A Fool's Errand,* ed. John Hope Franklin (Cambridge, Mass. 1961), passim; Frances R. Keller, *An American Crusade: The Life of Charles Waddell Chestnutt,* (Provo, Utah, 1978), 70.

6. Painter, *Exodusters,* 17-22; James M. McPherson, *The Aboli-tionist Legacy: From Reconstruction to the NAACP* (Princeton, 1975), 54-55.

7. August Meier, *Negro Thought in America, 1880-1915: Racial Ideologies in the Age of Booker T. Washington* (Ann Arbor, 1964), 12-16, and passim.

8. Painter, *Exodusters,* 110-17; Edwin S. Redkey, *Black Exodus: Black Nationalist and Back-to-Africa Movements, 1890-1910* (New Haven, 1969), 33-37.

9. The actual influence of Black legislators during Reconstruction has been summarized in Kenneth Stampp, *The Era of Reconstruction, 1865-1877* (New York, 1965), 167-71. For detailed explanations of government fiscal, monetary, and land-reform policies see Irwin Unger, *The Greenback Era: A Social and Political History of American Finance, 1865-1879* (Princeton, 1964); Robert Sharkey, *Money, Class and Party* (Baltimore, 1959). For a more detailed account of Black efforts at land and other reforms for the freedmen see Williamson, *After Slavery,* 85; Peter Kolchin, *First Freedom: The Response of Alabama's Blacks to Emancipation and Reconstruction* (Westport, Conn., 1972), 134-36; Ripley, *Slaves and Freedmen,* 50-58, 194-98; Carol K. R. Bleser, *The Promised Land: A History of the South Carolina Land Commission, 1869-1890* (Columbia, S.C., 1969), xiii, 19; Charles Vincent, *Black Legis-lators in Louisiana During Reconstruction* (Baton Rouge, 1976), 34, 98-111.

10. T. T. Allain is quoted in T. Thomas Fortune, *Black and White: Land, Labor and Politics in the South* (New York, 1884), 190-93. For Allain's continuing insistence on the moral and social value of free enter-prise see T. T. Allain, Broadside to Jane Addams, August 9, 1912, Jane Addams Papers, Swarthmore College. Isaiah Montgomery, "The Negro in Business," *Outlook,* LXIX (November 16, 1901), 733. Vernon L. Whar-ton, *The Negro in Mississippi, 1865-1890* (New York, 1965), 211-12. For the general picture see David C. Rankin, "The Origins of Black Leader-ship in New Orleans During Reconstruction," *Journal of Southern History,* XL, 3 (August 1974), 417-40; Thomas Holt, "Radical Blacks and Conser-vative Browns: The Voting Behavior of Negro Legislators in the South Carolina House of Representatives, 1868-1871," Paper delivered at the Annual Meeting of the Organization of American Historians, April 14, 1973.

11. Langston, *From the Virginia Plantation,* 504-06; John R. Lynch, *The Facts of Reconstruction* (New York, 1913), 267-73. Kenneth L. Kusmer, *A Ghetto Takes Shape, Black Cleveland, 1870-1930* (Urbana, Ill., 1976), 119-21. The thought and influence of the few Blacks active in labor organizations has not been well studied, though see Herbert Gutman, *Work, Culture and Society in Industrializing America* (New York, 1976), 121-208.

12. Blassingame, *Black New Orleans,* 79, 153-54; Kolchin, *First Freedom,* 157, 163-65, 167; Leonard I. Sweet, *Black Images of America,*

1784-1870 (New York, 1976), 3-5; Frederick Cooper, "Elevating the Race: The Social Thought of Black Leaders, 1827-1850," *American Quarterly*, XXIV, 5 (December 1972), 604-25; Floyd J. Miller, *The Search for a Black Nationality: Black Emigration and Colonization, 1787-1863* (Urbana, 1975), 121.

13.   David Walker, *An Appeal to the Colored People of the World*, (New York, 1965), 8, 19-20; Martin R. Delany, "The Condition, Elevation, Emigration and Destiny of the Colored People of the United States," abridged in Howard Brotze, ed., *Negro Social and Political Thought, 1850-1920* (New York, 1966), 5, 63-64; Lawrence J. Friedman, *The White Savage: Racial Fantasies in the Post-bellum South* (Englewood Cliffs, N.J., 1970), 140-43.

14.   Painter, *Exodusters*, 26; Langston, *From Virginia Plantation*, 283, 288; Roger A. Fischer, *The Segregation Struggle in Louisiana, 1862-1877* (Urbana, 1974), 78-79, 85-86; Kolchin, *First Freedom*, 141.

15.   George M. Frederickson, *The Black Image in the White Mind: The Debate on Afro-American Character and Destiny, 1817-1914* (New York, 1971), 49-50, 105; and the reflection of these views in Ray A. Billington, ed., *The Journal of Charlotte Forten* (New York, 1961), 49, 50, 53-54.

16.   Frederickson, *Black Image*, 97-129; McPherson, *Abolitionist Legacy*, 68-69.

17.   James McPherson, *The Negro's Civil War: How the American Negro Felt and Acted During the War for the Union* (New York, 1967), 134-35; Billington, ed., *Journal of Charlotte Forten*, 147, 153, 190. The freedmen developed an instant respect for Miss Forten as an "educated lady." See Elizabeth Ware Pearson, ed., *Letters from Port Royal, 1862-1868* (New York, 1969), 133 ff.

18.   Sprout, *"The Best Men,"* 29-42; George B. Tindall, *South Carolina Negroes, 1877-1900* (Baton Rouge, 1966), 22; Langston, *From Virginia Plantation*, 511; Montgomery, "Negro in Business," 733-34; McPherson, *Abolitionist Legacy*, 68.

19.   John Higham, *From Boundlessness to Consolidation: The Transformation of American Culture, 1848-1860* (Ann Arbor, 1969), 6-15; R. W. B. Lewis, *The American Adam: Innocence, Tragedy and Tradition in the Nineteenth Century* (Chicago, 1955), 13-27; George Frederickson, *The Inner Civil War: Northern Intellectuals and the Crisis of the Union* (New York, 1965).

20.   Richard Hofstadter, *Social Darwinism in American Thought* (Boston, 1944). Henry May, *Protestant Churches and Industrial America* (New York, 1948), emphasizes the importance of clerical, as opposed to academic or journalistic, leaders in molding popular opinion.

21.   W. H. Crogman, "Negro Education, Its Helps and Hindrances," *Proceedings and Addresses of the National Education Association*, XXII (Madison, 1884), 108. For an influential view of social evolution that interchanges *race* and *nationality* see Josiah Strong, *Our Country* (New York, 1885), 159-71.

22.   Stahl Patterson, "Increase and Movement of the Colored Population, I. Increase," *Popular Science Monthly*, XIX (September 1881), 666; Alexander Crummell, *A Defense of the Negro Race in America . . . from the Assaults and Charges of Reverend J. L. Tucker, of Jackson, Mississippi* (Washington, 1883), 24.

23.   Alexander Crummell to John W. Cromwell, April 25, 1877, Alexander Crummell Papers, Schomburg Collection, New York Public Library; Fortune, *Black and White*, 213-15; Crogman, "Negro Education," 107-09, 112-13.

24.   Painter, *Exodusters*, 147, 158-59.

25.   Allison Blakely, "Richard T. Greener and the 'Talented Tenth's' Dilemma," *Journal of Negro History*, LIX, 4 (October 1974), 306-07.

26.   The talk was reprinted in John M. Langston, *Freedom and Citizenship* (Miami, 1969), 232-58.

27.   William H. Chafe, "The Negro and Populism: A Kansas Case Study," *Journal of Southern History*, XXXIV, 3 (August 1968), 404-05.

28.   Langston, *Freedom and Citizenship*, 240.

29.   *Life and Times of Frederick Douglass*, 429-39.

30.   Painter, *Exodusters*, 243-250.

31.   Wilson J. Moses, *The Golden Age of Black Nationalism, 1850-1925* (Hamden, Conn., 1978), 90-91, correctly demonstrates the intellectual affinity between Douglass and Washington, with Fortune's concurrence, based primarily on their assessment of the freedmen and their secular and pragmatic views of social change. Moses's book was published after the drafting of this manuscript.

32.   George Washington Williams, *A History of the Negro Race in America, 1619-1880*, II (Cleveland, 1883), 534, 537-42; McPherson, *Abolitionist Legacy*, 102-03.

33.   Langston, *From the Virginia Plantation*, 235.

34.   W. E. B. DuBois, "The Negro in Literature and Art,"*Annals of the American Academy of Political and Social Science*, XLIX (September 1913), 235.

35.   "The Reminiscences of William Edward Burghardt DuBois," Columbia University, 1963, 88, 90.

36.   George Washington Williams to Henry Wadsworth Longfellow, July 29, 1875, Henry Wadsworth Longfellow Papers, Houghton Library, Harvard University.

37.   Williams, *History of Negro Race*, I, x, II, 553-84.

38.   Ibid., I, 114, 552; Benjamin Brawley, *A Social History of the American Negro*, reprint ed., (New York, 1971), xxiii; William V. Pooley to Frederick Jackson Turner, May 21, 1910, Frederick Jackson Turner Papers, Huntington Library, San Marino, Cal.; Henry Nash Smith, *Virgin Land: The American West as Symbol and Myth* (New York, 1957), 296-98.

39.   Williams, *History of Negro Race*, I. 115, 120-21; Williams, *A History of the Negro Troops in the War of the Rebellion, 1861-1865* (New York, 1888), 67.

40.   Williams, *History of Negro Race,* I, 333; John Hope Franklin, "George Washington Williams, Historian," *Journal of Negro History,* XXI (January 1946), 90.

41.   Williams, *History of Negro Race,* II, 528.

42.   Ibid., 462-64, 475-76, 552; Franklin, "Williams," 90.

43.   Slavery as a Black social institution has received its fullest treatment in Eugene Genovese, *Roll, Jordan, Roll: The World the Slaves Made* (New York, 1974), which tries to explain how the relationship between master and slave shaped the uses Blacks made of their cultural heritage, and in Herbert Gutman, *The Black Family in Slavery and Freedom* (New York, 1976), which explains the complex relationship between African traditions, the slave life cycle, and family structure. Gutman's emphasis on the stability and adaptability of Black families was described in essays and monographs by W. E. B. DuBois in the late 1890s and early 1900s.

44.   S. P. Fullinwider, *The Mind and Mood of Black America: 20th Century Thought* (Homewood, Ill., 1969), 18; Richard Greener to Archibald Grimke, April 28, 1913, Grimke to John F. Andrews, et. al., June 30, 1892, Archibald Grimke Papers, Howard University; Mary White Ovington to Joel Spingarn, December 20, 1915, Joel Spingarn Papers, New York Public Library.

45.   Fullinwider, *Mind and Mood of Black America,* 19; Archibald Grimke, *The Life of Charles Sumner: The Scholar in Politics* (New York, 1892), 152, 291. Grimke's assumptions about "human nature" are only implied in his biographies. They are clearly expressed in his fascinating essay, "The Sex Question and Race Segregation," in *Papers of the American Negro Academy,* Nineteenth Annual Meeting (Washington, 1916), 5-7.

46.   Archibald Grimke to John A. Andrew, et. al., June 30, 1892, Grimke Papers; Grimke, *William Lloyd Garrison: the Abolitionist* (New York, 1891), 391.

47.   Fortune's adamant opposition to the emigrationist schemes of the 1890s is noted in Emma Lou Thornbrough, *T. Thomas Fortune, Militant Journalist* (Chicago, 1972), 142. Durham's skeptical assessment of Blyden is noted in John S. Durham to Emmett Scott, March 6, 1913, Booker T. Washington Papers, Library of Congress.

48.   William Simmons, *Men of Mark: Eminent, Progressive and Rising* (Cleveland, 1887), 785-86; Thornbrough, *Fortune,* 23-34; Fortune, *Black and White,* 182-3; Seth M. Scheiner, *Negro Mecca: A History of the Negro in New York City, 1865-1920* (New York, 1965), 106-07.

49.   Chester M. Destler, "Western Radicalism, 1865-1901: Concepts and Origins," *Mississippi Valley Historical Review,* XXXI (December 1944), 348-49; Lee Benson, *Merchants, Farmers and Railroads: Railroad Regulation and New York Politics, 1850-1887* (Cambridge, Mass. 1955), 88, 94, 105-17.

50.   Henry George, *Progress and Poverty* (New York, n.d.), 167, 267-96, 408-21, 433-72.

51. Fortune, *Black and White,* 210-15, 241.

52. Sheldon Hackney, *Populism to Progressivism in Alabama* (Princeton, 1969), 33-35; C VannWoodward, *The Strange Career of Jim Crow,* 3d ed., (New York, 1974), 60-61. Lawrence C. Goodwyn, "Populist Dreams and Negro Rights: East Texas as a Case Study," *American Historical Review,* LXXVI (December 1971), 1435-1456.

53. Fortune, *Black and White,* 182, 190-93; Fortune, "Why We Organize a National Afro-American League," *The Afro-American Budget,* I, 8 (February 1890), 233, Pamphlet in Moorland Collection, Howard University. The Populist emphasis on cooperatives is stressed in Lawrence Goodwyn, *The Populist Movement, A Short History of Agrarian Revolt in America* (New York, 1978), xx-xxi, 55-93.

54. Thornbrough, *Fortune,* 116.

55. T. Thomas Fortune, "The Kind of Education the Afro-American Most Needs" (n.d.), 3-5, Moorland Collection; Fortune, *Black and White,* 124.

56. The ideological affinity between Douglass and Washington is stressed in Moses, *Golden Age of Black Nationalism* 90-100.

57. Fortune, *Black and White,* 87-90; Fortune, *Kind of Education,* 204, 209; Emma Lou Thornbrough, "The National Afro-American League, 1887-1908," *Journal of Southern History,* XXVII, 4 (November 1961), 497; T. Thomas Fortune to Booker T. Washington, September 21, 1891, Washington Papers.

58. Biographical data on Durham has been gathered from letters. See John S. Durham to Whitefield McKinlay, January 6, 1897, October 24, November 11, 1902, February 2, 1905, Carter Woodson Collection, Library of Congress; Roland P. Faulkner to Hollis Frissell, February 2, 1913 John S. Durham to Emmett Scott, March 6, 1913, November 19, 1915, Washington Papers. See also the brief obituary in *Crisis,* XLX, 4 (February 1920), 200.

59. Booker T. Washington to Robert Ogden, May 30, 1896, Robert Ogden Papers, Library of Congress; John S. Durham to Whitefield McKinlay, September 5, 1902, Woodson Collection.

60. John S. Durham, *To Teach the Negro History: A Suggestion* (Philadelphia, 1897), 7.

61. Ibid., 13-21.

62. Ibid., 15.

63. Ibid., 15; John S. Durham, "The Labor Unions and the Negro," *Atlantic Monthly,* LXXI (February 1898), 222-31.

64. Durham, *To Teach Negro History,* 6. Durham's fundamental notion, that ethnic pride is chauvinistic when taught apart from specific reference to social structures and group ideological interests, is reiterated in more sophisticated form in Orlando Patterson, *Ethnic Chauvinism: The Reactionary Impulse* (New York, 1977). In the preface (pp.9-11), Patterson notes the difficulty in understanding ethnicity as a social phenomenon lies "in the reluctance to treat the subject historically" and the failure to

recognize that "ethnicity is, above all, a form of commitment; it is an ideology, a faith; one that is often secular, but is also frequently a secular faith layered on a more profound religious faith."

65. John S. Durham to Emmett Scott, March 16, 1913, Washington Papers.

66. Note the marvelous letter of professional advice, philosophical perspective, and collegial encouragement in Alexander Crummell to Frazier Miller, July 26, 1894, Crummell Papers. Biographical material on Crummell can be found in Kathleen O'Mara Wahle, "Alexander Crummell: Black Evangelist and Pan-Negro Nationalist," *Phylon*, XXIX (1968), 388-89; Wilson J. Moses "Civilizing Missionary: A Study of Alexander Crummell," *Journal of Negro History*, LX, 2 (April 1975), 233-35.

67. Moses, *Golden Age of Black Nationalism*, 62, 64, 67.

68. Ibid., 64, 71; Crummell, *Defense of the Negro Race*, 26.

69. Alexander Crummell, "The Necessities and Advantages of Education Considered in Relation to Colored Men," Address delivered to the Hamilton Lyceum of New York City, July 4, 1844, ms. in Crummell Papers; Crummell, "The Dignity of Labor and its Value to a New People," Address to the Working Men's Club of Philadelphia, 1881, ms. in Crummell Papers; Josephus, pastor of Church of the Crucifixion, Philadelphia, to Alexander Crummell, November 30, 1872, Crummell Papers.

70. Wahle, "Crummell," 389.

71. Moses, "Civilizing Missionary," 241; Fullinwider, *Mind and Mood*, 10-11.

72. Alexander Crummell, *The Future of Africa* (New York, 1862), 218-19, 221, 234-35, 242-43; W. H. Hare, secretary of the Missionary Society of the Protestant Episcopal Church, to Alexander Crummell. April 25, 1872, Crummell Papers; Alexander Crummell to John E. Bruce, January 21, 1898, John E. Bruce Papers, Schomburg Collection; Robert July, *The Origins of Modern African Thought* (London, 1968), 107-09; Moses, "Civilizing Missionary," 239-40.

73. Alexander Crummell to John W. Cromwell, April 25, 1877, Crummell Papers; Crummell to John E. Bruce, October 30, 1896, Bruce Papers.

74. Crummell, "The Race Problem in America;" reprinted in Brotz, ed., *Negro Social and Political Thought*, 184; Crummell, *Defense of Negro Race*.

75. Alexander Crummell to J. W. Cromwell, June 15, October 15, 1897, Crummell Papers; Crummell to John E. Bruce, January 21, 1898, Bruce Papers; Paul L. Dunbar, "Negro Life in Washington." *Harper's Weekly*, XLIV (January 13, 1900), 40. For Dunbar's encounters with stereotypes see Dunbar to William Dean Howells, April 26, 1897, William Dean Howells Papers, Houghton; Dunbar to Brand Whitlock, December 26, 1900, Allen Nevins Collection, Columbia University.

76. Alexander Crummell to John E. Bruce, October 30, 1896, Bruce Papers; Crummell to John W. Cromwell, June 15, 1897, Crummell

Papers; William Crogman to Francis J. Grimke, September 24, 1894, in Carter Woodson ed., *The Works of Francis J. Grimke,* IV (Washington, 1944), 34-35.

77. "Prospectus for the American Negro Academy," (n.d.), Bruce Papers; Alexander Crummell to John W. Cromwell, October 5, 1897, Crummell Papers; Crummell, "Civilization, the Primal Need of the Race," Inaugural Address to the American Negro Academy, March 5, 1897, ms. in Crummell Papers.

78. Washington *Bee,* September 17, 1898; Washington *Colored American,* July 1, August 6, 1898.

79. For Crummell's influence see W. E. B. DuBois, *The Souls of Black Folk* (Greenwich, Conn., 1961), 157-65; William Ferris, *The African Abroad: Or His Evolution in Western Civilization Tracing His Development Under Caucasian Millieu* (New Haven, Conn., 1913), 206-08; Moses, "Civilizing Missionary," 245-47.

CHAPTER 2

1. W. E. B. DuBois, *The Souls of Black Folk* (Greenwich, Conn., 1961), 42-43.

2. August Meier, *Negro Thought in America, 1880-1915: Racial Ideologies in the Age of Booker T. Washington* (Ann Arbor, 1964), 101 and passim; Wilson Jeremiah Moses, *The Golden Age of Black Nationalism, 1850-1925* (Hamdon, Conn., 1978), 28.

3. Harold Cruse, *Rebellion or Revolution?* (New York, 1968), 84.

4. Moses, *Golden Age,* 96.

5. Louis R. Harlan, *Booker T. Washington: The Making of a Black Leader, 1856-1901* (New York, 1972), unpaginated preface.

6. James Clarkson to John E. Bruce, November 25, 1896, John E. Bruce Papers, Schomburg Collection, New York Public Library; C. VannWoodward, *Origins of the New South, 1877-1913* (Baton Rouge, 1951), 356-61; Meier, *Negro Thought,*110.

7. Washington's speech at the Southern Industrial Convention at Huntsville, Alabama, October 12, 1899, is reprinted in the Washington *Bee,* January 27, 1900. At that conference he, along with several southern white politicians, advocated literacy qualifications for the suffrage. See George W. Atkinson to Booker T. Washington, October 20, 28, 1899, Booker T. Washington Papers, Library of Congress. The support Washington had among philanthropists and southern white educators is noted in Louis R. Harlan, *Separate and Unequal: Public School Campaigns and Racism in the Southern Seaboard States, 1901-1915* (New York, 1968), 78n; Horace Mann Bond, *Negro Education in Alabama: A Study in Cotton and Steel* (New York, 1969), 217-25.

8. Howard Brotz, *The Black Jews of Harlem: Negro Nationalism and the Dilemmas of Negro Leadership* (London, 1964), 76.

9. "The Reminiscences of William Edward Burghardt DuBois," Columbia University, 1963, 150.

10. William Graham Sumner, "Discipline," *The Conquest of the United States by Spain, and Other Essays* (Chicago, n.d.), 15.

11. Cruse, *Rebellion or Revolution,* 85; Paulo Freire, *Pedagogy of the Oppressed* (New York, 1970), 21; Franz Fanon, *The Wretched of the Earth* (New York, 1966), 153-54.

12. Leslie A. Lacy, *The Rise and Fall of a Proper Negro* (New York, 1971), 151.

13. Harlan, *Booker T. Washington,* unpaginated preface.

14. In late May 1900, in a talk to the political elite at the Bethel Literary Society in Washington, D.C., Washington reiterated the importance of rehabilitation over agitation. The speech is reprinted in the Washington *Bee,* June 2, 1900. Rayford Logan, *The Betrayal of the Negro, From Rutherford B. Hayes to Woodrow Wilson* (New York, 1965) 306-07, interprets this speech as "the limit to which he was prepared to go in order to retain his position as the spokesman acceptable to Negroes, without alienating his staunch white supporters in the North and South."

15. Edith Armstrong Talbot, *Samuel Chapman Armstrong: A Biographical Study* (New York, 1904), 5, 8, 10, 14, 16, 27.

16. James M. McPherson, *The Abolitionist Legacy: From Reconstruction to the NAACP* (Princeton, 1975), 217.

17. Talbot, *Armstrong,* 101-06.

18. Ibid., 170-71; Samuel C. Armstrong to Lucious P. Fairchild, May 21, 1872, Lucious P. Fairchild Papers, Wisconsin State Historical Society.

19. Samuel C. Armstrong to John G. Whittier, October 9, 1891, John G. Whittier Papers, Houghton Library, Harvard University; Talbot, *Armstrong,* 171-74, 184, 187.

20. Samuel C. Armstrong to Ralph Waldo Emerson, May 27, 1874, Ralph Waldo Emerson Papers, Houghton; Armstrong to John G. Whittier, April 23, 1886, Whittier Papers; Theodore Clark Smith, *The Life and Letters of James A. Garfield* (New Haven, 1925), 802-03. Armstrong's racism is emphasized, without efforts to compare it to the "romantic" variety, in Henry A. Bullock, *A History of Negro Education in the South: From 1619 to the Present* (New York, 1970), 76.

21. Booker T. Washington, *Up From Slavery* (New York, 1941), 31, 36-37, 41; Robert R. Moton, *Finding a Way Out* (Garden City, N.Y., 1921), 145.

22. Booker T. Washington to Theodore Roosevelt, September 15, 1903, Theodore Roosevelt Papers, Library of Congress; Washington, *Up From Slavery,* 62-64; Constance McL. Green, *The Secret City: A History of Race Relations in the Nation's Capital* (Princeton, 1967), 143-44; E. Franklin Frazier, *Black Bourgeoisie: The Rise of a New Middle Class* (New York, 1965), 195-212; John S. Durham, *To Teach the Negro History* (Philadelphia, 1897), 14-15.

23. Washington, *Up From Slavery,* 67-71; William Armstrong to

Booker T. Washington, July 8, 1899, Robert Speer to Washington, September 19, 1902, Washington Papers.

24. Washington, *Up From Slavery,* 76-77; Booker T. Washington to Seth Low, June 18, 1907, Seth Low Papers, Columbia University; James G. Blaine, *Twenty Years of Congress: From Lincoln to Garfield* (Norwich, Conn., 1886), 167; Allen J. Goings, *Bourbon Democracy in Alabama, 1874-1890* (University of Alabama, 1951) 151, 159-60, 165-66; Burke Hinsdale, ed., *President Garfield and Education* (Boston, 1882), 254-55; William W. Rogers and Robert D. Ward, *August Reckoning: Jack Turner and Racism in Post-Civil War Alabama* (Baton Rouge,1973) 100-02.

25. Booker T. Washington, *The Story of the Negro,* II (New York, 1909), 10, 31; Harold Isaacs, *The New World of Negro Americans* (New York, 1964), 160-64; Carter Woodson, *The Miseducation of the Negro* (Washington, 1933), 20-23; Washington, "The Educational Outlook in the South," *Proceedings and Addresses of the National Education Association,* (Madison, 1884), 125-30.

26. Booker T. Washington, *The Future of the American Negro* (Boston, 1899), 5, 68-69; Washington, *Working With the Hands* (London, 1904), 17-18; Fanon, *Wretched of Earth,* 153; Peter Kolchin, *First Freedom: The Responses of Alabama's Blacks to Emancipation and Reconstruction* (Westport, Conn., 1972), 134-36.

27. Booker T. Washington, "The Influence of Negro Citizenship," *Proceedings of the National Educational Association* (Madison, 1900) 114-15; Washington, *My Larger Education: Being Chapters From My Experience* (New York, 1911), 178-79; Washington, *Story of Negro,* I: 119, II: Chap. III. For a criticism of contemporary social science's use of the theory of *cultural deprivation* see Charles A. Valentine, *Culture and Poverty: Critique and Counter-Proposals* (Chicago, 1968), 14-17, and passim.

28. Talbot, *Armstrong,* 186; Washington, *Up From Slavery,* 226-27; William Holtzclaw, *The Black Man's Burden* (New York, 1915), 217-18.

29. California State Board of Charities and Corrections, *First Biennial Report* (Sacramento, 1904), 24-31; Booker T. Washington, "Negro Education and the Nation" *Proceedings of the National Education Association,* XLVI (Winona, Minnesota, 1908), 93; Emmett Scott and Lyman Beecher Stowe, *Booker T. Washington: Builder of a Civilization* (New York, 1916), 67.

30. Booker T. Washington to Seth Low, April 15, 1911, Low Papers; Washington to Joseph R. Lee, ca. 1903, Washington Papers; Washington, *Working With the Hands,* 157; Scott and Stowe, *Washington,* 176-79.

31. Booker T. Washington to Dr. Prince A. Morrow, n.d., filed in Robert Park Correspondence for 1912, Box 61, Washington Papers; Merle Curti, *The Social Ideas of American Educators* (Totowa, N.J., 1968), 293; Lawrence Cremin, *The Transformation of the School: Progressivism in American Education, 1876-1957* (New York, 1961), 116-19; Talbot,

Armstrong, 170-1, 253-54; McPherson, *Abolitionist Legacy,* 208.

32. Booker T. Washington to Oswald Garrison Villard, November 16, 1904, Oswald Garrison Villard Papers, Houghton; Washington, *Working With the Hands,* 64; Washington, *My Larger Education, Being Chapters From My Experience* (Garden City, N.Y., 1911) 137; Richard Wright, *White Man, Listen!* (New York, 1964), 85.

33. Harlan, *Booker T. Washington,* 124.

34. Hollis Frissell to Robert Ogden, Sepember 2, 1896, and clipping on Washington's forthcoming article in the *Atlantic Monthly,* Ogden Papers, Library of Congress complains that Washington has appropriated the "Hampton Idea" slogan; Washington, *Up From Slavery,* 81, 94-95; Max Bennett Thrasher, *Tuskegee: Its Story and Its Work* (New York, 1901), 148-50; "Reminiscences of DuBois," 46.

35. Robert Park to Booker T. Washington, March 1, 1913, Washington Papers.

36. Washington, *Story of Negro,* II: 192.

37. Berenice Fisher, *Industrial Education, American Ideals and Institutions* (Madison, 1967), Chap. III; Washington, *Working With the Hands,* 63; McPherson, *Abolitionist Legacy,* 212-16.

38. Booker T. Washington to Charles Mason, October 11, 1915, with "Data on Students Entering Tuskegee Institute," Washington Papers. Booker T. Washington to Seth Low, June 18, 1907, Seth Low Papers, Columbia University.

39. Booker T. Washington to Ray S. Baker, January 31, February 7, 1907, Ray S. Baker Papers, Library of Congress; New York *Age,* March 15, 1908; Washington, *Up From Slavery,* 94-95, 227-28; Fred Shannon, *The Farmer's Last Frontier: Agriculture, 1860-1897* (New York, 1945), 165-69; Harlan, *Booker T. Washington,* 130.

40. Washington's use of the term *condition* is found in *Story of the Negro,* I: 136, and *Future of the American Negro,* 25-26. For his reference to Henry Ossawa Tanner see *Up From Slavery,* 202-03. See also Robert Ogden to Booker T. Washington, February 23, 1904, Charles Chestnutt to Washington, November 16, 1901, John Henry Adams to Emmett Scott, October 29, 1914, Scott to Adams, December 10, 1914, Washington Papers; Moses, *Golden Age,* 96.

41. William Baldwin to Booker T. Washington, November 7, 1898, Andrew Carnegie to Washington, November 30, 1906, Washington Papers.

42. Giles Jackson to Booker T. Washington, March 25, 1902, John S. Durham to Washington, May 2, 1902, Washington to Emmett Scott, August 7, December 16, 1905, Washington to Robert Moton, January 14, 1907, August 21, 1911, Washington to Jessee Bingha, July 25, 1915, Washington Papers; Booker T. Washington and W. E. B. DuBois, *The Negro in the South, His Economic Progress in Relation to His Moral and Religious Development* (Philadelphia, 1907), 59.

43. Isaiah Montgomery, "The Building of a Negro Town," in *Proceedings of the National Negro Business League: Its First Meeting*

(Boston, 1901), 100-03; Washington, *Story of the Negro,* II: 252; Iverson Sumners, "A Negro Town in Illinois," *Independent,* XLV (August 27, 1908), 465-68; Booker T. Washington to Oswald Garrison Villard, June 4, 1902, Villard Papers.

44. Booker T. Washington to Robert Ogden, May 30, 1896, Ogden Papers; Washington, *Future of the American Negro,* 73; Washington, *Up From Slavery,* 211; Samuel R. Spencer, *Booker T. Washington and the Negro's Place in American Life* (Boston, 1955), 116.

45. James Dockery to Booker T. Washington, June 30, 1903, James Ferrier to Washington, May 12, 1905, Washington to Ferrier, May 17, 1905, R. H. Thompson to Washington, April 13, 1914, Washington Papers; R. R. Wright, Jr., "The Negro in Times of Industrial Unrest," *Charities,* XV (October 7, 1905), 69-73.

46. In 1899 he had to go to Atlanta, where with the help of John Hope, W. E. B. DuBois and William Pledger, he petitioned the legislature to kill a bill calling for unique literary and property qualifications for Negro suffrage. See Booker T. Washington to T. Thomas Fortune, November 7, 1899, November 10, 1899, Washington Papers; See also Booker T. Washington to Oswald Garrison Villard, August 31, 1903, October 10, 1904, April 12, 1905, April 20, 1908, January 5, 1911, Villard Papers; Booker T. Washington to Ray S. Baker, July 23, 1907, Baker Papers; Washington, *Future of the American Negro,* 141-42, 153.

47. Booker T. Washington to Theodore Roosevelt, April 20, July 5, 1901, Theodore Roosevelt Papers; William McKinlay, *Speeches and Addresses: From March 1, 1897 to May 30, 1900* (New York, 1900), 166-70.

48. Archibald Grimke to John F. Andrews, et al., June 30, 1892, Archibald Grimke Papers, Howard University; Talbot, *Armstrong,* 272-74; Harlan, *Washington,* 164; Kelly Miller, *Radicals and Conservatives* (New York, 1968), 303.

49. Booker T. Washington to Theodore Roosevelt, April 20, 1901, Roosevelt to Washington, April 23, 1901, Washington to Roosevelt, April 27, July 5, August 2, September 1, 1901, Roosevelt Papers.

50. John Blum, *The Republican Roosevelt* (New York, 1962), 21, 43-46; Booker T. Washington to George Foster Peabody, November 23, 1901, George Foster Peabody Papers; Library of Congress; Booker T. Washington to Seth Low, June 18, 1907, Low Papers; Theodore Roosevelt, "Preface," in Scott and Stowe, *Washington,* xiii; Miller, *Radicals and Conservatives,* 295-96, 304.

51. Booker T. Washington to Theodore Roosevelt, October 4, October 7, October 17, November 6, December 17, December 24, 1901, Roosevelt Papers.

52. Booker T. Washington to Theodore Roosevelt, October 7, November 6, December 17, 1901, June 30, 1902, February 20, 1904, Thomas Platt to Roosevelt, February 24, 1904, Roosevelt Papers; Harlan, *Washington,* 311; Booker T. Washington to Woodrow Wilson, February 25,

1914, Woodrow Wilson Papers, Library of Congress; John Durham to Whitefield McKinlay, October 24, 1902, Carter Woodson Papers, Library of Congress.
53.   Booker T. Washington to T. Thomas Fortune, November 22, 1904, Washington to John Dancy, November 28, 1904, Washington Papers; Booker T. Washington to Whitefield McKinlay, November 8, 1906, Woodson Papers; Booker T. Washington to Oswald Garrison Villard, October 28, 1906, Villard Papers; Booker T. Washington to Theodore Roosevelt, January 5, 1902, July 29, 1904, January 4, 1906, Roosevelt Papers.
54.   George Plimpton to Booker T. Washington, October 11, 1890, Rose Cody to Washington, January 28, 1901, Angela Collins to Washington, August 22, August 30, 1902, H. A. Oakman to Washington, August 22, 1902, J. B. Dunn to Washington, August 4, 1903, Washington Papers; Washington to Francis J. Garrison, May 2, 1900, Garrison to Washington, May 8, 1905, Francis J. Garrison Papers, Schomburg Collection; Washington to Horatio N. Rust, December 23, 1895, H. N. Rust Collection, Henry Huntington Library, San Marino, California; H. L. Wayland to Robert Ogden, September 10, 1896, Ogden Papers; Washington, *Up From Slavery,* 129-30.
55.   Trustees are listed on Tuskegee letterheads. By 1909 they included Seth Low, George Foster Peabody, Paul Warburg, Robert Ogden, William C. Wilcox, H. H. Hanna, V. H. Tulane, and William Schieffelin. See also Booker T. Washington to Theodore Roosevelt, December 12, 1911, Roosevelt Papers; Edward C. Kirkland, *Dream and Thought in the Business Community, 1860-1900* (Ithaca, 1956), 87, 92-97.
56.   Booker T. Washington to Seth Low, July 12, 1897, August 20, 1906, February 16, 1909, "List of Legacies Due Tuskegee Through September, 1910," Low Papers; Booker T. Washington to George Foster Peabody, November 23, 1901, Peabody Papers; Robert R. Moton to Edgar Bancroft, September 25, 1916, Moton to William C. Wilcox, January 11, 1917, Moton to Bancroft, January 4, 1920, Bancroft Family Papers, Columbia University; Anson Phelps Stokes to W. E. B. DuBois, October 8, 1940, Anson Phelps Stokes Papers, Yale University; Spencer, *Booker T. Washington,* 115-16.
57.   W. N. Sheets to Booker T. Washington, June 7, 1901, Issac Fisher to Washington, August 2, August 18, August 19, 1902, Hugh Brown to Washington, March 15, 1902, August 25, 1904, Washington Papers; William Simmons, *Men of Mark: Eminent, Progressive and Rising* (Cleveland, 1887), 829-32, for biography of Corbin.
58.   W. E. B. DuBois to Oswald Garrison Villard, March 24, 1905 Villard Papers: Elliot Rudwick, *W. E. B. DuBois, A Study in Minority Group Leadership* (Philadelphia, 1960), 88-93, describes Washington's subsidies of the press. Rudwick is correct to note Washington's influence on editorial policy, but this control of political opinion (itself not complete) could not be translated into control of format or social values.

59. Emma Lou Thornbrough, "American Negro Newspapers, 1880-1904," *Business History Review*, XL (1966), 468-69, 478-79, 489; L. M. Hershaw, "The Negro Press in America," *Charities*, XV (October 7, 1905), 66-68.

60. Booker T. Washington to Emmett Scott, July 9, 1904, Fred Moore to Scott, November 11, 1907, Washington to Moore, March 28, March 29, July 20, 1910, Scott to Moore, September 5, September 23, 1910, Scott to George Knox, November 15, 1911, Knox to Scott, November 19, 1911, Washington Papers.

61. E. E. Cooper to Booker T. Washington, September 8, 1899, April 27, May 2, 1901, T. Thomas Fortune to Washington, August 20, 1902, January 6, 1906, Fred Moore to Emmet Scott, October 8, 1907, Moore to Washington, January 31, 1910, Washington Papers; Washington to Francis J. Garrison, May 20, 1905, Garrison Papers.

62. Robert Terrell to John E. Bruce, March 29, 1896, Booker T. Washington to Bruce, April 21, 1896, John E. Bruce Papers; E. E. Cooper to Washington, September 8, 1899, August 5, 1901, Washington Papers; Thornbrough, "American Negro Newspapers," 469.

63. W. E. B. DuBois to Oswald Garrison Villard, March 25, 1905, with series of letters and supporting "exhibits," Villard Papers; John C. Dancy to Booker T. Washington, December 16, 1904, Emmett Scott to Washington, December 16, 1904, Washington Papers; E. E. Cooper to Robert Terrell, August 11, 1904, Robert Terrell Papers, Library of Congress.

64. Booker T. Washington to T. Thomas Fortune, January 27, 1904, Fred Moore to Washington, March 23, 1910, Washington Papers; Washington to Oswald Garrison Villard, July 20, 1903, Villard Papers; Fortune, "The Negro Publisher," *Proceedings of National Negro Business League*, I: 159; Emma Lou Thornbrough, *T. Thomas Fortune: Militant Negro Journalist* (Chicago, 1972), 205, 220, 269, 308.

65. T. Thomas Fortune to Booker T. Washington, March 25, 1901, Emmet Scott to Washington, December 16, 1904, Washington Papers; New York *Age*, September 27, 1906.

66. Booker T. Washington to T. Thomas Fortune, November 22, 1904; Washington Papers; New York *Age*, January 26, February 2, 1905.

67. E. E. Cooper to Booker T. Washington, December 12, 1901, Emmett Scott to Washington, December 16, 1904, Washington to T. Thomas Fortune, January 27, 1904, Fortune to Washington, January 6, 1906, Washington Papers; New York *Age*, October 3, 1907; Thornbrough, *T. Thomas Fortune*, 296-97; August Meier, "Booker T. Washington and the Negro Press, With Special Reference to the Colored American Magazine," *Journal of Negro History*, XXXVIII (1953), 73-74; Gilbert Osofsky, *Harlem: The Making of a Ghetto: Negro New York, 1890-1930* (New York, 1971), 96-101.

68. Fred Moore to Booker T. Washington, November 11, 1907, Washington to Moore, March 28, 1910, Scott to Moore, September 5, 1910, Washington to Moore, June 7, June 10, 1911, Moore to Washington,

September 8, 1911, Moore to Scott, October 7, 1911, Moore to Washington, December 19, 1912, Washington to Moore, February 17, 19, November 18, 1913, Scott to James Weldon Johnson, December 28, 1915, Washington Papers; J. Max Barber to Mary Church Terrell, November 26, 1907, Mary Church Terrell Papers, Library of Congress; James Weldon Johnson, *Along This Way* (New York, 1933), 302-03; Meier, "Booker T. Washington and the Negro Press," 79-80.

69.   Booker T. Washington to Fred Moore, March 28, 1910, Moore to Washington, March 29, 1910, Emmett Scott to Moore, September 25, 1910, December 28, 1910, Washington to Moore, June 7, June 10, 1911, Scott to Lester Walton, March 27, 1913, Walton to Scott, March 31, 1913, Washington Papers; *Crisis*, VI (June, 1913), 65; Robert J. Alexander, "Negro Business in Atlanta," *Southern Economic Journal*, XVII (1951), 451-64.

70.   Fred Moore to Booker T. Washington, February 22, 1911, Washington to Moore, July 5, 1911, Lester Walton to Emmett Scott, May 2, 1913, Washington Papers; Osofsky, *Harlem*, 120, 133; Roi Ottley and Willaim J. Weatherby, *The Negro in New York: An Informal Social History, 1626-1940* (New York, 1969), 235.

71.   Lester Walton to Emmett Scott, March 31, 1911, Booker T. Washington to Fred Moore, December 18, 1911, June 12, 1913, Walton to Scott, July 9, September 28, 1913, Scott to Walton, September 19, 1913, Walton to Washington, December 14, 1913, Moore to Scott, October 8, 1907, Scott to Moore, October 10, 1907, Washington Papers; Louis R. Harlan, "Booker T. Washington in Biographical Perspective," *American Historical Review*, LXXVI (December, 1970), 1595-96, speculates on the sources of Washington's "secretive" nature.

72.   George B. Cortelyou to Booker T. Washington, May 6, 1899, Thomas J. Calloway to Washington, July 5, 1900, Washington Papers; W. E. B. DuBois to Willaim Monroe Trotter, May 20, 1905, Francis Broderick Notes to the W. E. B. DuBois Papers, Schomburg Collection; W. E. B. DuBois, *The Autobiography of W. E. B. DuBois* (New York, 1969), 221; DuBois, "The American Negro at Paris," *American Monthly Review of Reviews*, XXII (November 1900), 575-77.

73.   Washington *Bee*, August 11, 1900; *Proceedings of National Negro Business League*, I: 1-2, 7-8, 31, 33-34, 93.

74.   H. A. Rucker to Booker T. Washington. March 28, 1901, Giles Jackson to Washington, March 25, 1902, Washington to J. W. E. Bowen, April 22, 1905, Fred Moore to Washington, March 23, 1910, Washington to Moore, May 3, 1910, Washington to Andrew Carnegie, December 16, 1910, John Bertram (Carnegie's secretary) to Washington, December 29, 1910, Washington Papers; Booker T. Washington to Messrs. Cole and Johnson, September 22, 1905, James Weldon Johnson Papers, Yale University; Washington *Bee*, September 6, 1902, August 29, 1903; New York *Age*, June 29, August 17, 1905; Spear, *Black Chicago*, 86-87.

75. Louis R. Harlan, "Booker T. Washington and the National Negro Business League," in William G. Shade and Roy Herrenkahl, eds., *Seven on Black* (Philadelphia, 1969), 81-82; Washington *Bee,* September 6, 1902; Stephen R. Fox, *The Guardian of Boston: William Monroe Trotter* (New York, 1970), 24-25.

76. Booker T. Washington to Robert R. Moton, August 21, 1911, Robert Park to Emmett Scott, September 21, 1912, Washington Papers; *Proceedings of National Negro Business League,* I: 100-03, 182, 188, 196; New York *Age,* November 30, 1905.

77. E. E. Cooper to Booker T. Washington, November 1, 1901, Fred Moore to Washington, March 23, 1910, March 17, 1914, Samuel Courtney to Washington, April 19, 1915, J. S. Harrison to Washington, July 20, 1915, Washington to Jesse Bingha, July 25, 1915, Washington Papers; Charles Anderson to Robert Terrell, February 17, 1914, Robert Terrell Papers; Osofsky, *Harlem,* 95, 97.

78. Emmett Scott to Fred Moore, March 11, 1912, Booker T. Washington to Robert R. Moton, May 9, 1914, Moton to Washington, April 28, 1915, Washington to Moton, May 26, 1915, Moton to Scott, July 10, 1915, Scott to Moton, July 14, 1915, Washington Papers; Scott and Stowe, *Booker T. Washington,* 185. See Frazier, *Black Bourgeosie,* 157-61, for a harsh critique of the Business League as the proponent of the "myth" that small businesses could provide the lever for social mobility and economic security for Blacks. While Frazier, Like Washington, condemned the salaried middle class for its failure to promote a general economic and social rehabilitation of Black communities, he also saw the limitations in Washington's economic alternative—the bourgeosie.

79. Booker T. Washington to Ray S. Baker, March 16, 1907, Baker Papers.

CHAPTER 3

1. Elliott Rudwick, *W. E. B. DuBois: A Study in Minority Group Leadership* (Philadelphia, 1960); Stephen R. Fox, *The Guardian of Boston: Willaim Monroe Trotter* (New York, 1971).

2. C. Vann Woodward, *Origins of the New South, 1877-1913* (Baton Rouge, 1951), 356-61.

3. Here they have followed the views of Kelly Miller, *Radicals and Conservatives* (New York, 1968), 25-42, and Ray S. Baker, *Following the Color Line* (New York, 1964), 222-6. See Ralph Bunche, "A Brief and Tentative Analysis of Negro Leadership," Memorandum for the Carnegie-Myrdal Study (1940), 2, 14-15, Schomburg Collection, New York Public Library; Meier, *Negro Thought in America, 1880-1915* (Ann Arbor, 1953), 110, 198-200; Louis R. Harlan, "Booker T. Washington in Biographical Perspective," *American Historical Review,* LXXV (October 1970), 1581-99.

4. Booker T. Washington to Archibald Grimke, June 5, 1899, Archibald Grimke Papers, Howard University; Charles Chestnutt to Washington, November 16, 1901, Booker T. Washington Papers, Library of Congress.

5. Henry May, *The End of American Innocence: A Study of the First Years of Our Own Time, 1912-1917* (New York, 1959), vii-xi, and passim.

6. Wilson J. Moses, *The Golden Age of Black Nationalism, 1850-1925* (Hamden, Conn., 1978), 197-219.

7. Charles Valentine, "Voluntary Ethnicity and Social Change: Classism, Racism, Marginality, Mobility and Revolution, with Special Reference to Afro-Americans and Other Third World Peoples," *Journal of Ethnic Studies,* III (Spring 1975), 1-27.

8. On the social network of the politicians, journalists, and entertainers see John S. Durham to Whitefield McKinlay, January 6, 1897, and other letters in Carter Woodson Collection, Library of Congress; Edward E. Brown to Archibald Grimke, November 28, 1899, Grimke Papers; E. E. Cooper to John E. Bruce, April 24, 1899, John E. Bruce Papers, Schomburg Collection; Constance M. Green, *The Secret City: A History of Race Relations in the Nation's Capital* (Princeton, 1967), Chap. 7; Allison Blakely, "Black US Consuls and Diplomats and Black Leadership, 1880-1920," *Umoja,* 1 (Spring 1977), 1-16; Kenneth Kusmer, *A Ghetto Takes Shape, Black Cleveland, 1870-1930* (Urbana, Ill., 1976), 121-122.

9. Archibald Grimke to John F. Andrew, et al., June 30, 1892, Grimke Papers; Kelly Miller, "Migration and Distribution of the Negro Population as Affecting the Elective Franchise," American Negro Academy, *Occasional Paper 11* (Washington, 1905); W. E. B. DuBois, "Careers Open to College-Bred Negroes," in Two Addresses by Alumni of Fisk University (Nashville, 1898), 2-14; Samuel McCune Lindsay, "The American Negro," unpublished talk delivered at the University of Pennsylvania, 1897, Ms. in the Samuel McCune Lindsay Papers, Columbia University.

10. Paul L. Dunbar to Colonel Robert G. Ingersoll, February 12, 1897, Gumby Collection, Columbia University; John S. Durham to Whitefield McKinlay, January 6, 1897, October 14, 1902, Woodson Collection; Theodore Roosevelt to Robert Terrell, June 18, 1897, Robert Terrell Papers, Library of Congress; E. E. Cooper to John E. Bruce, April 24, 1899, Bruce Papers; John S. Durham, "The Labor Unions and the Negro," *Atlantic Monthly,* LXXXI (February 1898), 222, 226, 228-29.

11. John Dancy to Charles Anderson, May 4, 1906, John E. Bruce to Melvin Chisulm, May 8, 1906, Robert Terrell to Chisulm, May 9, 1905, T. T. Fortune to Chisulm, May 10, 1906, James Weldon Johnson Papers, Yale University; John R. Lynch, *The Facts of Reconstruction* (New York, 1913), 285-94; Vincent DeSantis, *Republicans Face the Southern Question: The New Departure Years, 1877-1897* (Baltimore, 1959), 129-31, 172-73; Washington *Bee,* December 4, 18, 1897.

12. Washington *Bee,* November 20, 1897, March 19, April 9, 1898, June 6, 1903.

13. Emmett Scott to John E. Bruce, September 23, November 18, 1895, Booker T. Washington to Bruce, April 21, 1896, John E. Bruce Ms., untitled, ca. 1900, Bruce Papers; Calvin Chase to Booker T. Washington, January 28, 1901, T. Thomas Fortune to Washington, October 5, 1901, E. E. Cooper to Washington, January 28, 1901, Washington Papers; John S. Durham to Whitefield McKinlay, October 14, 1902, Woodson Collection.

14. Harlan, *Booker T. Washington,* 256-57.

15. James S. Clarkson to Booker T. Washington, February 7, 1896, G. W. Atkinson to Washington, October 28, 1899, Grover Cleveland to Washington, December 3, 1899, Washington Papers; George F. Hoar to John E. Bruce, February 25, 1895, Clarkson to Bruce, November 25, 1896, Bruce Papers.

16. Miller, *Radicals and Conservatives,* 31-32; W. E. B. DuBois, "The Possibilities of the Negro: The Advanced Guard of the Race," *The Booklovers Magazine,* II (July 1903), 7-8; S. W. Bennet to Whitefield McKinlay, December 17, 1902, Woodson Papers; E. E. Cooper to Booker T. Washington, January 28, November 7, December 12, 1901, Washington Papers.

17. Samuel P. Hays, "The Politics of Reform in Municipal Government in the Progressive Era," *Pacific Northwest Quarterly,* LV (October 1964), 157-69; Lee F. Pendergras, "the Formation of a Municipal Reform Movement: The Municipal League of Seattle," *Pacific Northwest Quarterly* LXVI (January 1975), 12-25; Zane L. Miller, *Boss Cox's Cincinnati: Urban Politics in the Progressive Era* (New York, 1968), 114-16, 164-67; James B. Crooks, *Politics and Progress: The Rise of Urban Progressivism in Baltimore, 1895-1911* (Baton Rouge, 1968), 19, 93-95, 108-26, 195-221.

18. W. E. B. DuBois, "The Black Vote of Philadelphia," *Charities,* XV (October 7, 1905), 33-34; Miller, *Boss Cox's Cincinnati,* 165-67; Crooks, *Politics and Progress,* 8-9, 145; Frances R. Keller, *An American Crusade: The Life of Charles Waddell Chestnutt* (Provo, Utah, 1978), 244.

19. T. T. Fortune, "Why We Organize a National Afro-American League,"*The Afro-American Budget,* I (February 1890), 233-34; Emma Lou Thornbrough, "The National Afro-American League, 1887-1908," *Journal of Southern History,* XXVII (1961), 501.

20. Archibald Grimke to John F. Andrew, et al., June 30, 1892, Grimke Papers; Gilbert Osofsky, *Harlem: The Making of a Ghetto, Negro New York, 1890-1930* (New York, 1971), 160-61.

21. Washington *Bee,* August 27, December 24, 1898.

22. Washington *Bee,* November 4, 1899; Thornbrough, "National Afro-American League," 501-03; Booker T. Washington to Charles Anderson, February 25, 1911, Anderson to Emmett Scott, March 28, 1914, Washington Papers.

23. Fox, *Guardian of Boston,* 46-47.

24. Louis R. Harlan, *Separate and Unequal, Public School Campaigns and Racism in the Southern Seaboard States, 1901-1915* (New York, 1968), 75-101; Robert Ogden to Booker T. Washington, November 11, 1901, Washington Papers.

25. Booker T. Washington's control of Afro-American Council policy is indicated in Washington to E. H. Stewart, April 7, April 21, July 9, 1904, Washington Papers. Resentment at Washington's maniuplations is indicated in W. E. B. DuBois to Albert Bushnell Hart, October 9, 1905, Francis Broderick Notes to the W. E. B. DuBois Papers, Schomburg Collections; Charles Bentley to Archibald Grimke, March 20, 1905, DuBois to Grimke, March 21, 1905, Grimke Papers.

26. Washington *Bee,* January 8, March 26, 1898.

27. William S. Scarborough to Booker T. Washington, August 16, 1902, Washington Papers.

28. "The Reminiscences of William Edward Burghardt DuBois," Columbia University Oral History Project, 1963, p. 149

29. William Monroe Trotter to Ray S. Baker, October 5, 1907, Ray S. Baker Papers, Library of Congress.

30. Washington *Bee,* July 26, 1902, July 11, August 8, 1903; Booker T. Washington to Whitefield McKinlay, August 3, 1903, Woodson Collection. The incident and its aftermath are treated in detail in Fox, *Guardian of Boston,* 31-80. Booker T. Washington, *The Rights and Duties of the Negro* (n.p., 1903), is the published version of the Louisville talk.

31. The shortcomings of a Harvard education in the 1890s have been noted by W. E. B. DuBois, *Dusk of Dawn: An Essay Toward an Autobiography of a Race Concept* (New York, 1940), 40-41; Lawrence Veysey, *The Emergence of the American University* (Chicago, 1965), 87-96. John Durham to Whitefield McKinlay, September 5, 1902, Woodson Collection.

32. Booker T. Washington to Theodore Roosevelt, March 27, 1903, Roosevelt Papers, Library of Congress; James Hayes to Whitefield McKinlay, July 9, 1903, Woodson Collection; Washington *Bee,* January 10, January 24, June 13, June 27, August 9, 1903; John M. Langston, *From the Virginia Plantation to the National Capital* (Hartford, 1894), 490; Fox, *Guardian of Boston,* 82.

33. Washington *Bee,* October 17, October 31, December 19, 1903.

34. Emery T. Morris to Archibald Grimke, October 19, 1911, Grimke Papers; J. Milton Waldron to William G. McAdoo, March 12, April 5, 1913, William M. Trotter to McAdoo, March 12, 1913, William Gibbs McAdoo Papers, Library of Congress; Fox, *Guardian of Boston,* 111-12.

35. John S. Phillips to Booker T. Washington, April 29, 1910, Jon B. McKee to Washington, May 4, 1910, "Bert Williams" manuscript, May 5, 1910, Harry Burleigh to Washington, August 2, 1915, Washington Papers; Washington to James Weldon Johnson, August 29, 1904, Emmett Scott to Johnson, August 3, 1915, Johnson Papers; W. E. B. DuBois to Anson Phelps Stokes, August 22, 1940, Anson Phelps Stokes Papers, Yale

University; W. E. B. DuBois, "The American Negro At Paris," *The American Monthly Review of Reviews,* XXII (November 1900), 577.

36.   Paul L. Dunbar to Mrs. Dunbar, May 16, 1898, Paul L. Dunbar Papers, Schomburg Collecton; Paul L. Dunbar, "Negro Life In Washington," *Harper's Weekly,* XLIV (January 13, 1900), 40.

37.   E. E. Cooper to Booker T. Washington, December 17, 1901, Washington Papers; Paul L. Dunbar to Brand Whitlock, December 26, 1900, Allen Nevins Collection, Columbia University.

38.   Representative works of Blacks utilizing the style of social research and the emphasis on discrimination as the basis of Black problems in cities are William L. Bukley, "The Industrial Condition of the Negro in New York City," *Annals of the American Academy of Political and Social Science,* XXVII (May 1906), 590-96; R. R. Wright, Jr., "The Negro in Times of Industrial Unrest," *Charities,* XV (October 7, 1905), 69-73. See also,Lindsay, "American Negro," 7.

39.   On the struggle to obtain funding for research see Carter Woodson to Frederick Bancroft, November 26, 1927, Bancroft Family Papers, Columbia University; Carter Woodson to Benjamin Brawley, January 7, 1932, NAACP Papers, Library of Congress; W. E. B. DuBois to Board of Directors, Encyclopedia of the Negro, May 29, 1941, Stokes Papers; Dr. Guy Johnson, "My Recollections of W. E. B. DuBois," January 1976, Ms. supplied to the author.

40.   W. E. B. DuBois, "Race Traits and Tendencies of the American Negro, by Frederick Hoffman," *Annals,* IX (January 1897), 127-33; "Reminiscences of William Edward Burghardt DuBois," 134. Hoffman believed his work would materially assist Blacks. See Frederick Hoffman to John R. Shillady, January 31, 1918, NAACP Papers. See also Mary W. Ovington to W. E. B. DuBois, June 10, June 16, October 7, 1904, W. E. B. DuBois Papers, formerly in custody of Dr. Herbert Aptheker.

41.   W. E. B. DuBois, *The Philadelphia Negro: A Social Study* (Philadelphia 1899), 322-26.

42.   Ibid., 282-84, 296-97.

43.   Ibid., 177, 309-21.

44.   Ibid., 392-3; DuBois, "The Negroes of Farmville, Virginia: A Social Study," U.S. Bureau of Labor, *Bulletin No. 14* (January 1898), 37; id., "The Negro in the Black Belt: Some Social Sketches," U.S. Bureau of Labor, *Bulletin No. 22* (May 1899), 401, 416-17.

45.   DuBois, *Philadelphia Negro,* 395.

46.   W. E. B. DuBois to Booker T. Washington, April 1, 1896, September 22, October 31, 1898, February 17, 1900, Washington Papers; W. E. B. DuBois, "Results of Ten Tuskegee Conferences," *Harper's Weekly,* XLI (June 22, 1901), 641.

47.   Nick Chiles to Booker T. Washington, November 12, 1906, Washington Papers; Emmett Scott to Mary C. Terrell, March 22, 1904, Terrell to Mr. Pinckett, September 9, 1906, John Milholland to Terrell, September 17, 1907, Mary C. Terrell Papers, Library of Congress: [Mary

Terrell], "What it Means to be Colored in the Capital of the United States," *Independent*, LXII (January 24, 1907), 181-86; Terrell, "A Plea for the White South by a Colored Woman," *The Nineteenth Century and After*, LX (July 1906), 70-84; Kelly Miller, *Radicals and Conservatives*, 31-32; Archibald Grimke, "Why Disfranchisement is Bad," *Atlantic Monthly*, XLIV (July 1904) 72-81.

48. George Foster Peabody to Kelly Miller, October 4, 1903, Booker T. Washington to Emmett Soctt, December 16, 1905, Washington Papers; Scott to Mary C. Terrell, March 22, 1904, Hallie Queen to Terrell, January 2, April 16, 1909, Mary C. Terrell Papers; Thomas A. Church to Robert Terrell, November 15, 1915, Robert Terrell Papers, Library of Congress.

49. Edward E. Wilson, "The Joys of Being a Negro," *Atlantic Monthly*, LCVII (February 1906), 245-50.

50. Ethel Perry Chestnutt to Booker T. Washington, March 7, 1901, Charles Chestnutt to Washington, November 16, Novermber 25, 1901, Washington Papers; Charles W. Chestnutt, *Frederick Douglass* (Boston, 1899), 68; Keller, *American Crusade*, 188-91.

51. Frederick Douglass, "Why is the Negro Lynched?," in Phillip Foner, ed., *The Life and Writings of Frederick Douglass* IV (New York, 1955), 505.

52. Charles W. Chestnutt, *The Wife of His Youth and Other Stories of the Color Line* (Ridgewood, N.J., 1967), 93, 294, 313, 232.

53. Keller, *American Crusade*, 188-91.

54. Robert Bone, *The Negro Novel in America* (New Haven, 1965), 37; Sylvia Render, "Introduction," *The Short Fiction of Charles W. Chestnutt* (Washington, 1974), 48-49.

55. Charles W. Chestnutt, *The Marrow of Tradition* (Ann Arbor, 1969), 178-79, 189-90; Chestnutt, "Disfranchisement," in Booker T. Washington, et al., *The Negro Problem* (New York, 1969), 100; Russell Ames, "Social Realism in Charles Chestnutt," reprinted in Robert Hemenway, ed., *The Black Novelist* (Columbia, Mo., 1970), 27, suggests that Chestnutt used violence realistically while continuing the stereotyped characters.

56. W. E. B. DuBois, *The Souls of Black Folk* (Greenwich, Conn., 1963), 166-80; James Weldon Johnson, *The Autobiograpny of an Ex-Colored Man* (New York, 1912), 188-90; Archibald Grimke, "The Sex Question and Race Segregation," *Papers of the American Negro Academy* (Washington, 1916), 3-24.

57. Charles Chestnutt to Booker T. Washington, March 5, 1904, Washington Papers.

58. Charles Chestnutt, *The Conjure Woman* (Boston, 1899), passim, demonstrates how illiterate Blacks used folklore to manipulate whites. Render, ed., *Short Fiction of Chestnutt*, 18-19, summarizes the scholarship that suggests that Chestnutt wished to portray the dialect and folklore of the Fayetteville Negroes accurately.

59. Charles Chestnutt to W. E. B. DuBois, June 27, 1903, in Herbert Aptheker, ed., *The Correspondence of W. E. B. DuBois: Vol. 1, Selections, 1877-1934* (Amherst, 1973), 56-57; DuBois, "Careers Open to College-bred Negroes," 5; DuBois, "The Conservation of Races," in Howard Brotz, ed., *Negro Social and Political Thought, 1850-1920* (New York, 1966), 486-87. Lawrence J. Friedman, *The White Savage: Racial Fantasies in the Postbellum South* (Englewood Cliffs, N.J., 1970), 126-47, for a discussion of some of the ambiguities for Blacks who accepted white middle-class decorum.

60. Paul L. Dunbar to William Dean Howells, July 13, 1896, William Dean Howells Papers, Houghton Library, Harvard University.

61. John S. Durham to Whitefield McKinlay, October 14, 1902, Woodson Collection; James Weldon Johnson to Mrs. Johnson, January 30, 1914, Johnson Papers.

62. Harry Burleigh to Booker T. Washington, August 2, 1915, Washington Papers; Washington to James Weldon Johnson, January 3, 1913, Emmett Scott to Johnson, November 25, 1913, Johnson papers.

63. James Weldon Johnson, *Along This Way* (New York, 1933), 172-73; Mary White Ovington, *Half A Man: The Status of the Negro in New York* (New York, 1969), 127-36.

64. DuBois, *Souls of Black Folk*, 22, 42-54; W. E. B. DuBois to George F. Peabody, August 28, 1911, Peabody Papers, Library of Congress.

65. On DuBois and Turner see William Toll, "W. E. B. DuBois and Frederick Jackson Turner: The Unveiling and Preemption of America's 'Inner History,'" *Pacific Northwest Quarterly*, LX (April 1974), 66-78. On cultural Zionism see "The Spiritual Revival," *Selected Essays by Ahad-Ha-Am* (Philadelphia, 1912), 253-305. DuBois, *Souls of Black Folk*, 148-51. Moses, *Golden Age of Black Naitonalism*, 156-62, describes DuBois's adherence to *Ethiopianism*, a teleological philosophy that combines a belief in the decline in the materialistic West and the rise of a spiritual African race. DuBois, of course, combined a belief in a Black cultural Renaissance with careful sociological research and the virtues of democratic citizenship. Moses carries DuBois's Ethiopianism too far out of context and is probably not correct to assert that DuBois did not care to do careful sociology. The ambiguities in DuBois's thought are more carefully dissected in Arnold Rampersad, *The Art and Imagination of W. E. B. DuBois* (Cambridge, Mass., 1976), 68-69, 88-90, which emphasized the mythic qualities in *The Souls of Black Folk*.

66. DuBois, *Souls of Black Folk*, 23, 148; Fritz Stern, *The Politics of Cultural Despair: A Study in the Rise of the Germanic Ideology* (New York, 1965).

67. W. E. B. DuBois, "The Talented Tenth," in Washington, ed., *Negro Problem*, 61.

68. DuBois, *Souls of Black Folk*, 65-73; Chestnutt, *Wife of His Youth*, 311; Chestnutt, *Marrow of Tradition*, 190, 251. DuBois, ed., *The*

Negro American Family (Atlanta, 1908), 10-18, 42-45.

69.   J. Frank Armstrong to Booker T. Washington, July 1, 1903, Washington to Charles F. Smith, December 9, 1903, Washington Papers; W. E. B. DuBois to George F. Peabody, December 28, 1903, Peabody Papers.

70.   Jessie Fauset to W. E. B. DuBois, December 26, 1903, Hallie Queen to DuBois, February 2, 1907, in Aptheker, ed., *Correspondence of DuBois*, I: 66, 125-26; Johnson, *Autobiography of Ex-Colored Man*, 21.

71.   Rudwick, *DuBois*, 94-119; DuBois, *Autobiography*, 247-53.

72.   By 1913 the Music and Lecture Guild of New England engaged DuBois and Mary Church Terrell as well as Washington to speak on different aspects of Negro social conditions. See Alexina C. Barrell to Mary Church Terrell, June 30, 1913, Mary C. Terrell Papers.

73.   New York *Age*, March 9, 1905; William M. Trotter to W. E. B. DuBois, March 26, 1905, DuBois to Trotter, March 26, 1905, Broderick Notes; W. E. B. DuBois, "The Niagara Movement," *Voice of the Negro*, II (September 1905), 619.

74.   DuBois, "Niagara Movement," 620-22; Rudwick, *DuBois*, 94-95; Gunnar Murdal, *An American Dilemna* (New York, 1964), 742-43.

75.   L. M. Hershaw, "The Negro Press in America," *Charities*, XV (October 7, 1905), 67; Mary Church Terrell, *A Colored Woman in a White World* (Washington, 1968), 222-23.

76.   W. E. B. DuBois, "Debit and Credit," *Voice of the Negro*, II (January 1905), 677; Charles Chestnutt to W. E. B. DuBois, June 27, 1903, in Aptheker, ed., *Correspondence of DuBois*, I: 56-57.

77.   J. W. E. Bowen to Booker T. Washington, December 29, 1903, Bowen to Emmett Scott, February 13, 1904, J. Max Barber to Scott, March 3, 1904, Washington Papers; Kelly Miller, "The Negro as a Political Factor," *Voice of the Negro*, I (January / Febuary 1904), 18-22, 57-64.

78.   Emmett Scott to J. Max Barber, March 30, April 14, 1904, Barber to Scott, April 27, 1904, Washington Papers; Booker T. Washington to Theodore Roosevelt, June 14, 1904, Roosevelt Papers.

79.   J. Max Barber to Emmett Scott, July 18, 1904, Scott to Barber, July 20, 1904, J. W. E. Bowen to Scott, July 21, 1904, Scott to Barber, July 23, 1904, Scott to Booker T. Washington, July 23, 1904, Washington to Scott, July 23, 1904, Barber to George Cortelyou, August 27, 1904, Washington Papers; Washington to Theodore Roosevelt, June 14, July 29, 1904, Roosevelt Papers.

80.   Emmett Scott to J. W. E. Bowen, August 22, 1904, Bowen to Scott, September 26, 1904, Bowen to Booker T. Washington, October 19, 1904, Washington to Bowen, October 24, 1904, Bowen to Washington, November 9, 1904, Scott to Bowen, November 21, 1904, Washington to J. Max Barber, December 27, 1904, Scott to Wilford Smith, December 22, 1904, Smith to Scott, December 26, 1904, Washington Papers.

81.   "Shall We Materialize the Negro?" *Voice of the Negro*, II (March 1905) 194-96; John Henry Adams, "Rough Sketches: William

Edward Burghardt DuBois, Ph.D.," ibid., 176-81.

82.   "Tuskegee's Twenty-fifth Anniversary," *Voice of the Negro,* III (May 1906), 315-22; W. E. B. DuBois, "St. Francis of Assisi," *Voice of the Negro,* III (October 1906), 419-26; DuBois, "The Value of Agitation," *Voice of the Negro,* IV (March 1907), 109-110.

83.   W. E. B. DuBois to W. H. Talbert, June 13, 1905, DuBois to Albert B. Hart, September 9, 1905, DuBois to Secretaries of the Niagara Movement, September 13, 1905, Broderick Notes; "Address of the Georgia Equal Rights League," *Voice of the Negro,* III (March 1906), 175-77.

84.   The most prestiguous nonpartisan Black in the capital, Archibald Grimke, refused to join the Niagara Movement. See Charles Bentley to Archibald Grimke, March 30, 1905, and Grimke's penciled reply, Grimke Papers; Rudwick, *DuBois,* 107, 118.

85.   W. E. B. DuBois to Bishop Alexander Walters, April 7, 1908, Broderick Notes; William M. Trotter to Archibald Grimke, December 20, 1910, Grimke Papers; J. Max Barber to Mary Terrell, November 26, 1907, Mary C. Terrell Papers; Charles Crowe, "Racial Violence and Social Reform—Origins of the Atlanta Riot of 1906," *Journal of Negro History,* LIII (July 1968), 234-56.

86.   Crowe, "Racial Violence and Social Reform," 235-39.

87.   New York *Age,* September 6, September 27, October 4, 1906; *Following the Color Line* 18-19.

88.   "Interview with C. B. Wilmer and W. E. B. DuBois," January 31, 1907, Ray S. Baker Papers, Library of Congress.

89.   Mary W. Ovington to Ray S. Baker, November 12, 1906, Baker Papers.

90.   "Interview with Wilmer and DuBois,"

91.   Ibid.

92.   Edgar G. Murphy, *Problems of the Present South,* (New York, 1905) 78; Alfred Holt Stone, *Studies in the American Race Problem* (New York, 1908), 6, 212; Ulrich B. Phillips, "The Plantation as a Civilizing Factor," *The Sewanee Review,* XII (July 1904), 258, 263-67.

93.   "Interview with Wilmer and DuBois"; Stone, *Studies in American Race Problem,* 239-40.

94.   George M. Frederickson, *The Black Image in the White Mind: The Debate on Afro-American Character and Destiny, 1817-1914* (New York, 1971), 283-95.

95.   Edgar G. Murphy, "Shall the Fourteenth Amendment Be Enforced?" *North American Review,* CLXXX (January 1905), 127.

96.   Stone, *Studies in American Race Problem,* 14, 20, 74, 204; Murphy, *Problems of Present South,* 157, 184, 187.

97.   Stone, *Studies in American Race Problem,* 5-13; Murphy, *Problems of Present South,* 7-8; Edgar G. Murphy, *The Basis of Ascendancy* (New York, 1909), xv-xviii. On Stone's appointment at the University of Wisconsin in 1908 see Frederick Jackson Turner to Alfred Holt Stone, May 4, 1908, Turner to A. L. P. Dennis, May 4, 1908, Frederick

Jackson Turner Papers, Huntington Library, San Marino, California.

98. See the frivolous comments in Walter L. Flemming, "The Servant Problem in a Black Belt Village," *The Sewanee Review,* XIII (January 1905), 1-17.

99. "Interview with Wilmer and DuBois;" I. A. Newby, *Jim Crow's Defense, Anti-Negro Thought in America, 1900-1930* (Baton Rouge, 1968), 105, 126; W. E. B. DuBois, "The Economic Future of the Negro," *Publications of the American Economic Association,* series 3, no. 7 (February 1906), 222. DuBois's speech was followed by Alfred Holt Stone's comments on the incapacity of Blacks to succeed without white management.

100. W. E. B. DuBois to Guarantors of *Horizon,* September 1, 1909, DuBois to F. H. M. Murray, October 6, November 11, 1909, Murray to DuBois, February 8, 1910, DuBois to Murray, February 10, 1910, Murray to DuBois, March 7, 1910 and other letters, F. H. M. Murray Papers, Howard University.

101. W. E. B. DuBois to E. C. Williams, January 8, January 19, November 27, 1907, May 20, 1909, Joel Spingarn Papers, Howard University; A. K. Saga to John E. Bruce, March 25, 1907, John E. Bruce Papers; W. E. B. DuBois to Benito Sylvain, January 24, 1907, DuBois to Joseph Booth, February 5, 1907, Broderick Notes.

102. Oswald Garrison Villard to Booker T. Washington, December 13, 1910, February 7, 1911, Villard Papers; Oswald Garrison Villard to Mary C. Terrell, September 19, 1907, Mary C. Terrell Papers.

CHAPTER 4

1. "Booker T. Washington," *Crisis,* XI (December 1915), 82; John S. Durham to Emmett Scott, November 19, 1915, Booker T. Washington Papers, Library of Congress.

2. Horace Mann Bond, "Negro Leadership Since Washington," *South Atlantic Quarterly,* XXIV, 2 (April 1925), 120.

3. Julius Caldwell to Mary Church Terrell, August 9, 1916, Mary Church Terrell Papers, Library of Congress.

4. The publication of Ray S. Baker, *Following the Color Line* (New York, 1908) after the Atlanta race riot encouraged many Blacks to express their grievances. See W. E. B. DuBois to Ray S. Baker, April 3, May 2, 1907, Mary C. Terrell to Baker, April 14, 1907, Oswald Garrison Villard to Baker, May 17, 1907, Ray S. Baker Papers, Library of Congress; James Weldon Johnson to Brander Matthews, November, 1908, James Weldon Johnson Papers, Yale University.

5. DuBois's role is prefigured in Joseph Lundy to John E. Bruce, April 22, 1910, John E. Bruce Papers, Schomburg Collection, New York Public Library.

6. A summary of Ferris's professional career is found in Randall K. Burkett, *Black Redemption: Churchmen Speak for the Garvey Movement* (Philadelphia, 1978), 65-70.

7. William H. Ferris, *The African Abroad: Or His Evolution in Western Civilization, Tracing His Development Under Caucasian Milieu* (New Haven, 1913), 113, 280-1, 339; Washington *Bee*, January 8, 1898.

8. Ferris, *African Abroad*, 13-14, 25, 33; S. P. Fullinwider, *The Mind and Mood of Black America: 20th Century Thought* (Homewood, Ill., 1969), 22.

9. Ferris, *African Abroad*, 34, 190-1, 296-99.

10. Ibid., 909.

11. Ibid., 196 (quotation), 761-980.

12. *Crisis*, VII (January 1914), 147; Fullinwider, *Mind and Mood*, 22; Wilson J. Moses, *The Golden Age of Black Nationalism, 1850-1925* (Hamden, Conn., 1978), 211, 214, Orlando Patterson, *Ethnic Chauvinism: The Reactionary Impulse* (New York, 1977), 9-11.

13. James Weldon Johnson to Brander Matthews, November, 1908, Johnson Papers; Eugene Levy, *James Weldon Johnson: Black Leader, Black Voice* (Chicago, 1973), 127; James Weldon Johnson, *The Auto-biography of an Ex-Colored Man* (New York, 1912).

14. On Johnson's political activities see Emmett Scott to James Weldon Johnson, December 24, 1905, and on the receipt of his book see Scott to Johnson, November 25, 1913, Johnson Papers. See also Johnson to William S. Braithwaite, August 20, 1917, William S. Braithwaite Papers, Houghton Library, Harvard University.

15. [Johnson] *Autobiography*, 75-76, notes how the preoccupation with racial stereotypes constricted the imagination and creativity of the Blacks and the whites in the South. See also, Levy, *James Weldon Johnson*, 130-31.

16. [Johnson] *Autobiography*, 166-67.

17. Ibid., 200, 210.

18. James Weldon Johnson to Walter White, October 19, 1927, NAACP Papers, Library of Congress.

19. [Johnson] *Autobiography*, 157-67.

20. Levy, *James Weldon Johnson*, 137.

21. Wilbur Thierkield to James Weldon Johnson, November 30, 1933, Johnson Papers; [Johnson]*Autobiography*, 103-09.

22. "Fifty Years" is reprinted in James Weldon Johnson, ed., *The Book of American Negro Poetry* (New York, 1931), 130-33. For enthu-siastic reactions see Charles Chestnutt to James Weldon Johnson, January 18, 1913, Booker T. Washington to Johnson, January 3, 1913, Johnson Papers.

23. Booker T. Washington to Fred Moore, July 15, 1911, Washington Papers, Library of Congress.

24. W. E. B. DuBois to Robert U. Johnson, June 6, 1911, the Century Collection, New York Public Library; *Crisis*, II (September 1911),

200; Michael D. Biddis, "The Universal Races Congress of 1911," *Race,* XIII, 1 (July 1971) 37-38.

25.   DuBois view of London is indicated in W. E. B. DuBois to James Weldon Johnson, February 11, 1916, Johnson Papers; *Crisis,* II (September 1911), 360-3; Biddis, "Universal Races Congress," 41, 44.

26.   "Races," *Crisis,* II (August 1911), 157; "The Races Congress," *Crisis,* II (September 1911), 202, 207, 209.

27.   Elliott Rudwick, *W. E. B. DuBois: A Study in Minority Group Leadership* (Philadelphia, 1960), 46-47. DuBois's interest in working in a "center of culture" is expressed in DuBois to Booker T. Washington, April 10, 1900, Booker T. Washington Papers. Roger P. Heller to William Toll, July 21, 1971, letter in author's possession.

28.   Nannie Burroughs to James Weldon Johnson, July 22, 1921, Johnson to Burroughs, August 4, 1921, NAACP Papers.

29.   Louis Harlan, "Booker T. Washington in Biographical Perspective", *American Historical Review,* LXXV (October 1970), 1582-84; "The Reminiscences of William Edward Burghardt DuBois," Columbia University Oral History Project, 150.

30.   W. E. B. DuBois to L. M. Hershaw, July 13, 1909, DuBois to George W. Crawford, July 31, 1909, DuBois to "Dear Colleagues," September 27, 1911, Francis Broderick Notes, Schomburg Collection; W. E. B. DuBois to William English Walling, June 13, 1910, NAACP Papers; Oswald Garrison Villard and DuBois to John E. Bruce, August 3, 1912, John E. Bruce Papers; Mary W. Ovington to Joel Spingarn, November 7, 1914, Joel Spingarn Papers, Howard University; DuBois to James Weldon Johnson, November 1, 1916, Johnson Papers; W. E. B. DuBois, "The National Committee on the Negro," *Survey,* XXII (June 12, 1909), 407-09.

31.   Abram Harris to Joel Spingarn, July 27, 1934, Joel Spingarn Papers, New York Public Library; W. E. B. DuBois to Walter White, June 16, 1933, NAACP Papers. See W. E. B. DuBois, "The Economic Future of the Negro," *Publications of the American Economic Association,* series 3, (February 1906), 222.

32.   "Reminiscences of Roger Baldwin," 317; "Reminiscences of Carl Van Vechten," 331; "Reminiscences of George S. Schuyler," 118-19, 292-93, Columbia University Oral History Project. For Charles S. Johnson's view that Black culture in the rural South constituted a mere retention of practices discarded by more mobile whites see his *Shadow of the Plantation* (Chicago, 1934), 12, 151, passim.

33.   W. E. B. DuBois, *Disfranchisement* (New York, 1912), pamphlet advocating woman's suffrage, New York Public Library; John Haynes Holmes to Mary W. Ovington, July 4, 1910, Martha Gruening to May Nerney, July 22, 1913, NAACP Papers; Mary W. Ovington to Joel Spingarn, November 7, 1914, Joel Spingarn Papers, Howard University. W. E. B. DuBois to Mary W. Ovington, April 9, 1914, W. E. B. DuBois Papers, formerly in custody of Dr. Herbert Aptheker.

34.   Nancy J. Weiss, *The National Urban League 1910-1940* (New York, 1974), 68-70; The conflicts within the American Zionist Movement have been ably summarized in Melvin Urofsky, *American Zionism from Herzl to the Holocaust* (New York, 1976), 231-79.

35.   W. E. B. DuBois to Mary W. Ovington, April 9, 1914, W. E. B. DuBois Papers; Rudwick, *DuBois,* 165-78.

36.   Booker T. Washington to Oswald Garrison Villard, December 11, 1910, Washington Papers; Villard to Washington, December 13, 1910, Oswald Garrison Villard Papers, Houghton Library; National Negro Committee, *Race Relations in the United States* (New York, 1910), pamphlet distributed from 20 Vesey Street, notes in Broderick Notes.

37.   "Schuyler Reminiscences," 118-19, 293; May Nerney to James W. Johnson, March 9, 1915, Johnson Papers; Johnson to William S. Braithwaite, January 28, 1914, William S. Braithwaite Papers. See the excellent picture of DuBois and his Black staff in Herbert Aptheker, ed., *The Correspondence of W. E. B. DuBois, Selections,* 1877-1934, Vol. I (Amherst, 1973), 163.

38.   On the Urban League's ideological affinities to Booker T. Washington see Weiss, *National Urban League,* 60-64. Richard R. Wright, Jr., *87 Years Behind the Black Curtain* (Philadelphia and Nashville, 1965), 31, 47-48, 187-97; Allen H. Spear, *Black Chicago: The Making of a Negro Ghetto, 1890-1920* (Chicago, 1967), 112, 184; Gilbert Osofsky, *Harlem: The Making of a Ghetto, Negro New York, 1890-1930* (New York, 1968), 92-123; David Katzman, *Before the Ghetto: Black Detroit in the Nineteenth Century* (Urbana, 1973), 164-66.

39.   W. E. B. DuBois to James W. Johnson, November 18, 1915, Johnson to Benjamin Brawley, November 28, 1917, Johnson Papers; Johnson to William S. Braithwaite, August 20, 1917, Braithwaite Papers; John Dewey to Horace M. Kallen, March 31, [1915], Kallen to Albert Barnes, January 1, 1919, Kallen to Wendell Bush, January 9, 1919, Walter Lippmann to Henry Hurwitz, December 24, 1916 (copy), Horace M. Kallen Papers, American Jewish Archives, Hebrew Union College. Randolph Bourne, "Trans-National America," *Atlantic Monthly,* CXVIII (July, 1916), 86-97.

40.   Mary W. Ovington to W. E. B. DuBois, April 11, November 21, 1914, DuBois Papers; Vachel Lindsay to Joel Spingarn, November 2, 1916, Spingarn to Lindsay, November 6, 1916, Joel Spingarn Papers, New York Public Library; Natalie Burlin to George F. Peabody, March 31, July 27, 1918, George Foster Peabody Papers, Library of Congress.

41.   "The Cost of the *Crisis*," *Crisis,* XI (November 1915), 26.

42.   Ridgley Torrence to James Weldon Johnson, March 27, 1914, Johnson Papers; "A Pageant," *Crisis,* X (September 1915), 230-31; "The Star of Ethiopia," *Crisis,* XI (December, 1915), 90.

43.   Harold Cruse, *The Crisis of the Negro Intellectual* (New York, 1967), 38.

44. Booker T. Washington to Oswald Garrison Villard, May 2, 1908, Villard to Washington, May 4, 1908, Washington to Villard, March 4, 1911, Villard to Washington, March 22, 1911, Langdon Marvin to Villard, December 29, 1909, January 8, 1910, Villard to Marvin, January 11, 1910, Villard Papers; W. E. B. DuBois, *The Autobiography of W. E. B. DuBois* (New York, 1968), 256-57, 289.

45. Oswald Garrison Villard to Joel Spingarn, March 20, 1913, April 16, 1914, William S. Scarborough to Villard, September 18, 1914, Mary W. Ovington to Spingran, November 4, November 7, 1914, May Nerney to Spingarn, n.d., Francis Cardoza to Spingarn, December 18, 1914, Joel Spingarn Papers, Howard University; Oswald Garrison Villard to May Nerney, May 21, 1914, NAACP Papers; DuBois, *Autobiography*, 260-61.

46. W. E. B. DuBois to Oswald Garrison Villard, November 5, 1907, Villard to Thomas Featherstonaugh, November 20, 1907, Oswald Garrison Villard-John Brown Collection, Columbia University; Albert B. Hart to Oswald Garrison Villard, January 5, 1910, Villard Papers; [Oswald] Garrison Villard], "Harper's Ferry and Gettysburg," *The Nation*, LXXXIX (October 28, 1909), 425.

47. Oswald Garrison Villard to Booker T. Washington, January 27, 1908, Villard Paper; Villard to Mrs. Anne Brown Adams, December 13, 1907, Villard-Brown Collection; Richard C. Greener to W. E. B. DuBois, February 4, 1910, in Aptheker, ed., *Correspondence of DuBois*, I: 168-69.

48. Aptheker, ed., *Correspondence of DuBois*, I: 60-65.

49. Arnold Rampersad, *The Art and Imagination of W. E. B. DuBois* (Cambridge, Mass., 1976), 112.

50. W. E. B. DuBois, *John Brown* (Philadelphia, 1909), 247, 263, 344-46.

51. Oswald Garrison Villard, *John Brown, 1800-1859* (New York, 1910), 176, 187; DuBois, *John Brown*, 363-64.

52. Rampersad, *Art and Imagination*, 115; DuBois, *John Brown*, 363-64.

53. Felix Frankfurter to Jacob Billikopf, April 25, 1945, Felix Frankfurter Papers; Library of Congress; Oswald Garrison Villard to Booker T. Washington, December 13, 1910, Villard Papers; DuBois, *Autobiography*, 256-57.

54. W. E. B. DuBois to Mary W. Ovington, April 9, 1914, DuBois Papers; DuBois to Oswald Garrison Villard, March 18, 1913, Villard Papers.

55. W. E. B. DuBois to Mary W. Ovington, April 9, 1914, DuBois Papers; DuBois to John E. Mooreland, June 2, 1914, Joel Spingarn Papers, Howard University.

56. Mary White Ovington to Joel Spingarn, December 20, 1915, Joel Spingarn Papers, New York Public Library; W. E. B. DuBois to Charles Studin, August 21, 1914, Arthur Spingarn Papers, Library of Congress.

57. W. E. B. DuBois to William E. Walling, June 13, 1910, NAACP Papers; Ida Wells Barnett to Joel Spingarn, April 2, 1911, Joel Spingarn Papers, Howard University; Booker T. Washington to Fred Moore, March 31, 1914, Washington Papers.

58. Mary W. Ovington to Joel Spingarn, December 20, 1915, Joel Spingarn Papers, New York Public Library; Joel Spingarn to James Weldon Johnson, October 28, 1916, W. E. B. DuBois to Johnson, November 1, 1916, Johnson Papers; DuBois to Ovington, June 28, 1920, NAACP Papers.

59. Reverdy Ransom to Joel Spingarn, February 19, 1912, Jessie Fauset to Spingarn, February 2, 1913, John Hope to Joel Spingarn, September 24, 1913, Butler Wilson to Joel Spingarn, December 28, 1915, William Pickens to Joel Spingarn, January 11, 1916, Joel Spingarn Papers, Howard University; John Hope to Oswald Garrison Villard, August 30, September 5, 1915, Villard Papers; W. E. B. DuBois to Arthur Spingarn, Joel Springarn, Mary W. Ovington, December 16, 1915, Memo in Arthur Spingarn Papers.

60. Arthur Spingarn to Moorfield Storey, August 11, 1913, May Nerney to Arthur Spingarn, November 18, 1913, Arthur Spingarn Papers; W. E. B. DuBois to James Weldon Johnson, March 31, 1915, Johnson Papers; Grant McConnell, *The Decline of Agrarian Democracy* (New York, 1969), 44-54.

61. Woodrow Wilson to Oswald Garrison Villard, August 23, 1912, Villard Papers; "Editorial," *Crisis,* IV (August 1912), 181; for Wilson's background see Arthur Link, *Wilson: The New Freedom* (Princeton, 1956), 20-21.

62. Oswald Garrison Villard to ?, August 14, 1912, Villard Papers.

63. Josephus Daniels, *Diary,* April 11, 1913, Josephus Daniels Papers; Albert S. Burleson to F. T. Roche, February 18, 1913, Albert S. Burleson Papers; Woodrow Wilson to H. A. Bridgemen, September 8, 1913, Woodrow Wilson Papers; William G. McAdoo to Oswald Garrison Villard, October 27, 1912, William Gibbs McAdoo Papers, all the Library of Congress.

64. Woodrow Wilson to Oswald Garrison Villard, August 21, 1913, Wilson Papers; Arthur Spingarn to Wilson, August 27, 1913, NAACP Papers. Wilson's sense of himself as a southerner is best expressed in Wilson to Frederick Jackson Turner, April 4, 1900, Frederick Jackson Turner Papers, Henry Huntington Library.

65. Kathleen Wolgemuth, "Woodrow Wilson and Federal Segregation." *Journal of Negro History,* XLIV (April 1959), 158-73; Nancy J. Weiss, "The Negro and the New Freedom: Fighting Wilsonian Segregation," *Political Science Quarterly*, LXXXIV, (March 1968), 61-79; Constance McLoughlin Green, *The Secret City: A History of Race Relations in the Nation's Capital* (Princeton, 1967), 171-76. See also Charles Purvis to Whitefield McKinlay, August 11, 1913, Carter Woodson Collection, Library of Congress.

66.   John Skelton Williams to William G. McAdoo, July 25, 1913, MacAdoo Papers.

67.   Congressman Andrew J. Peters to Archibald Grimke, September 26, 1913, Archibald Grimke Papers, Howard University; Mrs. Charlotte Hopkins to May Nerney, July 25, 1913, John Ralph to Nerney, July 29, 1913, NAACP Papers; Charles Sumner Hamlin, diary of March 12, 1914, Charles Sumner Hamlin Papers, Library of Congress; Booker T. Washington to Robert Terrell, February 24, 1910, John R. Lynch to Terrell, March 10, 1910, Robert Terrell Papers, Library of Congress; Link, *Wilson*, 246.

68.   Mary W. Ovington to May Nerney, May 17, 1913, Joel Spingarn Papers, Howard University; Mrs. Carrie Clifford to Oswald Garrison Villard, July 16, 1913, Henry Baker to Villard, September 9, 1913, NAACP Papers.

69.   National Independent Political League (J. Milton Waldron) to William G. McAdoo, March 12, 1913, National Colored Democratic League (Bishop Alexander Walters) to McAdoo, March 10, 1913, National Independent Political League (William M. Trotter), to McAdoo, March 12, 1913, McAdoo Papers.

70.   Booker T. Washington to Bishop Abraham Grant, January 23, 1908, Carter Woodson Collection; W. E. B. DuBois to Bishop Alexander Walters, April 16, 1908, Broderick Notes; Mary W. Ovington to Joel Spingarn, February 22, 1911, Joel Spingarn Papers, Howard University; Minutes of Board of Directors Meeting, NAACP, May 2, June 6, 1911, October 11, 1912, NAACP Papers; Oswald Garrison Villard to Archibald Grimke, November 11, 1913, Grimke Papers; Mary W. Ovington, *The Walls Came Tumbling Down* (New York, 1947), 105.

71.   Oswald Garrison Villard to Alexander Walters, September 10, 1913, Minutes of Board of Directors Meeting, NAACP, November 6, 1913, NAACP Papers; May Nerney to Archibald Grimke, November 7, 1913, Grimke Papers.

72.   William M. Trotter to F. H. M. Murray, September 7, 1913, F. H. M. Murray Papers, Howard University; William M. Trotter to William G. McAdoo, July 21, 1913, Oswald Garrison Villard to McAdoo, August 15, 1913, McAdoo Papers; William M. Trotter to Secretary of NAACP, August 19, 1913, NAACP Papers, William M. Trotter to Joel Spingarn, February 2, 1913, Joel Spingarn Papers, Howard University.

73.   Stephen Fox, *The Guardian of Boston: William Monroe Trotter* (New York, 1970), 171-87. See also W. E. B. DuBois to Joel Spingarn, January 20, 1916, Joel Spingarn Papers, Howard University.

74.   William M. Trotter to F. H. M. Murray, September 7, 1913, Murray to Trotter, September 22, 1913 Murray Papers.

75.   William M. Trotter to Joel Spingarn, January 28, 1914, Joel Spingarn Papers, Howard University.

76.   "The Annual Meeting of the NAACP," *Crisis*, VII (February, 1914), 192-94; Fox, *Guardian of Boston*, 186-87.

77. J. Milton Waldron to William G. McAdoo, April 5, 1913, McAdoo Papers; Mary W. Ovington, Memo to May Nerney, May 17, 1913, Joel Spingarn Papers, Howard University.

78. F. H. M. Murray to William M. Trotter, September 22, 1913, Murray Papers; Neval Thomas to Joel Spingarn, July 21, 1913, Joel Spingarn Papers, Howard University.

79. May Nerney to Joel Spingarn, July 2, 7, 1913, Joel Spingarn, "Memo on D.C. Branch," July, 1913, J. Milton Waldron to Spingarn, July 12, 1913, Neval Thomas to Spingarn, July 21, 1913, Thomas Clarke to Spingarn, July 24, 1913, Thomas to Spingarn, July 27, 1913, Nerney, "Memo on D.C. Branch," July 31, 1913, Alphonso Stafford to Spingarn, August 1, 1913, Joel Spingarn Papers, Howard University; Minutes of Board of Directors Meeting, NAACP, August 5, October 7, 1913, NAACP Papers.

80. May Nerney to Archibald Grimke, September 17, 1913, Grimke Papers; Neval Thomas to Oswald Garrison Villard, May 13, 1928, Villard to Thomas, September 28, 1928, Villard Papers.

81. Archibald Grimke to Theodore Roosevelt, July 20, 1912, Roosevelt to Grimke, August 18, 1912, Richard Greener to Grimke, April 28, 1913, Grimke Papers; Grimke to NAACP, October 20, 1913, Grimke to May Nerney, March 8, May 17, 1914, NAACP Papers; Charles S. Hamlin, "Diary" March 12, May 12-24, 1914, Hamlin Papers, Hamlin to William G. McAdoo, November 21, 1914, McAdoo Papers; August Meier and Elliott Rudwick, "The Rise of Segregation in the Federal Bureaucracy, 1900-1930," *Phylon*, XXVIII (1967), 178-84. A break in the segregation in the Department of the Interior may have occurred in the late 1920s. See James Weldon Johnson to Moorefield Storey, October 13, 1927, NAACP Papers.

82. Arthur Schomburg to John E. Bruce, November 24, 1911, Schomburg to Mrs. Bruce, July 26, 1914, John E. Bruce Papers; W. E. B. DuBois to Kelly Miller, December 9, 1915, Kelly Miller Papers, Howard University.

83. W. E. B. DuBois, "The African Roots of War," *Atlantic Monthly*, XLVII (May, 1915), 707-14, reprinted in Meyer Weinberg, ed., *W. E. B. DuBois, A Reader* (New York, 1970), 360-71.

84. Ibid., 361-62; W. E. B. DuBois, *The Negro* (New York, 1970), 89, 140.

85. DuBois, *The Negro*, 45, 61, 142; id., "African Roots," 365-66; V. I. Lenin, *Imperialism: The Highest Stage of Capitalism* (Moscow, n.d.), 5, 136-40.

86. DuBois, *The Negro*, 145-56; id., "African Roots," 368-70; W. E. B. DuBois to Robert U. Johnson, April 4, 1913, Century Collection.

87. Horace M. Kallen "Nationality and the Jewish Stake in the Great War," 9, pamphlet in Hebrew Union College Collection; id., "Democracy Versus the Melting Pot," *The Nation*, C (February 25, 1915), 217, 219.

88. Kallen, "Democracy Versus the Melting Pot," 194; Horace M. Kallen to Wendell Bush, February 13, 1919, John Dewey to Kallen, March 31, (1915), Kallen Papers; H. L. Mencken to Alain Locke, February 10, (?), Horace M. Kallen to Locke, July 8, 1935, Alain Locke Papers, Howard University.

89. DuBois, *The Negro,* 132-34.

90. John Higham, *Send These to Me, Jews and Other Immigrants in Urban America* (New York, 1975), 106-07, 209-11.

91. The tension between the process of free choice and the compulsions of ethnic loyalty in Kallen's thought are indicated in Patterson, *Ethnic Chauvinism,* 167.

92. Horace M. Kallen to Hera Morgan, April 3, 1958, Kallen Papers.

93. George Shepperson, "Introduction" to *The Negro,* xx-xxv; Letter from Francis Grimke in *Crisis* (June 1916), 83.

CHAPTER 5

1. Richard Wright, *White Man, Listen!* (Garden City, N.Y., 1964), 98. See also, Chinweizu, *The West and the Rest of Us* (New York, 1975), 16; Nathan Huggins, *Harlem Renaissance* (New York, 1971), 6-7.

2. Arno Mayer, *Wilson vs. Lenin, Political Origins of the New Diplomacy, 1917-1918* (Cleveland, 1964), 301, 380-83.

3. Theodore Kornweible, Jr., *No Crystal Stair, Black Life and "The Messenger," 1917-1928* (Westport Conn., 1975), 18-19.

4. Walter White to James Weldon Johnson, September 15, 1921, Johnson to M. A. N. Shaw, January 10, 1923, Cyril Briggs to Johnson, July 18, 1923, NAACP Papers, Library of Congress.

5. George E. Haynes, *Trend of the Races* (New York, 1922), 154.

6. Booker T. Washington to Oswald Garrison Villard, March 21, 1913, Oswald Garrison Villard Papers, Houghton Library, Harvard University; Oswald Garrison Villard to Booker T. Washington, February, 1913, Washington to Villard, February 17, 1913, Villard to Washington, April 4, 1913, Booker T. Washington Papers, Library of Congress.

7. Samuel R. Spencer, Jr., *Booker T. Washington and the Negro's Place in American Life* (Boston, 1955), 178, 190-91, notes that Washington became more critical of discrimination in his later life but finds only personal frustration—not a changing perception of Blacks and their proper relationship to whites.

8. Booker T. Washington, *The Man Farthest Down: A Record of Observation and Study in Europe* (New York, 1912), 13.

9. Booker T. Washington to Robert Park, December 2, 1910, Washington Papers.

10. Washington, *Man Farthest Down,* 77, 163, 293, 315.

11. Booker T. Washington to Robert Park, May 24, 1911, Washington Papers; Mary Church Terrell, *A Colored Woman in a White*

World (Washington, 1968), 67, 84-87; W. E. B. DuBois, *Dusk of a Dawn: An Essay Toward An Autobiography of a Race Concept* (New York, 1968), 45-47; "Starvation and Prejudice," *Crisis,* II (June, 1911), 62-64; "The Man Farthest Down," *Crisis* II (July, 1911), 105-06, 125; "Opinion," *Crisis,* VI (May, 1913), 21-22.

12. Washington, *Man Farthest Down,* 91, 100.

13. Booker T. Washington, "How Denmark Taught Itself Prosperity and Happiness," *The World's Work,* XXII (June, 1911) 14486-94; Washington, *My Larger Education: Being Chapters From My Experience* (New York, 1911), Chap. 11.

14. Robert Park to Booker T. Washington (ca. May 15, 1911), Washington to Park, June 30, 1911, Washington Papers.

15. Washington, *My Larger Education,* 284. Note the advertisements for Black dolls in *Crisis,* II (July, 1911), 131, and succeeding issues. For a discussion of the role of art in illuminating the cultural tensions between Africa and "the West," see James Baldwin, *Nobody Knows My Name* (New York, 1963), 31-32.

16. Robert Park to Booker T. Washington, May 11, 1911, Monroe Work to Washington, June 23, 1913, Washington to Work, June 27, 1913, Washington Papers; Washington to Carter Woodson, October 3, 1915, Carter Woodson Papers, Library of Congress; W. E. B. DuBois to Anson Phelps Stokes, August 22, 1840, Anson Phelps Stokes Papers, Yale University; Washington, *Man Farthest Down,* 101.

17. Emmett Scott to James Weldon Johnson, December 28, 1915, Washington Papers.

18. Booker T. Washington to Robert Park, July 24, 1914, Park to Washington, August 1, 1914, Washington to Andrew Carnegie, January 4, 1915, Washington Papers; Washington, *Up From Slavery* (New York, 1940), 70.

19. Booker T. Washington to Robert Park, August 14, 1914, Washington Papers.

20. Emmett Scott and Lyman Beecher Stowe, *Booker T. Washington: Builder of a Civilization* (New York, 1916), 311. See also Booker T. Washington, "The Basis of Race Progress in the South," in A. M. Trawick, ed., *The New Voice in Race Adjustment* (New York, 1914), 26, 28-29.

21. Booker T. Washington to Carl Kelsey, May 24, 1914, Washington to George Ward (city commissioner, Birmingham, Alabama) July 13, 1914, Washington Papers; Booker T. Washington, "My View of Segregation Laws," *New Republic* (December 4, 1915), 113-14.

22. Hollis Frissell to Oswald Garrison Villard, December 9, 1916, Villard Papers; Philip J. Alston to Booker T. Washington, April 12, 1915, Samuel Courtney to Washington, April 19, 1915, Washington to Alston, April 25, 1915, Robert Moton to Washington, May 5, 1915, Washington Papers; Emmett Scott to James Weldon Johnson, August 3, 1915, James Weldon Johnson Papers, Yale University. For a general discussion of

stereotyping in films see Daniel J. Leab, "The Gamut from A to B: The Image of the Black in Pre-1915 Movies," *Political Science Quarterly,* LXXXVIII (March 1973), 53-70.

23.   W. E. B. DuBois, "Booker T. Washington," *Crisis,* XI (December 1915). DuBois did not learn of Washington's article in the *New Republic* until 1946. See DuBois to Anson Phelps Stokes, December 18, 1946, Stokes Papers.

24.   Woodrow Wilson to Joel Spingarn, July 31, 1916, W. E. B. DuBois, "First Dictated Draft of the Purposes of the Amenia Conference," (1916), Joel Spingarn Papers, Howard University; Elliott Rudwick, *W. E. B. DuBois, A Study in Minority Group Leadership* (Philadelphia, 1960), 184.

25.   W. E. B. DuBois, *The Amenia Conference; An Historic Negro Gathering* (Amenia, New York, 1925), 18; Rudwick, *DuBois,* 186-87; Eugene Levy *James Weldon Johnson: Black Leader, Black Voice* (Chicago, 1973), 182. Benjamin Brawley, *A Social History of the American Negro* (New York, 1921), 365-66, mentions the Universal Races Congress of 1911 and the Pan-African Congress of 1919 as major events in which DuBois participated but does not mention Amenia. Florette Henri, *Black Migration Movement North, 1900-1920* (Garden City, N.Y., 1976). John Hope Franklin, *From Slavery to Freedom, A History of Negro Americans* (New York 4th ed., 1976), 335, notes that Amenia led to "a calm but firm unanimity among Negro leaders" to work for various reforms. The conference itself did not achieve this, and men like DuBois, Moton, and Fred Moore moved in different ideological directions.

26.   Joel Spingarn to James Weldon Johnson, October 28, 1916, W. E. B. DuBois to Johnson, November 1, 1916, Johnson Papers; John C. Napier to Spingarn, August 6, 1918, Roy Nash to Spingarn, October 4, 1925, Neval Thomas to Spingarn, August 13, 1925, John Hope to Spingarn, October 12, 1925, Joel Spingarn Papers, New York Public Library; James Weldon Johnson, *Along This Way: The Autobiography of James Weldon Johnson* (New York, 1933), 308; Terrell, *Colored Woman,* 195.

27.   Emmett Scott to Joel Spingarn, July 11, 1916, Fred Moore to Spingarn, July 20, 1916, William Monroe Trotter to Spingarn, August 23, 1916, Joel Spingarn Papers, Howard University.

28.   DuBois, *Amenia Conference,* 17.

29.   "Announcement of the Amenia Conference," August 24-26, 1916, Mary Church Terrell Papers, Howard University; Spingarn to James Weldon Johnson, August 17, 1916, Johnson Papers.

30.   DuBois, *Amenia Conference,* 14-15; *Crisis,* XIII (April 1917), 285; XIV (May 1917), 9-10, 18-19; XVIII (June 1919), 90-91; Rudwick *W. E. B. DuBois,* 188.

31.   Rudwick, *W. E. B. DuBois,* 186; Stephen R. Fox, *The Guardian of Boston: William Monroe Trotter* (New York, 1971), 204 agrees with Rudwick.

32. Ralph J. Bunche, *A World View of Race* (n.p., 1936), 81-84. For a discussion of how Bunche's generation criticized its elders like DuBois, James Weldon Johnson, and Benjamin Brawley see James O. Young, *Black Writers of the 1930s* (Baton Rouge, 1973), 35-63.

33. Neval Thomas to Joel Spingarn, August 13, 1925, Joel Spingarn Papers, New York Public Library.

34. *Report of the National Advisory Commission on Civil Disorders* (New York, 1968), 239-42.

35. *Crisis*, XII (May, 1916), 10; XII (July, 1916), 142; [George E. Haynes] *The Negro At Work During the World War and During Reconstruction* (Washington, 1921), passim.

36. George E. Haynes,"Negroes Move North I. Their Departure from the South," *The Survey*, XL, 5 (May 4, 1918), 116-18; Kelly Miller, *An Appeal to Conscience: America's Code of Caste a Disgrace to Democracy* (New York, 1918), 48-50, 90-92; Miller, *The Disgrace of Democracy: An Open Letter to President Woodrow Wilson* (Washington, 1917), 4; Robert Russa Moton, "The American Negro and the World War," *The World's Work*, XXXVI (May, 1918), 77; Emmett J. Scott, *Negro Migration During the War* (New York, 1920), 19, 22-25.

37. [Haynes] *Negro at Work*, 12-15; Nancy J. Weiss, *The National Urban League*, 1910-1940 (New York, 1974), 89-90, 108-111.

38. Haynes, "Negroes Move North," 116-18; Scott, *Negro Migration,* 14-18, 92; Charter Woodson, *A Century of Negro Migration* (Washington, 1918), 169-74.

39. Kelly Miller, "The Economic Handicap of the Negro in the North," *Annals*, XXXVII (May, 1906), 81-88.

40. George E. Haynes, "Conditions Among Negroes in the Cities," *Annals*, XLIX (September 1913), 105-06, 108.

41. Scott, *Negro Migration, 6.*

42. Woodson, *Century of Migration,* 182; James Booker to Carter Woodson, July 5, 1920, Woodson Collection.

43. Haynes, "Negroes Move North," 120-21; Scott, *Negro Migration*, 83-92.

44. Scott, *Negro Migration,* 30; Haynes, "Conditions Among Negroes," 119; Miller, *An Appeal to Conscience, 69.*

45. Carter Woodson, *The Miseducation of the Negro* (Washington, 1933), 58-59.

46. W. E. B. DuBois, "The Passing of Jim Crow," The Independent, 91 (July 14, 1917), 54. See also DuBois "The Economic Future of the Negro," *Publications of the American Economic Association,* series 3 (February 1906), 222, 228.

47. For full accounts of the riots see Elliott Rudwick, *Race Riot at East St. Louis, July 2, 1917* (New York, 1972); William Tuttle, Jr., *Race Riot, Chicago in the Red Summer of 1919* (New York, 1974).

48. "East St. Louis," *Crisis,* XIV, 5 (September 1917), 219-38.

49. "Memphis or East St. Louis?" *Crisis, XIV*, 3 (July 1917), 113.

50.   Walter White, "Chicago and Its Eight Reasons," *Crisis,* XVIII, 6 (October 1919), 293-97.

51.   James Weldon Johnson, "The Riots," *Crisis,* XVIII, 5 (September 1919), 243. See also George E. Haynes, "The Opportunity of Negro Labor," *ibid.,* 236.

52.   *Crisis,* XIV (June, 1917), 59; Moton, "American Negro and World War," 77.

53.   Kelly Miller, *Segregation, the Caste System and the Civil Service* (Washington, 1914), Pamphlet in the Howard University Library.

54.   August Meier, "The Racial and Educational Philosophy of Kelly Miller, 1895-1915," *Journal of Negro Education,* XXIX (Spring 1960), 121-27.

55.   Kelly Miller, "The Effect of the European War upon the Colored Race," *The Decennial Brief of the Mu-So-Lit Club of Washington, D.C.* (November 12, 1915), 1, Pamphlet in the Howard University Library.

56.   Kelly Miller, *The Negro Sanhedrin: A Call for a Conference* (Washington, 1923), 16; Miller, *Radicalism and the Negro* (Washington, 1920), 10-11.

57.   Cyril Briggs to James Weldon Johnson, July 18, 1923, NAACP Papers; Kelly Miller, *The Negro's Place in the New Reconstruction* (Washington, n.d.), where internal evidence suggests it was published during the Peace Conference, argues that Negroes must use moral suasion to convince whites that they have the same human interests.

58.   W. E. B. DuBois, "War and the Colored Races," *The Decennial Brief,* 1.

59.   *Crisis,* XVII (January 1919), 110.

60.   *Crisis,* XII (September 1916), 216.

61.   Benjamin Brawley, *A Short History of the American Negro* (New York, 1913), 156, 194.

62.   Benjamin Brawley, *Africa and the War* (New York, 1918), 35. Note the comment of Ray S. Baker, *What Wilson Did At Paris* (New York, 1922), 27, that the German colonies were "the jackpot of the great game."

63.   Brawley, *Social History of American Negro,* 386. For a general discussion of the new Negro mood see pages 372-89. DuBois, Brawley, and Johnson should not be criticized too severely for oversimplifying the relationship between Black Americans and Africa. If World War I convinced Black intellectuals of their need to escape from the tutelage of white Americans, World War II convinced them of the vanity in seeing themselves as "tutors" of Africa. See the sensitive discussion in Baldwin *Nobody Knows My Name,* 49-54.

64.   A. Philip Randolph and Chandler Owen, *Terms of Peace and the Darker Races* (New York, 1917), 3-4, 8.

65.   Ibid., 8, 13, (quotation), 16-17.

66.   Ibid., 27-29.

67.   W. E. B. DuBois, "The Negro Takes Stock," *New Republic,* XXXVI (January 2, 1924) 143; DuBois, "The Position of the Negro in the

American Social Order; Where Do We Go From Here?" *Journal of Negro Education*, VIII (1939) 565.

68. *Crisis*, XII (June, 1916), 74; XII (August, 1916), 169; XII (September, 1916), 217; Brander Matthews, "The Decline and Fall of Negro Minstrelsy," in Matthews, *A Book About the Theater* (New York, 1916), 219-33. Note the comments on the pernicious effects of minstrelsy on the white image of the Negro in James Weldon Johnson, *Negro Americans, What Now* (New York, 1934), 91-92, and in Robert Russa Moton, *Finding a Way Out* (Garden City, N.Y., 1921), 60. For the passing of the "old time darky" see Edgar G. Murphy, *Problems of the Present South* (New York, 1905), 85.

69. J. Rosamond Johnson to Joel Spingarn, February 8, 1917, Joel Spingarn Papers, New York Public Library; George Foster Peabody to Kelly Miller, February 8, 1915, Kelly Miller Papers, Howard University; George Foster Peabody to Franz Boaz, June 10, 1918, George Foster Peabody Papers, Library of Congress.

70. E. Azalia Hackley to George Foster Peabody, August 4, 1918, Peabody Papers.

71. Newton Baker's role in the diverting of Colonel Charles Young is revealed in Newton Baker to Woodrow Wilson, June 26, July 7, 1917, Newton Baker Papers, Library of Congress. Baker's general attitude is revealed in George Foster Peabody to Oswald Garrison Villard, February 3, 1932, Villard Papers. See also Margaret Woodrow Wilson to George Foster Peabody, July 15, 1918, Newton Baker to Peabody, August 8, 1918, Natalie Burlin to J. Rosamond Johnson, August 22, 1918, Joseph E. Blanton to William Aery, September 9, 1918, Peabody Papers.

72. Natalie Burlin to George Foster Peabody, September 6, 1918, James Weldon Johnson to Burlin, October 18, 1918, Peabody Papers; Lawrence W. Levine, *Black Culture and Black Consciousness* (New York, 1977), 168-69.

73. Natalie C. Burlin to George Foster Peabody, March 31, 1918, January 24, 1921, Peabody Papers; *Crisis*, XVII (December 1918), 76; "Black Music and Its Future Translation into Real Art," *Current Opinion* (July 1917), 26-27.

74. James Weldon Johnson to Benjamin Brawley, November 28, 1917, March 28, 1932, Johnson Papers; *Crisis*, XIV (June, 1917), 80-81; Levy, *James Weldon Johnson*, 302-03; Harold Cruse, *The Crisis of the Negro Intellectual* (New York, 1967), 35-39.

75. Benjamin Brawley to William Stanley Braithwaite, December 25, 1917, William S. Braithwaite Papers, Houghton Library; Elsie Clews Parsons to Mrs. James Weldon Johnson, May 2, 1922, Johnson Papers.

76. Rudwick, *W. E. B. DuBois*, 235; George Padmore, *Pan-Africanism or Communism* (New York, 1972), 96. See also Owen Charles Mathurin, *Henry Sylvester Williams and the Origins of the Pan-African Movement, 1869-1911* (Westport, Conn., 1976), 162-3, and Chinweizu, *The West*, 111, 115-83.

77.   *Crisis,* XVIII (May, 1919), 7; James Weldon Johnson, "Africa at the Peace Table and the Descendants of Africans in our American Democracy," in Johnson and Horace Meyer Kallen, *Africa and the World Democracy* (New York, 1919), 14.

78.   DuBois, "Negro Takes Stock," 144-45.

79.   *Crisis,* XXII (November, 1920), 5.

80.   Praise of the *Journal of Negro History* appears in *Crisis,* XIII (December, 1916), 61. DuBois's explanation of his relationship with Scott appears in *Crisis,* XVIII (May, 1919), 11. Carter Woodson to NAACP Board, May 8, 1920; W. E. B. DuBois, "First Report on Trip to the Peace Conference," January 1919, NAACP Papers.

81.   DuBois, "First Report," manuscript in NAACP Papers.

82.   Ibid.

83.   W. E. B. DuBois to Chairman of the Board of Directors, NAACP, January 12, 1919, NAACP Papers.

84.   *Crisis,* XVIII (June 1919), 64, 72.

85.   *Crisis,* XVII (March 1919), 220; *Crisis,* XVIII (June 1919), 70. Note, however, a defense of General Ballou as an officer undertaking an "experiment" who should not be judged too harshly for his stern discipline in Robert Russa Moton to Newton Baker, March 18, 1919, Baker Papers.

86.   *Crisis,* XVIII (June 1919), 59.

87.   Herbert Aptheker, ed., *The Correspondence of W. E. B. DuBois, I, Selections, 1877-1934* (University of Massachusetts Press, 1973), 231, notes that several volumes were prepared but never published. No volume analyzing the significance of Black participation in the war, including especially the political and cultural significance of the changing Black self-perception among Black Americans, West Indians, and Africans, has appeared. Jack D. Foner, *Blacks and the Military in American History* (New York, 1974); Chapter 6 includes a very thin discussion of World War I.

88.   Emmett J. Scott, *The American Negro in the World War* (n.p., 1919), accepts the official American government view that the war grew from racial and nationalistic animosities in Europe.

89.   W. E. B. Dubois, *Darkwater, Voice From Within the Veil* (New York, 1969), 66.

90.   Johnson, "Africa at the Peace Table," 13-16.

91.   *Crisis,* XVII (February 1919), 174; Horace Meyer Kallen, *The Structure of Lasting Peace: An Inquiry into the Motives of War and Peace* (Boston, 1918), 149; Horace M. Kallen to Wendell Bush, January 9, 1919, Horace M. Kallen Papers, American Jewish Archives, Hebrew Union College.

92.   *Crisis,* XVII (March 1919), 224-25; XVII (April 1919), 271-73; Baker, *What Wilson Did,* 35.

93.   *Crisis,* XVII (February 1919), 165; Johnson, "Africa at the Peace Table," 18.

94. *Crisis*, XVII (April 1919), 273; Raymond J. Sontag, *A Broken World, 1919-1939* (New York, 1971), 4-7; Walter Lippmann, *The Political Scene: An Essay on the Victory of 1918* (New York, 1919), 68-69, 100-13; DuBois, "Negro Takes Stock," 144-45.

95. DuBois, *Dusk of Dawn,* 276-88; Johnson, "Africa at the Peace Table," 19.

96. Ida Gibbs Hunt to Mary W. Ovington, January 10, 1920, M. C. Slaughter to James Weldon Johnson, July 26, 1921; Butler Wilson to Ovington, July 30, 1921, NAACP Paper.

97. W. E. B. DuBois to James Weldon Johnson, July 28, 1921, F. Edward Taylor to Walter White, August 26, 1921, NAACP Papers.

98. Moorefield Storey to Arthur Spingarn, November 4, 1920, Arthur Spingarn Papers, Library of Congress; James Weldon Johnson, *Self-Determining Haiti* (New York, 1920), 31.

99. Walter White to Mary W. Ovington, September 12, 1921, NAACP Papers.

CONCLUSION

1. Horace Mann Bond, "Negro Leadership Since Washington," *The South Atlantic Quarterly,* XXIV, 2 (April, 1925), 120.

2. Cyril V. Briggs to James Weldon Johnson, July 18, 1923, NAACP Papers, Library of Congress, Harold Cruse, *The Crisis of the Negro Intellectual* (New York, 1967), 75-76.

3. Theodore Vincent, *Black Power and the Garvey Movement* (Berkeley, 1975), 129. Kenneth L. Kusmer, *A Ghetto Takes Shape, Black Cleveland, 1870-1930* (Urbana, Ill., 1976), 231-32.

4. Bond, "Negro Leadership," 122-23.

5. Joel Spingarn to George E. Haynes, August 11, 1926, Albert B. Hart to Haynes, September 7, 1926, William Harmon Foundation Papers, Library of Congress.

6. Abram L. Harris, "The Negro Problem as Viewed by Negro Leaders," *Current History,* XVIII, 3 (June 1923), 413-14. See mutual respect for one another in W. E. B. DuBois to James Weldon Johnson, December 20, 1929, NAACP Papers, and Abram Harris to Joel Spingarn, July 27, 1934, Joel Spingarn Papers, New York Public Library.

7. George E. Haynes, *The Trend of the Races* (New York, 1922),

8. Ibid., 21.

9. Mary B. Brady, Director of Harmon Foundation, to Samuel McCune Lindsay, April 6, 1928, Samuel McCune Lindsay Papers, Columbia University.

10. Alain Locke, "The New Negro," in Locke, ed., *The New Negro* (New York, 1968 ed), 4.

11. W. E. B. DuBois to Alain Locke, October 9, 1924, Alain Locke Papers, Howard University.

12. Locke, "New Negro," 12, 14.

13. Alain Locke, "The Negro Speaks for Himself," *The Survey,* LII (April 15, 1924), 72.

14. Locke, "New Negro," 7.

15. Haynes, *Trend of the Races,* 92; Locke, "New Negro," 14.

16. Horace M. Kallen, *Zionism and World Politics: A Study in History and Social Psychology* (London, 1921), 138-39. Kallen also emphasized the completion of practical projects in Palestine, but he was among the few Zionists at the time to emphasize the importance of relations with Arabs.

17. Edward R. Kantowicz, *Polish-American Politics in Chicago, 1888-1940* (Chicago, 1975), 163-64; Josef J. Barton, *Peasants and Strangers: Italians, Rumanians, and Slovaks in an American City, 1890-1950* (Cambridge, Mass., 1975), 83, 85-90, 152-53; Humbert Nelli, *The Italians in Chicago, 1880-1930: A Study in Ethnic Mobility* (New York, 1970), 222-42.

18. Carl Osthaus, "The Rise and Fall of Jesse Bingha, Black Financier," *Journal of Negro History,* LVIII, 1 (January 1973), 48-49.

19. Franz Boas, "The Problem of the American Negro," *Yale Review,* 2nd ser., x (January 1921), 390.

20. H. L. Mencken to Alain Locke, February 10, ?, Locke Papers; James Weldon Johnson, *Along This Way* (New York, 1933), 305.

21. Arthur Spingarn to Archibald Grimke, November 28, 1925, Archibald Grimke Papers, Howard University; Nathan Huggins, *Harlem Renaissance* (New York, 1971), 98-116; Langston Hughes, *The Big Sea: An Autobiography* (New York, 1940), 270-72, exonerates Van Vechten.

22. Frederick L. Hoffman to Carter Woodson, March 17, 1920, copy in Arthur Spingarn Papers, Library of Congress.

23. Lothrop Stoddard, "Negative Speech," in "Shall The Negro be Encouraged to Seek Cultural Equality?" *Report of the Debate Conducted by the Chicago Forum,* March 17, 1929, pamphlet in Schomburg Collection, New York Public Library. See the more sustained argument, with extensive discussion of "biracialism," in Lothrop L. Stoddard, *Re-Forging America: The Story of Our Nationhood* (New York, 1927), 273, 276, 284-324.

24. W. E. B. DuBois, "Affirmative Speech" and "Closing Statement," in *Report of Debate.*

25. Cruse, *Crisis of the Negro Intellectual,* 35-63; Huggins, *Harlem Renaissance,* 3-12, 305-06.

26. James Weldon Johnson, "The Dilemma of the Negro Author," *The American Mercury,* XV (December 1928), 481.

27. W. E. B. DuBois, *Education and Work* (Washington, 1930), Pamphlet in Schomburg Collection.

28. Richard Wright, *American Hunger* (New York, 1979), 43-45.

| Index